Geta

Mozambique

MIKE COPELAND

SUNBIRD
PUBLISHING

First published in 2006

2 4 6 8 10 9 7 5 3 1

Sunbird Publishers (Pty) Ltd
2nd Floor, Design Centre, 179 Loop Street
Cape Town, 8001

www.sunbirdpublishers.co.za

Registration number: 1984/003543/07

Publisher: Natanya Mulholland
Editor: Sean Fraser
Design and layout: Catherine Coetzer
Cartographer: John Hall
Editorial adviser: David Bristow
Production: Andrew de Kock

Reproduction by Unifoto (Pty) Ltd, Cape Town
Printed by Tien Wah Press (Pte), Singapore

ISBN 1 919 93830 3

In the research and writing of this guide, I was assisted by so many kind and friendly people: Janice at O Lar Do Ouro, the Hotel Cardosa staff, Joao des Neves of The Mozambique Advisor, Michelle at Casa Lisa, Leo of Praia do Sol, Dries and Charles from Paindane, Dave and Jill at Barra Lodge, the Inhambane Tourism Association, Grant of Pomene Lodge, Carol from Vilankulo Beach Lodge, Marion and Dave in Beira, James at Catapu, Russell of the Blackfoot Bar, Genevieve in Pemba, Laura on Ibo Island, Doogles in Blantyre, Emilio at Tiger Lodge, Cahora Bassa and Guy at DaimlerChrysler for the loan of a super-capable Jeep. Warm thanks to you all. I also tip my cap to that early pioneer of tourism in Mozambique, Senhor Alves.

Noticed on a menu at Sylvia Shoal:

If God had not invented the Oceans,
The Portuguese would have.

Mike Copeland
Cape Town, January 2006

I dedicate this book to Pats, companion and partner on all my visits to Mozambique.

Contents

MAPS

MAP KEY

Note: Some maps are not to scale.

⊨	Accommodation	+	GPS coordinates point		Post office
⬭	Baker	i	Information		Resort / Beach
$	Bank	⚲	Mechanic		Restaurant / Bar
⊕	Bus terminus	⊕	Medical centre / hospital		Road, main route
▲	Camping	⚖	Monument		Road
🎥	Cinema	P	Parking		Shops
🗿	Curios / craft shops	✳	Place of interest		Telephone
⚲	Diving centre / shop	Ⓦ	Place of worship		Train station
⛽	Garage, petrol / diesel	☀	Police station		

HOW TO USE THIS BOOK

The first 10 chapters are filled with background information on Mozambique, its history, people and natural environment. Advice is offered on planning your trip, getting to your destination, staying healthy, and other practical aspects of travelling to and around Mozambique. Some of the advice and recommended equipment is only applicable for the less-developed parts of the country and should not be necessary if you are staying in and around the larger towns in the south. Chapters 11 to 16 cover the southern half of the country – up the coast from the border with South Africa's KwaZulu-Natal province to the Save River, north of Vilankulo. Coastal resorts and islands make this the most visited section of Mozambique. The following six chapters describe the lesser-known but equally beautiful northern coastline – from Mozambique's second-largest city, Beira, up to the Ruvuma River and the border with Tanzania. Ilha de Moçambique, the World Heritage Site and jewel in a string of offshore islands, is the must-see destination in this section. The next chapter heads inland through the Niassa province and Malawi to Tete, and the book ends with some useful words and phrases in Portuguese.

This guide can be used to plan and travel the entire length of Mozambique, either with your own vehicle or using public transport. Bus routes and fares, road conditions and fuel availability,

accommodation and food – it's all here. I start in the south and work my way north, so if you are travelling in the opposite direction – from north to south – you will just have to hold the book upside down!

It was difficult to decide which currency to quote in this book. In the south, prices are often quoted in South African rands (R) because most visitors come from that country. Further north, American dollars ($) is the preferred currency as visitors could come from anywhere. The rand and dollar, however, tend to fluctuate, whereas prices in the local currency, metical (MT), are remarkably stable (the average exchange rate during the research of this book was 3200 MT to the rand and 20000 MT to the dollar). As a result, I have decided to quote prices in meticais (plural), and have rounded them off to the nearest 1000. It is flattering to note that the Mozambique government recently made this offficial policy. Therefore, a hotel room listed here at 400 MT is equal to 400000 meticais, or R125 or $20. The exception to this is that prices in South Africa are quoted in rands and for Zimbabwe and Malawi in US$.

Telephone numbers are listed as you would dial them in Mozambique (including the area code), and Malawian and South African telephone numbers are preceded by the international and regional dialling codes.

Introduction

Mozambique is bouncing back. Holiday-makers are returning to the beautiful beaches and coral reefs, the restocked game parks and the legendary big-game fishing so popular in local waters. From five-star luxury in the south, to wild, no-star adventures up north, Mozambique has something for everyone. Investors, too, are returning and finding that there is profit to be made in the reconstruction and development of the country now that 40 years of strife have well and truly ended. Streets are being cleaned up and buildings renovated and painted, although bureaucracy and red tape may still make it difficult for Mozambicans to beautify their properties.

Those who remember 'the old days' will still recognise a lot in the new Mozambique. You are still likely to bump into a neighbour from Jo'burg in Maputo, or your neighbour from Harare in Beira. The beer is cold and refreshing and the prawns delicious, plentiful and cheap. The nightlife in Maputo is wild, and the tide still goes out so far that, to go for a swim, you need first to go for a jog.

Most of the tourism originates from South Africa – even non-African visitors usually enter via that country – which means that most tourists travel no further than Vilankulo and the Bazaruto Archipelago. It is a great pity (although some may consider it a blessing) that the wild-and-wonderful north is not visited by more tourists. In this guide, I have tried to cover all the regions as comprehensibly as possible and urge you to explore them all.

Mozambique is one of the fastest growing tourist destinations in Africa, if not the world. It is changing fast and guide books can't always keep up with the developments. So please feel free to let me know where this book needs updating or improving.

If you have ambitions to travel further afield in Africa (and I think everyone should), look out for my other book, *Getaway Guide – Cape to Cairo*. And if you want to drop me a line, my address is mcopeland@telkomsa.net

Mozambique's flag is a busy affair made up of three horizontal bands, from top: green, white-edged black and yellow. Into the middle band, they have manage to fit a red triangle, yellow star, open white book and a crossed rifle and hoe in black!

Facts, figures and highlights 1

Mozambique is a long, narrow and predominantly tropical country on the eastern seaboard of southern Africa. Its coastline is washed by the warm waters of the Indian Ocean, while inland it is bordered by six countries – Malawi, Zambia, Zimbabwe, Swaziland, Tanzania and South Africa.

The Indian Ocean stretches along Mozambique's entire eastern boundary, and plays an important role in the local economy.

The fantastically shaped mountains around Cuamba dominate the scenery in the northern parts of Mozambique.

Size

With the exception of the Tete and Niassa provinces, most of Mozambique lies within 300 kilometres of its 2 500-kilometre coastline. At 801 600 square kilometres, it is about the size of the UK and France combined and, compared to its neighbours, it is more than twice the size of Zimbabwe and a little over two-thirds the size of South Africa.

Topography

Most of Mozambique comprises a low-lying coastal plain that lies at less than 350 metres above sea level, rising to mountains and plateaus along the Malawi and Zimbabwe borders. Two of southern Africa's major rivers, the Limpopo and Zambezi, flow through the country, as well as the Save, Lurio and Rovuma. There is also over 200 kilometres of Lake Malawi coastline in the extreme North West.

Climate

Mozambique lies mostly within the tropics and has a mild, humid climate with southern summer rainfall (October to March). The average maximum January temperature for Beira is 32°C with a minimum of 24°C, while for July it is 25°C and 16°C respectively. The south, towards Maputo, is slightly cooler, and heading north, a little warmer. For a five-day forecast of weather almost anywhere in the world, go to www.weather.com

Cities and towns

Maputo is the capital, but it is fairly isolated down south. Other main towns are: Beira, Nampula, Pemba, Inhambane, Xai-Xai, Tete, Quelimane and Nacala. There are 10 provinces: Maputo, Gaza, Inhambane, Sofala, Manhica, Zambezia, Nampula, Cabo Delgado, Niassa and Tete.

Language

The official language is Portuguese (see Chapter 25 – Portuguese words and phrases). Arabic, Makonde and Swahili are spoken in the north, while pidgin Fanagalo (learnt by workers on the South African mines) is still spoken and understood in the south. There are also a number of vernacular Bantu languages, and English is becoming more understood as tourism grows.

Population

The population is estimated to be just over 20 million (resulting in a fairly low population density of 25 people per square kilometre), with the densest habitation around Maputo. There are 16 main ethnic groups, including Makua, largely in the north and the largest; Makonde, also from the north and famous for their carvings; Sena from the central provinces; and Shangaan, dominant in the south. The mortality rate of children under five (27.3%) is said to be the highest in the world, and the average life expectancy is a pessimistic 45 to 50.

Currency

The metical (MT) is the official currency. The plural is meticais (pronounced *meticaysh* and usually quoted in mils (thousands). At the time of researching this book, the rate of exchange was 3 200 metacais (written for the purposes of this book as 3,2 MT) to the South African rand, and 20 000 (20 MT) to the US$. The Moz government recently decreed that 1 000 'old' MT will equal one 'new' MT, effectively dropping three zeros off the price of everything. This may lead to confusion as some prices may be quoted in old MT, others in new MT. Beware! Although the MT has been fairly stable, inflation and the fluctuating rand and dollar mean that you should check the latest exchange rates prior to departure. Whenever possible, change your money at a *cambios* money exchange office. They are private, secure, effeciently run and offer the best rates. Banks also offer good rates, but can be frustratingly slow. If stuck, change at your hotel, a shop or garage. But avoid street hustlers – you could easily be ripped off. For an easy-to-use currency converter, check out www.xe.com

Time

Time in Mozambique is Universal Time plus 2 – the same as all of its neighbours (except Tanzania, which is one hour earlier). In the far north of Mozambique, you may come into contact with Swahili Time. This is a confusing way of counting 12 hours of actual daytime as a day and 12 hours of night-time as the night. In other words, whereas our day officially starts at midnight (while it is, in fact, still dark), the day in Swahili Time starts at sunrise, our 6 am. As a result, 10 am for the Swahili is 4 pm in the afternoon for us (16 hours after the start of our day, but only 10 hours after the start of the Swahili day), and 4 am is 10 pm at night for us – told you it was confusing!

Visa requirements

All visitors, except South Africans and Malawians, require visas, which should be obtained in advance at a

Mozambique is holiday country and families swim, fish and sail along its seaboard.

Mozambiquan embassy, high commission or consulate. A single-entry tourist visa is valid for 60 days from date of issue for a maximum stay of 30 days. Same-day visas cost $13 (R85), next-day visas $10 (R65), and if you are prepared to wait a week, only $5 (R45). Visas are also available at borders for $25 (R171), but those issued at Ponta do Ouro and other small border posts can only be used to exit from that border post again (a proper visa is a barcoded form pasted into your passport). Check for the latest visa information at www.the-gsa.co.za

Government

Mozambique is a multiparty democracy, with 250 elected representatives in a national assembly. There are two main parties, Frelimo and Renamo, and about a dozen minor ones. Renamo enjoys support in the centre of the country, while Frelimo is strong in the south and north. Elections were last held on 1 December 2004. They were peaceful, free and fair, giving Frelimo 62% of the vote and 160 seats, and Renamo 30% and 90 seats. President Armando Guebuzo (Frelimo) succeeded Joaquim Chissano as Head of State.

Tourist highlights

The most impressive destination must be Ilha de Moçambique, a World Heritage Site that was the country's original island capital. The solid old fortress of São Sebastião (St Sebastian), Governor's Palace, quaint streets and old houses make this the unpolished gem of the African east coast. Other interesting islands are Ibo, in the Querimbas, Bengueru off Vilankulo and Inhaca off Maputo. Although both the history and architecture are fascinating, most visitors come for the fishing, diving and swimming – the Querimbas and Bazaruto archipelagos, Pemba, Vilankulo, the Inhambane area and Ponta do Ouro are world famous for their reefs, channels and golden beaches. And don't forget the music and nightlife of Maputo!

History and economy

2

The tragedy of African history is that the really interesting stuff has been lost. Impermanent documentation, or none at all, makes it difficult to trace what actually happened prior to the arrival of the European powers. Fortunately, though, the East Coast of Africa was well connected to the Indian Ocean trading routes and is mentioned in early travel writing.

The grand entrance to the old dockyard on Ilha de Moçambique.

As early as the 1st century AD, a Greek-Egyptian captain wrote of the trade between Red Sea ports, Arabia, East Africa and India. Rome was linked to China along this network of inter-mediaries. By the 9th and 10th centuries, the unifying effect Islam was having on Arabia helped trade in the Indian Ocean region to flourish, and by the 13th century, the entire East African seaboard was linked by a string of thriving ports and city-states – Mogadishu, Brava, Malindi, Pemba, Zanzibar, Mombasa, Mafia, Kilwa and Sofala, the port for Monomatapa's gold in the far south. No one bothered going further south, as trade there was regarded as being of no value. Iron implements, cloth, glass and beads were brought south to exchange for ivory, gold and slaves. Populated by skilled traders who decorated their substantial dwellings with carpets from Isfahan and porcelain ware of Sung China, a unique culture developed – Swahili, a blend of Arab and African. The famous early traveller, Ibn Battuta, who visited Mombasa in 1330, found a peaceful, well-organised and flourishing city.

Enter the Portuguese

The ancient system of trade was rudely interrupted in the late 15th century when Europe decided to break the stranglehold the Ottoman Turks had on the Red Sea route to the East. It was the Portuguese, the greatest seafaring nation at the time, who first sailed around Africa and pio-neered a new route. First Bartholomeu Diaz and then Vasco da Gama clawed their way around the Cape and on to the riches of India.

With their superior ships and trained soldiers, the Portuguese destroyed the

Visitors shop for the colourful fabric worn as *capulanas* by local women.

Subsistence fishing is an important activity in hungry Mozambique.

established African coastal trade. Da Gama ravaged Mombasa, D'Almeida burned Kilwa and Da Cunha ruined Brava and Zeila. With the precious metals of Monomatapa their main interest, the Portuguese set up forts at Sofala (1505) and the island of Moçambique (1507). Then, using the mighty Zambezi River as a highway into the interior, they established a fort at Tete and traders ventured up the Mazoe River to attend the gold fairs at what is now Mount Darwin in Zimbabwe.

The southern point of Portuguese influence was Bahia de Lagoa (Delagoa Bay, and later to become the city of Lourenço Marques), with the offshore island of Inhaca serving as a fortified outpost. Feeling safe on islands, they set up a fort on Ibo in the Querimbas Archipelago and, in 1558, built the São Sebastião fortress on Moçambique Island, from where they ran their southern African sphere of influence.

Portugal continued to dominate trade between India and Europe in spite of strong competition from the Dutch, English and French. The São Sebastião fort withstood a number of sieges by the Dutch at the beginning of the 17th century, the first battles fought between European powers on southern African soil. (In fact, had the Dutch been successful, they would not have needed the Cape of Good Hope as a stopover en route and so changed the course of African history.)

But the Portuguese rule on the East African coast was greedy and corrupt. Influential positions were bought and sold, and governors and captains traded for their own profit. Powerful traders built up large estates with private armies, and skirmished with each other as well as with indigenous peoples. Around the middle of the 17th century, the slave trade in Mozambique picked up, with the bulk of this human cargo

The doors of this small shop may have closed a long time ago, but business continues.

going to Brazil, another Portuguese colony. In 1696, the fall of the mighty Fort Jesus in Mombasa to Arab Omani forces signalled the end of Portuguese influence north of the Rovuma River, and trade was concentrated in the south. The slave trade continued to grow during the 17th century, as did the trade with Monomatapa. Gold, copper, tin, iron and lead were carried off as tribal wars were instigated and puppet chiefs gained support.

Portuguese East Africa

The 19th century was a time of consolidation and stabilisation for the fledgling country as borders were set during the frantic Scramble for Africa. Treaties were signed with Oom Paul Kruger of the Zuid-Afrikaansche Republiek, which allowed him a railway line and access to the port of Lourenço Marques (made the official capital of Mozambique in 1898), and similar concessions were granted to the British in Nyasaland

(now Malawi) for the use of Beira. Boundries were drawn with Britain in the south and west, and with German East Africa in the north, and the country of Mozambique (then known as Portuguese East Africa) took on its modern shape. Huge foreign charter companies were granted rights to trade and the territory began to prosper.

During the first half of the 20th century, thousands of settlers *colonatos* poured into the colony from the motherland, and Mozambique boomed under the iron fist of the Portuguese dictator, Salazar. Modern towns with red-roofed buildings, boulevards and bandstands sprung up. The *assimilado* system granted Portuguese citizenship to an African if he could meet certain strict requirements. Labour, however, was still regarded as a resource to be exploited, and most able-bodied local men ended up working on the South African mines, to the benefit of the South African and Portuguese governments.

Winds of change

In 1951 Mozambique was made an overseas province of Portugal, but the winds of change were blowing through Africa, and resistance to colonial rule was growing. In 1962, Frelimo, the Mozambique Liberation Front led by Eduardo Mondlane, launched its first military campaigns. By 1966, the north of the country was largely under their control, but the war dragged on until the overthrow of Antonio de Oliveira Salazar in Portugal in 1974. Portugal's new socialist government swiftly granted its colonies independence and Mozambique became a People's Republic in 1975 under the leadership of Samora Machel.

The country was in a bad shape after the civil war, a situation aggravated by the wholesale exodus of Portuguese skills and capital. Mozambique supported the Zimbabwe African National Union (ZANU) in their struggle to liberate Rhodesia, and the African National Congress (ANC) in their attempts to do the same in South Africa. The governments of these two countries, in turn, did their utmost to destabilise their new neighbour and supported, trained and equipped the Mozambique National Resistance (Renamo).

This was a sad time for southern Africa, and matters only improved in the early 1990s when South Africa restricted Renamo's support and Mozambique switched from Marxism to a market economy. A peace agreement was signed between Renamo and Frelimo in 1992, and this was followed by full elections in 1994. A comfortable win for Frelimo confirmed Joaquim

It is said that the name Mozambique is derived from Musa Mbiki, the name of the Sultan of Ilha de Moçambique when the Portuguese arrived there in the 15th century. It makes one wonder if South Africa's President Mbeki could not possibly have East African island roots!

Chissano as president. The most recent elections, regarded by observers as peaceful, free and fair, were held in December 2004. They gave Frelimo 62% of the vote and Renamo 30%.

Rebuilding Mozambique

Since 1994, the country has made great strides and what was once the 'poorest country in the world' is now regarded as the 'fastest growing economy in the world'. The inflation rate is down and Mozambique is attracting more foreign investment than any other sub-Saharan country. Sasol (South Africa's massive oil-from-coal project) has invested $1 billion in the Pande gas fields near Vilankulo, while many Zimbabweans who lost their farms to land reform in that country are now resettling in Mozambique and setting up tobacco plants and other enterprises.

Tourism is flourishing and the badly damaged infrastructure is being rebuilt. All of this creates sorely needed employment to complement the subsistence fishing and dry-land agriculture that currently dominates – cashew nuts, mandioca, maize, mangoes, peanuts and coconuts being the most common crops cultivated here.

3 People and culture

It is an unfortunate fact of life that those who are poor and repressed are usually good, honest and decent people, and it is the rich and powerful nations, who have all the means and rights that a strong democracy guarantees, that become arrogant, greedy and aloof. Mozambicans have suffered a long struggle for independence, a bitter civil war and a strict Marxist government and they are good, honest and decent people. They are also happy and relieved just to be allowed to lead normal lives and work hard to get ahead. Respect plays an important part in the social fabric of Mozambican life and age is revered. It's an old-fashioned system that demands that you, the visitor, show respect in order to gain respect.

With the hostilities of war behind them, Mozambicans – particularly the children – have learnt to smile again.

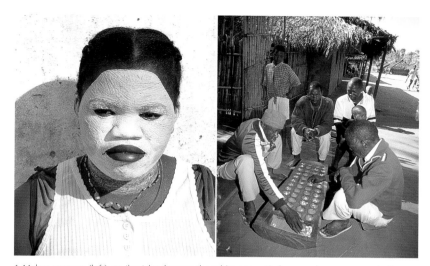

A Makua woman (left) on Ibo Island wears the white cosmetic face mask so common in the region. Men gather around for a game of *Bao* (right).

With a population of just over 20 million, Mozambique is not too densely populated. There are 16 main ethnic groups speaking a variety of languages and dialects, with Portuguese the official language. But, because of the protracted war and disruption of education, only about a quarter of the population speaks Portuguese. The education system is still inadequate, but improving. Under Portuguese rule, the Roman Catholic Church was closely linked to the state and was thus blamed for colonial abuses. After independence, a backlash against the Church saw the destruction and expropriation of many churches and their holdings and a subsequent drop in the practise of Christianity. With Islam strong in the north, the current estimate is that 35% of Mozambicans are Christian, 30% Muslim and the rest animists. The new government is strictly secular.

Arts and crafts

Woodcarvings are the most visual of the crafts practised by local craftsmen, sandalwood being the preferred medium in the south and ebony in the north (test for fake ebony by smelling for shoe polish or rubbing a damp finger over the wood for dye). The Makonde tribe in the northern Cabo Delgado province is famous for its carved masks. Clay pots, grass mats and batik prints are all finely crafted and make excellent souvenirs. As do the colourful cloths, called *capulanas*, worn by women around their waists. Just about any tailor at the local market will be able to make up any sort of garment you want from a piece of this brightly printed cloth.

On the menu

Mozambican food is usually quite spicy with chilli pepper (peri-peri) being the main culprit. The most basic dish is maize meal served with a stew of fish, meat or beans. Usually for sale in markets and at bus stops, it is very cheap. Snack bars will serve coffee, cold drinks and beer with your omelette, burger or prego (thin steak) roll. Chicken grilled flat, basted with a peri-peri sauce and served with chips is available anywhere anytime. Good, fresh and reasonably priced seafood is a feature of most restaurants, with prawns and calamari the most popular. Genuine local specialities such as Cozido a Portuguese (meat, dumplings, cabbage and rice) and Galinha a Zambeziana (chicken with lime, garlic and peri-peri) are hard to find, but well worth looking for.

Mineral water and the ubiquitous Coke and orange cold drinks are available all over, as are the excellent Mozambican beers: 2M (Dois em), Manhica and Laurentina. The Portuguese wine sold locally is not very good, but better South Africa wine is often available.

Postscript: I am not an advocate of handing out used clothing, sweets (especially the dangerous practice of throwing them out the car window to kids as you drive by) and other gifts to local people along the way. It reinforces a culture of begging and living off handouts, while at the same time creates an expectation that all travellers will do the same. Of course, should you befriend someone, or would like to show your appreciation for a special favour, then by all means be generous. But I have always found that local people best appreciate just being treated in an honest, friendly and non-condescending way. This nurtures a more natural and equal friendship between local and visitor.

Northern Mozambique's Makonde tribe are best known for their fine carvings.

The natural world 4

Mozambique is effectively split in half by the mighty Zambezi River (although some may argue that the divide is further south at the Save). Infrastructure, development and tourism blossoms in the south, while the north remains gloriously off the beaten track and unspoiled. Coastal dunes line the entire length of the country, giving way to tropical forests, miombo woodland and savanna inland. Coral reefs teem with fish just offshore, supporting a local fishing industry that relies on beach-built dhows (although far too many foreign trawlers carry off the biggest catches).

Boasting an extraordinary natural heritage, it is Mozambique's vast and diverse sea life that is the most impressive.

In the wild

Although there are six proclaimed national parks and five game reserves in Mozambique, the once abundant wildlife has been severely depleted by years of civil war, subsistence hunting, logging and poaching. There is hope on the horizon, however, with the planning of Transfrontier Conservation Areas (TFCAs). Facilitated by The Peace Parks Foundation, which boasts as its patron Nelson Mandela and inspired by the late Anton Rupert, TFCAs will link existing game reserves to form huge mega-parks. The game from well-stocked (and in the case of Kruger's elephants, overstocked) reserves will be allowed to migrate into poorly stocked areas. Annual migrations to make use of the best grazing will again be possible. Tourists will be able to travel between countries, and local communities will benefit from employment and the sustainable harvesting of natural resources. Sounds like an unobtainable dream? Well, it's working in the Kgalagadi, so why not here? Check out the website www.dolimpopo.com

While the Morromeu Reserve on the Zambezi delta is well known for its outstanding birdlife, and draws ornithologists from around the world, the Reserva do Gili, between Quelimane and Nampula, survives really in name only. Many of the parks and reserves are protected only by their isolation, but at least they do still exist and might rise again sometime in the future.

Maputo Elephant Reserve

The Maputo Elephant Reserve (see page 56), on the coast south of the capital, is struggling to make a comeback. Roads have already been improved, game rangers have been appointed and about 300 elephants call the reserve home, but the reserve still needs to be properly fenced as the elephants tend to roam and clash with local villagers. The plan is to link this reserve to the Tembe Elephant and Ndumo game reserves in South Africa by a TFCA.

Limpopo National Park

The national park of Banhine (see page 56), north of Maputo, will also be linked by way of a TFCA to form a new Peace Park that is being created along with South Africa's Kruger National Park and Gonarezhou National Park in Zimbabwe. The land between the Limpopo and Elephantes rivers, including the huge Massingir Dam, has been declared Mozambique's newest national park (the Limpopo National Park in 2001) and, together

> ### The birdlife in Mozambique
> has faired better than the mammals and is still excellent, although – as is the case almost worldwide – habitat degradation remains a problem. A combination of coastal, grassland, forest, riverine, wetland and mountain areas harbour over 900 documented species, including many endemics such as the green-headed oriole and Gunning's akalat.
> The Mozambique Bird Atlas Project has an interesting website: www.aviandemographyunit.org

Following severe degradation during the war, the wildlife is slowly recovering.

with a large chunk of bridging land, links the other reserves into one large transfrontier park. This will allow the proper migration of game and the alleviation of elephant overcrowding in Kruger. Some boundary fences have come down and game is being translocated. Already a new border gate has been built near Olifants Camp on the South African side in the Kruger National Park, but cannot be opened until the Mozambicans complete their side of the border post. At the moment, the only route through this area is via the Pafuri border gate in northern Kruger and down the Limpopo to Mapai. (See Chapter 9 for details.)

Zinave

The national park of Zinave, on the southern bank of the Save River northwest of Vilanculo, has no infrastructure and very little game, but because it is so isolated and sparsely populated it will probably survive well enough until the new super transfrontier park, of which it will also be a part, is created. To find out more about the activities of the Peace Parks Foundation, visit their website at www.peaceparks.org

Gorongosa

Gorongosa National Park (see pages 56 & 125), northwest of Beira, is another wildlife area in Mozambique that deserves a positive report. Dating back to the early 1920s, when it started as a small 1 000-square-kilometre reserve, it was not until 1951 that the first tourist accommodation was built at Chitengo. Declared a national park in 1961, it was increased in size to 5 300 square kilometres. Over the next couple of decades, it became world famous for its abundance of big game, but the civil war and poaching of the 1980s wiped out almost all the animals and destroyed the park's infrastructure. The headquarters of Renamo were located here, which also meant extensive land mining. In 1995, with the help of the European Union, an emergency programme was drawn up to rehabilitate this African jewel. Since then, the area has been demined, the headquarters at Chitengo are being restored, and importantly, game rangers are being trained and are out combating the once-wholesale poaching. The park reopened for visitors in 1998 with efficient, dedicated staff. The numbers of game are on the increase and one can easily see warthog, waterbuck, impala, duiker and a variety of birds. The Carr Foundation of the USA has since become involved

Mozambique is a bird-watcher's paradise.

and animal relocation is planned, as is the upgrading of Chitengo camp site with new ablutions and the building of more bungalows. It is nice to see a game park coming back from the brink of annihilation. (See Chapter 18.)

Niassa

The vast Niassa Reserve along the southern bank of the Rovuma River is reported still to have large numbers of game – buffalo, wild dog, lion, a variety of antelope and as many as 14 000 elephant! A group of private investors, working in partnership with Mozambican government, has done considerable work up there. There is talk of expanding the park's boundaries and creating buffer zones where hunting may be permitted. There is also a possibility of stringing together a transfrontier park that could include conservation areas in Tanzania and Malawi. Driving to the park's headquarters on the eastern boundary at Mecula is extremely difficult and there are virtually no internal roads. Contact the Sociedade da Reserva do Niassa at e-mail telemedia.3@online.no or gmadal@teledata.mz

Bazaruto

The best-known and most-visited marine park in Mozambique is the Bazaruto National Park (see page 111), which includes the islands and reefs off Vilankulo. Protected since 1971, the five islands are home to duiker, bushbuck, freshwater crocodiles and over 180 bird species, while the reefs harbour dugongs, whales, dolphins, turtles and 2 000 fish species.

On the road 5

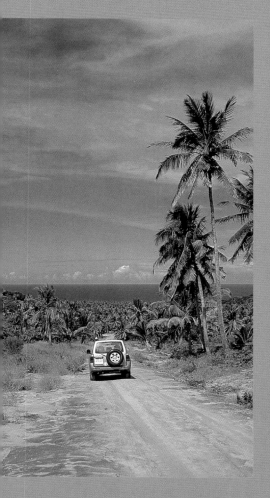

The best time to visit Mozambique is during the cooler, less-humid winter months from May to October – the threat of malaria is lower then, also. But, whatever time of the year you visit, try to avoid the overcrowding and higher prices during the South African school holidays. Most visitors to Mozambique come from neighbouring South Africa or Zimbabwe. They visit the southern half of the country and spend their time enjoying the beaches, islands, watersports and fishing. A fortunate few will travel the full length of Mozambique, either as part of a trans-African trek or southern African round trip.

Most of the roads leading down to the coast are quite rough and undeveloped.

From South Africa

From KwaZulu-Natal, in the south, it is possible to enter Mozambique along the coast, via Ponta do Ouro, or through Swaziland. From Gauteng, in the west, it's a comfortable run down to Maputo via the border at Komatipoort. Either way, your destination will be Maputo. With its bustling markets, vibrant nightlife and easy access to the offshore island of Inhaca, the capital should keep you busy for a good few days.

For the first-time visitor with a week or two at his or her disposal, a meander up the coast as far as Vilankulo would be the best introduction to Mozambique. The coastal towns of Xai-Xai and Inhambane have the basic necessities and infrastructure to visit the beach resorts that dot the coast here, and Vilankulo offers the opportunity to cross to the islands of the Bazaruto Archipelago. (See also Chapter 16.)

From Zimbabwe

Visitors from landlocked Zimbabwe will travel via Mutare and probably head for Mozambique's second-largest city, Beira. This route also provides easy access to the slowly recovering Gorongosa National Park to the north, and the offshore islands of Bazaruto to the south.

However, for the complete Mozambican experience, you should also visit the north, and the ultimate is to travel the entire length of the country from Ponto do Ouro in the south to the Rovuma River in the north. This route hugs the coast as far as Inhassoro, then heads inland to cross the Save River, past Gorongosa National Park

Having your own transport gives you untold travelling freedom.

and across the Zambezi, back to the coast at Ilha de Moçambique, Pemba and finally completely off the beaten track to the mouth of the Rovuma River with Tanzania beyond. You could keep heading north until you hit Cairo, or you could turn around and swing through Malawi and back south via Zambia and Zimbabwe. What a great trip that would be! (See also Chapter 23.)

Travelling around

You don't have to drive your own vehicle in Mozambique, and sometimes it's better not to. The advantages of having your own wheels are obvious – speed, comfort, security and, of course, convenience. The advantages of using public transport (hitching or free rides are not really an option in Moz) are less obvious, but also important. You will get to see and experience Mozambique and its people in a most wonderful way. Living at the level of the locals, you will not be considered a threat, nor will they be jealous of you and your possessions. You will be shown courtesy and kindness and learn more about the people, their customs, traditions and language. You will feel a part of the rhythm of Africa. (See also Chapter 3.)

Road travel

The roads down south are fairly good, although potholed, and if you stick to the tar, two-wheel drive is sufficient to get you around. Many of the sandy tracks down to the coast, however, are strictly for 4x4s. The further north you go, the rougher conditions become, and the tougher your vehicle

VEHICLE SPARES AND TOOLS

Cut back on this list if you are not straying too far off the beaten track.

- The workshop manual for your vehicle
- Full set of socket, ring and open spanners (compatible with your vehicle)
- Selection of screwdrivers (large and small, Phillips and flat)
- Pliers and vice grip
- Set of Allan keys (compatible with your vehicle)
- Shifting spanner and monkey wrench
- Hammer
- Spade
- Axe or saw
- Hacksaw
- File
- Wheel spanner
- 2 jacks (one high-lift)
- Tyre levers (long and strong)

- Puncture repair kit (including patches, gaiters, plugs and solution)
- Tyre pump or on-board compressor
- Pressure gauge, valves and valve tool
- 2 spare tyres and tubes
- Battery jumper cables
- Fanbelts (one universal)
- Engine oil, gearbox oil and brake fluid
- Q20 spray and grease
- Gasket silicon and contact adhesive
- Towrope
- Jerry cans (if no on-board auxiliary tank)
- Siphon pump or funnel for water or fuel
- Selection of nuts, bolts, washers and self-tapping screws
- Assortment of rope, string and wire

- A selection of plastic cable ties
- Electric wire, fuses, connectors and light bulbs
- Set of spark plugs (and spanner), points and condenser (petrol only)
- Set of fuel, air and oil filters
- Spare radiator and fuel hoses with clamps
- Insulation, masking and filament tape
- Pair of warning/hazard triangles (legal requirement)
- Fire extinguisher (a good one, no toys!)
- Spare set of keys (do not keep these inside the vehicle)
- And if you *know* your vehicle has a particular weakness, make sure you carry the appropriate replacement parts.

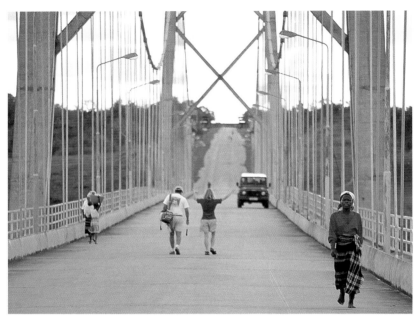

North of Vilankulo you reach the enormous Save River Bridge.

should be. Compared to so many other African countries, Mozambique's roads are uncrowded, the drivers quite courteous, and their vehicles in fairly good condition. The only drawback to driving here is dealing with the traffic police, the *transitos*. Many of them are like highway robbers and will create an offence and then fine foreign drivers. They are, however, being curbed by a government that wants to encourage tourism, so if you have not committed an offence, stand up for your rights and argue. Try not to hand over any documents or licences to a *transito*, or you could well be his hostage until he returns them.

Travel light – don't be tempted to take the kitchen sink, and try to avoid a roofrack or trailer. Remember that the more you take, the more effort you have to expend in carrying, maintaining and protecting your possessions.

Spare parts are not easily available, particularly for new exotic models. The cities of Maputo and Beira have agencies for most of the better-known marques, but out in the country you are more likely to find parts for old-model Land Rovers and Toyotas. Service and check your vehicle and all equipment before you go. New, untried and untested gear could let you down. Fortunately, Mozambican mechanics are great 'fixers' and their ability to get you going again will always surprise.

Fuel is quite freely available in the south, but as you venture further north it is advisable to carry spare fuel in jerry cans or an extra fuel tank. Diesel is slightly easier to obtain than petrol (and cheaper) and unleaded petrol is not always available. (If the nozzle of a leaded fuel pump will not fit your non-leaded tank, poke a long screwdriver or thin iron rod down your tank's filler pipe to open the obstructing flap.) Average prices of fuel per litre in Mozambique is 15 MT for diesel and 18 MT for petrol (leaded and unleaded). Emergency fuel is often sold in 20-litre yellow plastic drums at the roadside along stretches where there are no garages for kilometres. Remember, the Portuguese word

---

OFF TO MOZAMBIQUE

Fly-in packages

Air Holidays, tel: +27-(0)11-803-8223, fax: +27-(0)11-803-8076, e-mail: reservations@airholidays.co.za, website: www.airholidays.co.za
Top Holidays, tel: +27-(0)12-362-6406, fax +27-(0)12-362-6407, e-mail: reservations@tophols.com, website: www.tophols.co.za
Tropical Air Tours, tel: 21-32-5078, fax: 21-32-5082, e-mail: tropical@tvcabo.co.mz

Yacht charters

Barra Yacht Charters, tel: +27-(0)11-314-3355, fax: +27-(0)11-314-3239, e-mail: reservations@barralodge.co.za, website: www.barralodge.co.za
Island Quest, tel: +27-(0)11-802-5695; e-mail: info@islandquest.co.za, website: www.islandquest.co.za

Overland bus tours

Unusual Destinations, tel: +27-(0)11-706-1991, fax: +27-(0)11-463-1469; e-mail: info@unusualdestinations.com, website: www.unusualdestinations.com
Karibu Safari, tel: +27-(0)31-563-9774, e-mail: karibu@karibu.co.za, website: www.karibu.co.za

Sunway Safaris, tel/fax: +27-(0)11-803-7400, e-mail: sunway@icon.co.za, website: www.sunway-safaris.com

Booking agents and travel advisors

Mozambique Advisor, tel: 21-30-9477 or 82-302-0530, fax: 21-30-2054, e-mail: mozambique@adviser.co.mz, website: www.adviser.co.mz

Mozambique Connection, tel: +27-(0)11-8034185, fax: +27-(0)11-803-3861, e-mail: res@mozcon.com, website: www.mozcon.com

Mozambique Accommodation Solutions, tel: +27-(0)11-403-3648 or +27-(0)82-344-9265, fax: +27-(0)11-403-6732, e-mail: mozaccm@netactive.co.za

Mozambique Tourism, tel: +27-(0)11-803-9296 or +27-(0)11-234-0599, e-mail: travel@mozambiquetourism.co.za, website: www.mozambiquetourism.co.za

Mozambique Tours, tel: +27-(0)31-303-2190, e-mail: mit@iafrica.com, website: www.mozambiquetravel.co.za

A 4x4 vehicle is essential on Mozambique's rural roads after heavy rains.

for petrol is *gasolina*, diesel is *gasoleo* and don't ask for *petroleo* unless you particularly want paraffin…

Don't venture into Mozambique without good tyres. The best all-round tyres for load, speed and reliability on bad roads are truck tyres – radial or cross-ply. A high-ply rating is also important, especially for the sidewalls. And rather choose a high-profile than a low-profile tyre, as the best footprint for sand is long rather than wide. The higher profile will also give you better ground clearance.

And what about taking your motor-bike? Sure. If it's a good strong off-roader like a BMW F650, Honda's new Transalp 650 or Yamaha's old faithful Teneres, you can have a lot of fun in Moz. But take care, there's a lot of sand, and anything can happen on an African road. When you're on a bike, you're not protected by the vehicle's bodywork!

Safety in numbers?

One choice you will have to make way upfront is whether to travel alone, with a companion, in a group or in convoy with others. This is a very personal decision. Most purist travellers love to immerse themselves in the culture of a foreign country, and if you're travelling alone on public transport, nothing will dilute this experience or come between you and the locals. On the other hand, more gregarious travellers like the companionship, fun and security of groups or convoys. Make up your own mind, but don't be afraid to try something new. Oh, and pick your companions carefully – the success of your trip will depend on it.

What to pack 6

Take only what you *know* you will need, and not what you *think* you might need. Take only the necessities, and remember, the only thing you can never take enough of is money. If you're backpacking and using public transport on your travels, then obviously you have to be even more brutal in cutting down to the bare minimum.

A good storage system makes packing easy.

Documents

These are the most important items in your luggage. Without documents you can't cross borders, and you'll need them for yourself and your vehicle.

Your **passport** should be valid for at least three months after you expect to use it, and it should have at least two pages for each country you intend to visit – one for the visa and one for the entry and exit stamps. There seems to be a direct correlation between the importance of the country and the size of its rubber stamps – the less significant the country, the larger the stamps (and the bigger the tantrum of the border official when there is no clean page to use it on).

At time of writing, **visas** were required by all visitors to Mozambique, except South Africans and Malawians. Obtain one in your home country before arriving in Moz – visas are available at borders, but it's better to get one before you start your trip. In South Africa you can apply at any one of the following places:

Mozambique Consulate-General,
18 Hurlington Road, Illovo, Johannesburg, tel: +27-(0)11-327-2942, fax: +27-(0)11-327-2945

Mozambique Consulate,
11th Floor, Pinnacle Building, 8 Burg Street, Cape Town, tel: +27-(0)21-426-2944, fax +27-(0)21-426-2946

Mozambique Consulate,
5th Floor, 320 West Street, Durban, tel: +27-(0)31-304-0200, fax: +27-(0)31-304-0774

Mozambique Consulate,
64 Bester Street, Nelspruit, tel: +27-(0)13-752-7396, fax: +27-(0)13-755-1207

The following institutions are also able to assist with visas:

Mozambique National Tourist Co.,
10th Floor, Noswell Hall, 3 Siemens St., Braamfontein, tel: +27-(0)11-339-4900, fax: +27-(0)11-339-7295

Mozambique Connection,
1st Floor, Hing Yip, Cnr 9th & Wessels, Rivonia, tel: +27-(0)11-803-4185, fax: +27-(0)11-803-3861 e-mail: mozcon@pixie.co.za

The Visa Shop,
6th Floor, Thibault House, Thibault Square, Cape Town, tel: +27-(0)21-421-1059, fax: +27-(0)21-421-1065, e-mail: visashopcpt@worldspan.co.za

The Visa Shop (above) also has branches in Durban and Johannesburg. Further afield, Mozambique has representation in the following countries:

France: 82 Rue Lougier, F-75017, Paris, tel: 1-476-49132, fax: 1-426-73828.

Germany: Adenauerallee 46, D 53113, Bonn, tel: 228-224-024, fax: 228-213-920.

Malawi: Commercial Bank Building, Lilongwe, tel: 265-784-100
(Same-day transit visas are available for travel through the Tete Corridor to Zim.)

Tanzania: 25 Garden Avenue, Dar es Salaam, tel: +255-22-51-67843

United Kingdom: 21 Fitzroy Square, London, W1P 5HJ, tel: (0)171-383-3800

United States: 1990 M St, NW 570, Washington, tel: 202-293-7146, fax: 202-835-0245

Zambia: Villa 46, Mulungushi Village, Lusaka, tel: 1-250-468.

Zimbabwe: 156 Rhodes Avenue, Harare, tel: 4-790-837

Normal processing time for visas is seven working days, but they can be issued quicker on payment of a premium. Single-entry tourist visas are valid for entry within 60 days, and allow you to stay in the country for 30 days. For the latest information on visas visit www.the-gsa.co.za

Never travel without a **yellow fever certificate** – you're not always asked to show it, but that's better than being delayed and having to endure an inoculation on the border.

When it comes to **vehicle documentation**, a South African driver with a South African vehicle only needs the registration papers, or a certified copy thereof (and, very important, a letter of authorisation on an official letterhead if the vehicle is not being driven by the registered owner).

Visitors driving vehicles from non-neighbouring countries will need a **Carnet de Passage**. This internationally recognised document (issued by your local automobile association) facilitates customs formalities when crossing borders with a vehicle, and guarantees the payment of duties and taxes in the

event of the vehicle not leaving the country again. The motoring organisation that issues it will then have to pay the duties, and demand reimbursment from you, the owner of the vehicle – so make sure that your vehicle leaves Mozambique when you do! If you are South African and need a carnet for countries further north, contact:

Automobile Association (AA) of South Africa, tel: +27-(0)861-11-1994, e-mail: aasa@aasa.co.za, website: www.aasa.co.za

One page, in triplicate, is required for each country. One section is stamped and retained at the border on entry, the second is stamped on exit and the third is your proof of entry and exit. Please note that this does not free you from paying the local road taxes and third-party insurance. The AA in South Africa will also help foreigners, but with more stringent financial requirements.

Third-party insurance covers damage, injury or death to another person or property in Mozambique), and must be carried by all visiting vehicles. This is available at the border ($25 or R150; trailers $12 or R70). Cover is limited to R1 000 000 – with an excess of R1 000.

While **vehicle insurance**, covering theft of the vehicle, is recommended, it is not a necessity. Most South African motor-insurance policies include Mozambique in their territorial limits, but check yours to be sure.

Drivers' licences issued in neighbouring countries are recognised, but it might be a good idea to bring an international driver's licence issued by your local automobile association.

Keep every scrap of paper accumulated at the border post safely in a file, as you will be asked to show your documentation if stopped by an official (and you will be!).

Maps and guidebooks

If you're reading this, then you already have the best guidebook available. (Sorry, I had to squeeze that in!) Also check out the Bradt *Guide to Mozambique* by Philip Briggs, Lonely Planet's *Mozambique* and Footprint's *Guide to Mozambique* by Mike Slater. For maps, I recommend the National Geographic *African Adventure Atlas*. A magnificent encyclopaedia-like book that has only one problem – it's thick and heavy. Get a copy of Map Studio's *Illustrated Atlas of South, Central and East Africa* to travel with. Michelin's *Map Number 955* on central and southern Africa is also very good. At www.multimap.com you'll be able to find general maps.

GPS and navigation

A GPS is not generally necessary for coastal holidays in southern Mozambique. And you could even get by without one in the north, but I have listed GPS coordinates for those not-so-easy-to-find places. A small handheld GPS will give your position anywhere on earth to within 10 metres. Clever people can plot courses and create waypoints, but for dummies like me it's just reassuring to know where I am, and that I'm taking the right turn-off. Mount it on the dashboard of the vehicle and connect it to a powerpoint with an adaptor. An external antenna will improve the instrument's accuracy.

Photography

There is as great a variety of subjects to photograph in Mozambique as anywhere in the world, so be sure to take plenty of film or memory sticks. Unless you're a professional, don't take too much equipment. Travel light and be ready for anything, anytime.

Try to take your photographs in the early morning and late afternoon – the strong African sun washes out colour in the middle of the day and could give you very bland photographs. If at all possible, try to take your time. Get in close – the subjects of so many shots are simply too small and too far way otherwise, and are lost as a result. Stand so that the light source is behind you and selectively expose and focus for your main subject. Don't be shy to use your flash as fill-in if the subject is not well lit, even during the day. Then compose your shot.

Always make sure that people are comfortable with you photographing them. Try to engage them in conversation first, then motion with the camera that you want to take a shot of them and gauge their reaction. Usually, if you have just bought something from them in a market, or if they are showing off something of which they are proud, you will have no problem.

Although you might want to give sweets or pens to the people you photograph, you will probably also be asked for money. Try to resist the temptation as it creates the impression that travellers are an easy source of income. And don't promise to send them a copy of the photograph unless you honestly intend to.

Never photograph anything that might be considered of military importance, and show sensitivity at religious sites. Develop an eye for colourful detail – the intricate jewellery worn by women or unusual items for sale at a market often make better photographs than the overall shot.

TRAVEL WARDROBE

Here is a suggested clothing list:

♦ 2 pairs trousers or skirts: light cotton is comfortable and washable and trousers with zip-off legs can double as shorts. Zips on the pockets make life a little more difficult for pickpockets. Denim jeans aren't ideal as they're bulky, difficult to wash and even more difficult to dry quickly

♦ 4 shirts: I prefer collared shirts to T-shirts – they're smarter, cooler and have pockets (best with buttons)

♦ 2 pairs shorts: it gets hot in Moz and you can also swim in them

♦ Socks and underwear: they're light and easy to pack, so take at least 4 sets

♦ Sweater: take a lightweight sweater for the evenings, or a light rainproof jacket if visiting during the rain season

♦ Shoes: a pair of light boots or walking shoes, as well as a pair of sandals or thongs

♦ Cap or hat

♦ Towel and bathing costume

TOILETRIES

♦ Soap and shampoo

♦ Toothbrush and toothpaste

♦ Hairbrush and nail clippers

♦ Toilet paper

♦ Sanitary towels and/or condoms

♦ Shaving kit

♦ Sunblock

♦ Mosquito repellent

EXTRAS

♦ Backpack: If you are using public transport, take a good strong internal-framed one with a zipped flap to turn it into a carry bag; otherwise a small daypack will do for excursions to the beach or market

♦ Multipurpose tool or Swiss Army knife (remember not to stow this in your hand luggage if flying)

♦ Torch and spare batteries

♦ Matches or lighter

♦ Notebook and pen

♦ Travel guidebooks and maps

♦ Watch with built-in alarm

♦ Reading material (bird and mammal reference books, and some recreational reading)

♦ Plugs and adaptors to run or recharge electrical gear

♦ Pocket calculator (for navigation and currency calculations)

♦ Sunglasses and reading glasses

♦ Contact-lens cleaner and spare spectacles

♦ Binoculars

♦ Diving or snorkelling gear (or any other sporting equipment)

♦ Photographic gear (see page 34)

For good close-ups of animals or birds, you will need a powerful tele-photo lens. Get as close as possible with your vehicle, without leaving the road or disturbing the animal; switch off the engine so as not to cause camera vibrations and sit patiently waiting for something interesting to happen. Photos taken on a beach or over water are prone to glare and overexposure.

If you are hoping to sell your photographs, some publications still prefer slides. Otherwise, digital or print film is fine. Rather wait until you are home to have your film developed.

So, basically all you will need is a camera (a 28–90mm or similar lens is ideal on a 35mm camera), memory sticks or film (100 ASA is good for all-round work) and spare batteries.

Communication

Some people just have to stay in touch with everything they are trying to get away from. Family, friends and business back home can survive without you – relax! But, if you really must hook up with your 'past life', then a **cellular phone** is probably best.

Another communications option you might want to use is **e-mail**. Register an international Internet address on Hotmail or Yahoo and look out for Internet cafés (listed, where available, under towns). For a list of internet cafés in most major cities around the world – and their physical addresses – click on www.cybercafes.com

If you are to be cut off from these means of communication, consider **two-way radios**. These are available as inexpensive, portable 'walkie-talkies',

which are usually restricted to line-of-sight reception. Vehicle-based Citizens' Band (CB) radios are still reasonably inexpensive, work well up to 10 kilo-metres and are ideal for keeping a convoy connected. An HF or VHF radio, which is expensive, will connect you to the world. (The latter two require licences.) An added advantage of the HF radio is that it can be linked via a very hi-tech modem to your laptop (another can of worms!), which then allows you to send and receive e-mails via **Bushmail**. Bushmail hooks up via a radio signal to the Internet and, hey presto, you're fully connected, no matter how deep you are in the bush. Contact Jim Drummond (the man who never sleeps!) on tel: +27-(0)11-794-5249 or e-mail: jim@bushmail.net. But, the ulti-mate form of communication is a **satel-lite phone** – improving all the time, and still very expensive, it will connect you from anywhere to anywhere.

Clothing and personal gear

The beauty of travelling in Mozambique, and most of Africa, is that the weather is mild and you don't need to pack for extreme temperatures. Choose clothing that will not show dirt, and will wash and dry easily. Clothing should not offend local customs and religions.

A useful tip to make the chore of laundry a little easier (if travelling in your own vehicle) is to seal dirty clothes with water and soap powder in a buck-et with lid. Stashed anywhere aboard a bouncing vehicle all day will have them as clean as the proverbial whistle and will just need a good rinse before hanging out to dry.

Eating and sleeping

7

It is tempting to try to be self-sufficient. Camping and cooking for yourself is comfortable, pleasurable and predictable. But, it's also good to experience the lifestyles and flavours of the country and its people in the hotels, pensãos, restaurants and cafés – they are the pulse of Mozambique.

Accommodation may be rustic, but the setting is usually idyllic.

It is a misconception that Mozambique's tourist industry is slowly recovering to its previous levels – it's actually recovering very fast, and already way ahead of what it ever was in its 'heyday'. World-class hotels such as the Polana in Maputo and the Pemba Beach Hotel in Pemba will satisfy the fussiest multimillionaire tourist, while the many backpacker lodges dotted around the country are just what the budget traveller looks for. In even the 'lowest' of establishments, the staff are knowledgeable and courteous, the rooms are almost always neat, with fresh bedding, and the bathrooms clean and tiled. Unfortunately, the water and electricity supply is occasionally interrupted, so check this when booking into a place (the more expensive hotels have stored water and standby generators). Also check whether the air-con and fans work and how noisy they are. One aspect of Mozambique's buildings that does leave a lot to be desired is the state of the electrical installations – some can be quite dangerous, so take care. The newer hotels and camps are usually the best because they are generally in good nick. However, maintenance is not a high priority, so even these (and especially the reed-and-palm-frond huts) can reach their 'sell-by date' quite quickly, and can become quite dilapidated within a year or two. Remember, too, that quoted prices may be negotiable, particularly if you travel out of season. Breakfast is often included in the room rate, so check when booking in. There are many privately owned and unlicensed lodges offering accommodation in Mozambique. When advertised, promoted and usually paid for outside of the country, it means that local people do not benefit and legitimate operators lose business. If they are not properly registered and licensed, then I have not listed them. Other establishments only operate during the high season and close up out of season – these places might also not be listed.

Going camping

Camping gear and equipment are hard to find in Moz, so bring what you need. Don't be tempted to 'free-camp', no matter how attractive and isolated the spot looks. You will probably be gawked

---

CAMPING CHECKLIST

The following is some of the equipment you might need, but because comfort is such a personal thing, try not to be too influenced by my suggestions on choice of gear:

◆ Tent with a built-in mosquito net (vehicle roof-top tents are easy and safe)

◆ Camp stretcher and/or foam mattress

◆ Sleeping bag and inner sheet

◆ Pillow

◆ Light, folding camp chairs and table

◆ Lamp (first choice should be a fluorescent type that works off your vehicle's battery)

◆ Clothesline and pegs

◆ Washbasin and soap

Note: some camp sites have electrical points

---

at, possibly robbed and definitely fined if caught by an official, because it is illegal. Stay over at properly run sites with adequate security for yourself and your vehicle. You will also sleep much better if you choose a spot high on a ridge. The breeze up there will not only keep you cool, but also keep the mosquitoes at bay. Rumours have claimed that camping has been banned in Mozambique. This is not true, and there are many legal camp sites all over the country. The authorities have, however, closed some sites where the owners have licences to operate a hotel or lodge, but not a camp site as well. Some of these operators have now circumvented this problem by renting you a small reed hut or shaded area – putting up a tent next to it is then perfectly acceptable!

OUTDOOR COOKING CHECKLIST

- ◆ Cooker and fuel
- ◆ Ice-box or small fridge (the compressor type is best)
- ◆ Barbecue grid in a bag
- ◆ Sack of wood or charcoal
- ◆ Firelighters and matches
- ◆ Pot (a traditional black, cast-iron pot is ideal for cooking over a fire)
- ◆ Frying pan and kettle
- ◆ Plates and bowls
- ◆ Chopping board and a sharp knife
- ◆ Mugs and/or glasses
- ◆ Cutlery and can opener
- ◆ Washing-up bowl, soap and cloth
- ◆ Paper towels and refuse bags
- ◆ Water supply in containers

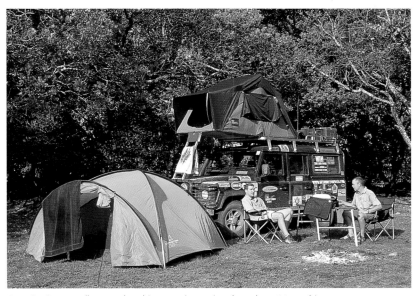

Camping is generally a good and inexpensive option throughout Mozambique.

The comforts may be basic, but welcome after a day on foot.

GRUB'S UP!

You may want to consider some of the following cooking ingredients:

Durables

* A selection of canned meats, fish and vegetables (just a few for emergencies – they're heavy)
* A selection of dehydrated foodstuffs (taste first – some are disgusting!)
* Breakfast cereal or muesli mix
* Sugar
* Powdered milk
* Tea and/or coffee
* Powdered isotonic drink
* Crisp bread or crackers
* Biscuits or rusks
* Salt, pepper, herbs and spices
* Stock cubes and garlic
* Dried fruit and nuts
* Rice and pasta
* Cooking and salad oil
* Honey or jam
* Peanut butter and/or Bovril
* Bottled water, cold drinks and beer

Semi-durables

* Bread
* Potatoes, onions, cabbage and carrots
* Apples and oranges
* Cheese and margarine
* Bacon and salami

Perishables

* Meat
* Eggs
* Salad
* Tomatoes
* Soft fruit

COUNTING THE COST

Some prices charged at Shoprite supermarkets in Mozambique:

- Loaf white bread — 11 MT
- Mineral water (1 litre) — 9 MT
- Can of beer — 15 MT
- Bottle Coke (500 ml) — 9 MT
- Longlife milk (1 litre) — 27 MT
- Washing powder (1 kg) — 70 MT
- Lettuce — 4 MT
- Potatoes (1 kg) — 21 MT
- Onions (1 kg) — 18 MT
- Frozen chicken (1 kg) — 39 MT
- Boerewors (1 kg) — 89 MT
- Beef mince (1 kg) — 99 MT
- Eggs (1 doz) — 32 MT
- Bully beef (300 g) — 35 MT
- Cooking oil (750 ml) — 34 MT
- Tea (100 bags) — 75 MT
- Instant coffee (250 g) — 52 MT
- Sugar 1 kg — 18 MT
- Rice (1 kg) — 20 MT

On the menu

Restaurant menus are remarkably unimaginative and similar in selection and price in Mozambique. This is simply because all menus must be passed and registered with the local authorities, and it's a hassle to have them changed. If you get tired of chicken and fish, ask your waiter whether there are specials on offer. Prices in the cheaper restaurants – where the locals might eat – range from 65 MT to 75 MT for a plate of chicken and chips or fish and rice, for example. In the more tourist-oriented establishments the same food could cost double, but be better presented. The selection could be bigger, too, with prawns for around 180 MT and pizza at 120 MT. If you will be cooking for yourself, fresh fruit, vegetables, beer, fish and even meat are available. There are some well-stocked supermarkets, and local produce is generally cheap and usually of a high standard. So, don't bring too much – you would be denying yourself the adventure of local food. Restaurant food up north is a spicy mix of Middle Eastern, Indian and Portuguese cuisine, but down south, where tourist tastes are catered for, the menus are all alike – flat chicken, steak and seafood. All along the coast, good and fresh seafood is always available, and the bread and rolls baked across the country are some of the best in Africa. Fresh fruit, vegetables and cashew nuts are sold everywhere, as are cold drinks, mineral water and excellent local beer.

Packing your food

How do you fit it all in? The most basic packing system is a set of plastic ammo boxes. They are strong and seal quite well, but they have their drawbacks. They can't lock, may not be strong enough and are always under a pile of other equipment when you need something. Steel trunks overcome some of these problems, but are still heavy and bulky. The answer is a custom-made packing system that fits into the back of your vehicle and consists of a series of drawers that pull out without disturbing your other equipment – but be warned, they aren't cheap.

8 Health and safety

Mozambique is a minefield of diseases, germs and nasty bugs, but don't let worrying about them spoil your trip. With a little preparation and care, you should be able to avoid most of them. Of course, Mozambique has real minefields too and a number of nasty bugs of the human kind, but these are also relatively easily avoided.

The danger of malaria increases in the wet season, when mosquitos breed both quickly and rampantly.

Consult the professionals

If you plan an extended, off-the-beaten-track trip, see your doctor or travel clinic for advice and shots at least six weeks before you leave. You may need to have a dental check-up, and organise a supply of any special medication you require. If you wear glasses or contact lenses, take spares and sufficient cleansing solution.

Doctors in Mozambique are resourceful and have a sound knowledge of local diseases, even though they often lack effective drugs and equipment. If you are diving, or there is a dive shop nearby, ask them for help or advice as they will have had specific medical training. Your hotel manager should also be able to refer you to the best local facilities.

That said, however, medical facilities tend to be better in South Africa, so if possible, seek treatment there. And remember to inform your doctor where you have been and what you have done; this will help his or her diagnosis. If you can't get to a doctor, go to www.health24.com, where you can ask a doctor health-related questions on-line.

Immunisation

A yellow-fever vaccination is essential and is valid for 10 years. Tetanus is a serious wound infection, so its vaccination is a must too. Also discuss cholera, hepatitis, typhoid, polio, tuberculosis, meningitis and rabies with your doctor before you depart. The list may be scary and you will probably not encounter any of these, but let your doctor guide you in what you need.

Medical insurance

Don't visit Mozambique without adequate medical insurance, the type that evacuates you if necessary. Your existing medical aid might already cover you and some vehicle insurance policies also include this cover. If not, consult a travel agent or contact the companies listed below.

Netcare 911, Cape Town, tel: +27-(0)21-952-2663, fax: +27-(0)21-592-2661, e-mail: traumalink6@worldonline.co.za, website: www.netcare911.co.za

Europ Assist, Johannesburg, tel: +27-(0)11-254-1000, fax: +27-(0)11-254-1110 e-mail: assist@europ-assistance.co.za

Along the way

Sensible eating, drinking and personal hygiene will determine your general wellbeing throughout your trip. You should be in tune with your body and know how far you can push it, and how much dirt and infection it can fight off. Travellers from within Africa tend to have a stronger immunity against local germs, and can usually eat and drink almost anything. Visitors from outside the continent, however, should take greater care with what they eat and drink and might have to stick to bottled water and well-cooked food.

Most of the towns and villages in Mozambique follow the rather sensible

> Travellers with even a slightly sensitive constitution would do well to remember the wisdom of 'peel it, boil it or leave it'.

system of slaughtering their meat and picking their fruit and vegetables early each morning. These are then all sold and consumed the same day, which allows little time for food to go off or become contaminated.

Water in some towns and resorts is okay to drink, but check first. Otherwise, drink bottled water or even soft drinks – but beer is still best!

Tummy trouble

Hopefully, you will suffer from nothing more serious than diarrhoea during your visit to Mozambique. Most of us drink or eat something that does not agree with us at some time or another. The best thing to do is to rest up somewhere comfortable and safe, stop eating, avoid alcohol and drink plenty of clean fluids.

If you have it bad, you will need an oral rehydration fluid. This sounds very impressive, but is really just sugar, salt and water – so a flat Coke with some salt added, or a Bovril drink with sugar should do the trick.

Only use blockers such as Imodium or Lomotil as a last resort; they simply stop the body from excreting the bacteria that is causing your discomfort and so prolong the agony.

Malaria

This disease is endemic in Mozambique, so it's best to take precautions wherever you are going to be. Your first defence against malaria is to avoid being bitten by mosquitoes. You don't need to know which type (the *Anopheles*), or sex (female) carries the infection, or what strain of malaria is most deadly

> **HOMEMADE REHYDRATION SOLUTION**
>
> ◆ ½ teaspoon salt
>
> ◆ ½ teaspoon baking soda
>
> ◆ 8 teaspoons sugar
>
> ◆ 1 litre clean water

(*Plasmodium falciparum*) – all mosquitoes look and sound the same, and you should treat all strains as potentially hazardous to your health.

Mozzies are most active between dusk and dawn, so it makes sense to wear long pants, long-sleeved shirts and socks, and use insect repellent in the evenings, especially if you are spending time outdoors. And when you go to bed, sleep under a net or an overhead fan.

With malaria, prevention is definitely better than cure so it's advisable to take a course of prophylactic drugs. The problem is that the malaria-carrying mosquito has built up an immunity to so many of the drugs that have been thrown at it over the years. Forget about using chloroquine or Paludrine on their own anymore. Doxycycline is okay, but has light sensitivity as a side-effect, and Larium can cause you to have some really strange dreams. Malarone (aka Malazone or Melanil) and Deltaprim are new to the market and have fewer side-effects, as is a Chinese herbal treatment called Quinghoasu.

The symptoms of malaria are fever, sweating and shivering. Fortunately, most rural doctors and clinics can recognise and treat it – usually with a good dose of quinine (10 Nivaquine tablets usually work pretty well for me – four right away, two after about eight hours, and then two on each of the following two days). Coartim, plus a course of antibiotics, is another good cure. In an emergency – you can't get to a doctor and have none of the above – pop a few malaria pills of any sort other than the ones that you were taking for prevention.

Malaria is, however, a serious matter and it's best to consult a knowledgeable doctor or travel clinic for the latest recommendations before you go.

Bilharzia

Just visible to the naked eye, the bilharzia worm infects freshwater snails in lakes and rivers. If you enter the water or wash in it, the worm could decide that you are a better host than the snail and bore into your skin – and then multiply there!

Running water is safest, but still be sure to dry yourself well after bathing. Symptoms are a high fever and blood in the urine. Bilharzia sounds scary, but your doctor can prescribe a quick and effective cure.

HIV/AIDS

While the list of bugs and diseases common to Mozambique shouldn't spoil your trip (few will ever be encountered), there is one that needs special mention – HIV/AIDS. If you're not careful in Mozambique, you are very likely to contract it and it will indeed kill you. So, no unprotected sex, no dodgy blood transfusions, and no using non-sterile needles, for whatever reason.

PLAYING IT SAFE

Basic first-aid kit

- First-aid manual
- Malaria prophylactic tablets
- Aspirin or paracetamol (for fever and pain and also to gargle for a sore throat)
- Antiseptic for disinfecting cuts and abrasions
- Adhesive bandages (both strips and rolls)
- Gauze bandages and cotton wool
- Antihistamine for allergies and to ease the itch from bites and stings
- Thermometer (standard body temperature is 37° C)
- Insect repellent
- Analgesic eye drops
- Analgesic ear drops
- Scissors and tweezers
- Safety pins
- Water purification tablets (a few drops of iodine also work)
- Sealed and sterile syringes and needles
- Sunblock and burn gel
- Throat lozenges
- Flu remedy

Optional extras

- Malaria cure
- Antibiotics
- Vitamin tablets
- Diarrhoea tablets
- Rehydration mixture
- Multivitamins

9 Getting there & getting around

Surrounded by so many countries, Mozambique is accessible from virtually every corner. Southern Mozambique is normally entered from South Africa through Komatipoort, while the north is reached from Zimbabwe via Mutare. But with Swaziland, Malawi, Tanzania and even Zambia sharing borders with Mozambique, there are many other options.

You will always find some mode of transport – even if it's only a bicycle.

Getting there by road

From South Africa Most overland traffic enters from South Africa at Komatipoort through the Lebombo/ Ressano Garcia border post (open 06h00–19h00). The other popular entry point from South Africa is up the coast from KwaZulu-Natal via Ponto do Ouro (08h00–17h00). Adventurous overlanders sometimes cross through Pafuri (08h00–16h00) in the north of the Kruger National Park, but have the problem of crossing the sometimes very deep drift across the Limpopo River lower down at Mapai in Mozambique. The other border posts in the south are from Swaziland via Goba or Namaacha (07h00–17h00). There are daily bus links between Johannesburg and Maputo at around R220 single and R400 return. Look out for Translux and Intercape.

From Zimbabwe Zimbabweans have to enter either through Mutare on their way down to Beira, or via Nyamapanda to Tete. There is no direct bus service between Zimbabwe and Mozambique – mini-buses operate on both sides, but you will be required to walk across the border.

From Malawi Travellers can choose between Zobue and on to Tete, via Milanje and down to Quelimane, Nayuchi to Cuamba, or Mandimba to Cuamba and on to Nampula and Ilha de Moçambique. All these borders are open 06h00 – 18h00.

From Tanzania Tanzania has a couple of small bush border posts, the biggest being on the coast at the mouth of the Rovuma River (06h00–17h00), which forms the border between these two countries.

Overland routes

From South Africa Working clockwise from the south, the first overland route is from KwaZulu-Natal in South Africa via the coast to enter Mozambique at Ponta do Ouro. Get onto the N2 from Johannesburg/Ermelo in the north or from Durban in the south, turn off to Jozini and travel north to Kosi Bay. Once you have crossed the border, you will need a 4x4 to negotiate the dunes to the resort of Ponta do Ouro, and the road is also pretty rough via Bela Vista on to Maputo.

An interesting alternative overland route for 4x4 drivers entering via South Africa is through the northeastern corner of the Kruger National Park at Pafuri. Once you have crossed into Mozambique, a scenic dirt road runs south along the Limpopo River to the deepwater drift at Mapai. You then have the choice of travelling east all the way through the bush to Vilankulo, or continuing south to join the Mozambican EN1 at Macia.

From Swaziland There are two routes into Moz from Swaziland. The southern one, via the border at Goba, is little used now and joins the Namaacha route. The main border crossing is in the north of Swaziland at Namaacha and follows a reasonable tar road down to Boane and on to Maputo via Matola. The Lebombo/Ressano Garcia border post through Komatipoort is by far the most popular overland route between South Africa (and Swaziland) and Moçambique. The road from Johannesburg or Pretoria goes through Witbank and down the N4 through the lush forests and pretty scenery

THE MAPUTO CORRIDOR LOGISTICS INITIATIVE

In an effort to improve the operational efficiency at borders and promote corruption-free border crossings, the Maputo Corridor Logistics Initiative (MCLI) has issued a pamphlet to assist travellers using the Lebombo/Ressano Garcia border post. First, they advise that you obtain your visa (if needed) from a Mozambican consular office before making your way to the border (although visas are obtainable at Ressano Garcia) and that you buy insurance and change money legally at the Border Country Inn Complex just before Lebombo (these services are also available at the border). The following is a list of the procedures you must follow to cross into Mozambique:

In South Africa

1. Collect your gate pass on which both the vehicle registration number and the number of people in the vehicle will be recorded.
2. Park in the designated area, whereafter all passengers disembark and proceed to the frontier office.
3. The driver of the vehicle reports to the Vehicle Registration Desk and presents the original vehicle registration document (or official copy). An authorising letter (on an official letterhead) is also required if you are not the owner of the vehicle.
4. The driver completes form DA 341 and hands it, together with the gate pass, to the official at the Vehicle Registration Desk, who then stamps both documents.
5. All passengers proceed with their passports and the gate pass to the South African Immigration Desk where the passports will be stamped.
6. Drive to the exit gate, hand in your gate pass, and proceed to the Mozambican frontier gate.

In Mozambique

1. Collect your gate pass on which both the car registration number and the number of people in your vehicle will be recorded.
2. Park in the designated area, wherafter all disembark and proceed to the frontier office.
3. If you did not obtain Mozambican vehicle insurance beforehand, purchase this at one of the insurance offices on site for 500 MT or R150 (valid for 30 days).
4. If you do not have a visa, report to the Migracao Desk and apply for one. It costs 350 MT (R171) and takes 10 minutes (if not crowded).
5. If you do have a visa, report to the Migracao Desk with your passport/visa and 40 MT (R12).
6. Each person will be required to fill in the Mozambican entry form you will receive from the official.
7. The passport is stamped, but make sure you receive a receipt for the 40 MT (R12).
8. The driver of the vehicle reports to the Vehicle Registration Desk with the original vehicle registration docu-ment (or official copy). An authorising

letter (on an official letterhead) is required if you are not the owner of the vehicle.

9. Present the DA 341 (from the South African side) and gate pass (from the Moz side) and have both stamped.

10. Pay 27 MT (only MTs are acceptable). The stamped form is your receipt.

11. Return to your car and request an officer (usually dressed in a blue uniform with orange pull-over) to inspect your vehicle and its contents, after which he will stamp your gate pass.

12. Proceed in your vehicle to the gate, hand over the gate pass, and drive through.

Note: If you are carrying anything that requires customs declaration and documentation (such as expensive camera equipment, laptops and the like), present yourself to both the South African and Mozambican customs desks when passing through the border. And should you experience any bribery or corruption, phone the MCLI in South Africa, tel: +27-(0)80-000-1190 or in Mozambique, tel: 21-307437. The website of the MCLI is www.mcli.co.za

of Mpumalanga (toll costs are R120). Nelspruit is the last large town before skirting the Kruger National Park to Komatipoort. The busy Lebombo border post is reasonably hassle-free, and then it's a quick effortless ride down the new toll road to Maputo (a toll of 68 MT is payable about halfway down and another 12 MT near Maputo).

From Zimbabwe Zimbabwe's main access into Mozambique is via Mutare. There is a good tarred road down from Harare via Marondera to Mutare. The border post at Machipanda is seldom busy and you should have no problems. Heading east to Beira on Mozambique's EN6 is a piece of cake, with the options of turning north to Tete, or getting onto the EN1 to either move south to Vilankulo and on to Maputo, or north to Gorongosa, Nampula and beyond.

From Zambia Zambia's short border with Mozambique has only one small, little-used border crossing at Cassacatiza, which links the South Luangwa region with Tete.

From Malawi Malawi's busiest link with Mozambique is the Zobue/Mwanza border post between Tete and Blantyre, but it is really just a corridor from Zimbabwe to Malawi. Another route runs from Blantyre, through the Milange border post and down to the coast around Quelimane. Other alternatives are via Liwonde to the Nayuchi border post, or from Mangochi to Mandimba. Both these routes will take you through Cuamba and on to Nampula in northern Mozambique. For backpackers with no vehicles, there is one more adventurous way of entering Moz from Malawi – across Lake

Malawi on the ferry to Likoma Island followed by a short boat ride Cobue in Mozambique. You would then make your way down via Lichinga, Mandimba and Cuamba to Nampula to eventually relax on Ilha de Moçambique.

From Tanzania The Rovuma forms a formidable border between Tanzania and Mozambique, as there are no bridges across this river. A small bush border post allows dugout canoe crossings at Masuguru, and at Mwambo – at the mouth of the Rovuma – there is a car ferry. This is one of Africa's wilder border crossings, not because it is dangerous, but because it is so off the beaten track. You can't depend on fuel availability or road conditions and can never be entirely sure that the ferry is running, but it is a challenge well worth tackling. (See also Chapter 22)

Public transport

Most of the above-mentioned borders are serviced by public transport of some sort. Fast, international bus routes run between Johannesburg and Maputo or through the Tete corridor between Zimbabwe and Malawi.

Johannesburg–Maputo Intercape Mainliner: tel: +27-(0)861-28-7287, e-mail: info@intercape.co.za, website: www.intercape.co.za; Translux: tel: +27-(0)11-774-3333, fax: +27-(0)11-774-3318, website: www.translux. co.za. Panthera Azul: tel: 21-49-2837 or +27-(0)11-337-7438, e-mail: pantazul @netactive.co.za

Harare–Beira There is no direct, non-stop bus between these two destinations. Take local transport to Mutare and then from the border to Beira.

Beautiful, tropical Pangane Beach in the north of Mozambique.

Tete Corridor Intercape and Translux (see page 49).

Some international overland safari companies visit Mozambique:

Karibu Safari: tel: +27-(0)31-563-9774, e-mail: karibu@karibu.co.za

Getting there by air

Scheduled air links with Mozambique are mainly through South African Airways, TAP (Air Portugal) and Linhas Aereas de Moçambique (LAM) airlines. There are also a number of air charter companies. Departure tax at airports is $20 for intercontinental, $10 for regional and $5 for domestic flights, payable in dollars or rands.

Mozambique's two main international airports, at Maputo and Beira, are served by a number of scheduled airlines. The Portuguese airline TAP flies from Lisbon (via Madrid), while the local Mozambican airline, LAM, flies regularly to and from Johannesburg, as does SAA. LAM flies to Harare in Zimbabwe and Lilongwe in Malawi (Air Malawi serves the Blantyre-to-Beira route), and shares the route to Manzini in Swaziland with Royal Swazi Airlines. Lesotho Airlines flies from Maseru to Maputo, while the Angolan airline flies there from Luanda. You can even arrive from Rio on Brazilian airline VARIG. Schedules change all the time, so check on the latest info with your travel agent.

Several private charter flight companies fly in and out of Mozambique from South Africa:

Charlan Air Charter, tel: +27-(0)11-701-3920, fax: +27-(0)11-701-3921, e-mail: charters@charlan.co.za
King Air Charter, tel: +27-(0)11-701-3250, fax: +27-(0)11-701-3288,
e-mail: king.air@mweb.co.za
National Airways Corporation, tel: +27-(0)11-267-5100, fax: +27-(0)11-701-3646; website: www.nac.co.za
Nelair Charters, tel: +27-(0)13-741-2012, fax: +27-(0)13-741-2013,
e-mail: coret@nelair.co.za,
website: www.nelair.co.za

Getting there by sea
Although Mozambique has a long coast line and many ports, there is no regular coastal passenger service. If you are persistent, you might be able to buy passage on one of Nedloyd's *ro-ro* ships that sail up and down the coast – speak to Manhica Freight in Maputo or Beira.

Several shipping companies do, however, offer cruises to Mozambique from South African ports. As attractive and enjoyable as these excursions are, they cannot really be regarded as options to get into the country, as it's not possible to break your journey for a stayover in Moz. These cruise companies change from year to year, but one of the established ones is:

Starlight Cruises, tel: +27-(0)11-807-5111.

Another option – if you really must arrive by sea – is to hang around the yacht club in Durban or Richards Bay until you find a yacht that is heading north and needs crew. Another exciting ocean option is between the southern Tanzanian port of Mtwara and the northern Mozambican port of Mocimboa da Praia. Local trading dhows sail these waters and, although I've never heard of anyone who's ever done it, you could always be the first! Let me know if you do…

Getting there by rail
It is also possible – but only just – to enter Mozambique by train. The South African main line, on Spoornet's Shosholoza Meyl, runs between

> If you are involved in an accident, you will have to present your third-party insurance, driver's licence and vehicle papers. You will need to inform the insurance company immediately and will be required to make a statement at the nearest police station.

CROSSING BORDERS

The following are just a few personal suggestions on the protocol to follow when crossing the border.

◆ Approach the border slowly and sedately – make no commotion or disturbance.

◆ Park sensibly in the correct areas without blocking others.

◆ Dress properly – at least sandals, shorts and shirt – and don't wear a hat, cap or sunglasses.

◆ Wait your turn – unless it's a complete free-for-all.

◆ Greet and smile at all officials – act politely and never make snide, whispered comments, or laugh.

◆ Expect polite treatment, but don't make an international incident out of official rudeness – it is only you who will suffer.

◆ Have all documents ready, but you don't have to be super-organised – this only seems to challenge officials into asking for something you don't have!

◆ Make sure you have been to both immigration and customs and have all the stamps and documentation (including insurance) you will need to show at the next roadblock.

◆ Don't smuggle anything – you may be searched and will have to bear the consequences.

◆ Avoid all bribery – even if strongly hinted at. You have a right to be fairly treated.

◆ Don't take photographs.

◆ Once formalities have been completed, don't rush off, and be ready to stop if asked.

Johannesburg and Komatipoort daily, and costs between R110 and R330. A shuttle bus then makes the connection between Komatipoort and Maputo. This service has, however, proven quite dangerous, with the likelihood of theft.

For the adventurous traveller who wants to try one of the wildest train border crossings in Africa (and possibly the world!), head for Liwonde in Malawi for the trip to Cuamba via the border at Entre Lagos. This little-known rail route between Liwonde through the border at Nayuchi goes to Cuamba and down to Nampula in northern Mozambique. It is a rough ride in box cars and not for the fainthearted (see Chapter 23).

Chancing it

Of necessity, I've listed some pretty dodgy border posts and entry routes here and, if you're feeling adventurous, then give them a go. But, take local advice first, because anything can happen – and usually does!

Getting around by road

Although Mozambique's roads are improving all the time, there are still bad potholes, sandy tracks and muddy wallows. Your vehicle is probably worth a lot of money and it's your only way around the country and home again, so drive carefully and look after it. The traffic police, *transitos* (who a wear navy-and-white uniforms), are only allowed to stop you for traffic violations and will also ask to see your papers. Stick to the speed limit (especially in towns), don't cross a solid white line, and follow all road signs. Civil police (who wear grey-and-white uniforms) may also stop you to inspect your documents, so always carry your passport, driver's licence, vehicle registration documents, temporary import permit and third-party insurance. Wear your seat belt (passengers, too), carry two warning triangles and wear shoes and a shirt when driving. If threatened with a fine, it is okay to argue politely and determinedly, especially if the fine is not warranted. Say, 'Sorry, *non comprendo*,' plead povery and offer an ice-cold Coke with a smile. Fines start at 1 000 MT (R350), and if you do need to pay one, demand an official receipt. Avoid driving at night and keep a sharp lookout for pedestrians and stray animals at all times. Hoot a lot – you are held liable if you hit a pedestrian without hooting.

Towns are quite well signposted with street names and numbers, but this is not true of the countryside. You can probably average 600 kilometres a day on tar and half that on reasonable dirt. Like all of its neighbours, driving in Mozambique is on the left.

Public transport

The main intercity bus routes are between Maputo and Beira, Beira and Tete, and Beira and Nampula. The largest Mozambican bus companies are Olivieras, Virginia and TSL. Express buses are fast and direct, while the non-express ones stop at small towns along the way. Unlike other African countries, which have designated bus stations, Mozambique's buses leave from the company's office or depot (see listings in towns).

Off these main routes, and for shorter hauls between small towns, local buses ply the roads. Where conditions become too rough for these smaller buses (which are sometimes no more than benches in the back of a truck), light pick-ups and trucks run. Minibuses and light pick-ups are known collectively as *chapas* (pronounced 'shappas') in Moz and run almost anywhere, in towns and out in the countryside. Remember, this is Africa – people are on the move, and if a vehicle has wheels, someone will take you where you want to go (for a fee, of course).

Getting around by boat

Ferry boats from Maputo take you across the bay to Catembe or out to Inhaca Island. It is also possible to take a short ferry ride between Inhambane and Maxixe, and various kinds of boats will get you to the islands of the Bazaruto Archipelago from Vilankulo and to the islands of the Querimbas Archipelago, north of Pemba.

Getting around by air

The Mozambican airline, LAM, runs scheduled flights between Maputo, Beira, Tete, Quelimane, Nampula, Pemba and Lichinga. Fares range between 3 200 MT and 6 000 MT. Most charter companies operate from outside Moz (see listings page 51), but a couple that are local include:

San Air, Quelimane, tel/fax: 24-21-3085
STA, Nampula, tel: 26-21-4653.
Unique Air Charters, Maputo, tel: 21-46-5592, fax: 21-46-5525
Air Viatur, Pemba, tel: 72-221-4310

10 Practical information

One's first visit to Mozambique can be a bit of a culture shock. It is so different from other southern African countries and even unlike its Central and East African neighbours. But, relax, Mozambicans are friendly and laid-back. The following information should ease your way into and around the country.

Mozambique's waters are most famous for their game fishing.

Too many shells means that far too much fishing has been taking place here.

For easy reference, the following categories are listed alphabetically.

Activities

Birding The world's most popular pastime is well catered for in Mozambique. Unlike the wild animals, which were decimated during the civil war, birdlife survived reasonably intact. The country's wide variety of habitats and climatic conditions support a large number of species. From the mangrove swamps and offshore islands to the montane forests of Namuli, endemics abound. Unfortunately, there is a big gap in scientific knowledge and literature on Mozambique's birds, a shortcoming the Mozambique Bird Atlas Project is attempting to rectify. The project also publishes two field guides, *Birds of the Maputo Special Reserve* and *Birds of the Niassa Reserve*. Find out more on the website www.aviandemographyunit.org

Diving Warm, clear water, near-pristine coral reefs and an abundance of sea life make Mozambique a divers' paradise. Snorkelling, scuba diving and spearfishing are all catered for by numerous dive operations up and down the coast. Some of the best sites are at Ponta do Ouro, Inhaca Island, Zavora, Paindane, Jangamo, Tofo, Barra, Morrungulo, Pomene, the Bazaruto Archipelago, Pemba and the Querimbas Archipelago. With smaller, colourful reef fish like fusiliers, coachmen, snapper and goldies, and game fish such as kingfish, barracuda and brindlebass, as well as turtles, mantas, dolphins, dugongs and whales, I wasn't lying when I said it was paradise! Bring your own gear, hire on the spot or – if you've never dived before – take a dive course and enter a whole new world. There are, however, a few rules and regulations of which you should be aware: divers' tax is 150 MT, spearfishing is not allowed with scuba gear, shellfish season is from 1 July to 31 December annually, and the lobster and crab season is from 1 November to 28 February.

Fishing The Mozambique coastline is famous for its game fishing. The clear, blue waters teem with king mackerel, dorado, wahoo, kingfish, bonito and yellowfin tuna. Boats can be launched or chartered from fishing resorts almost anywhere along the coast – Ponta do Ouro, the Inhambane coast, Pomene, Bazaruto Archipelago and Pemba are particularly good. The sailfish season peaks from June to August, but summer is the best time if it's marlin you're after. Angling from the shore can also be productive, saltwater fly-fishing is increasing in popularity and catch-and-release is encouraged. Driving on the beaches is banned (the fine is a hefty 5 000 MT), except at strictly controlled boat-launch sites. A marine tax of 600 MT is payable to the local marine officer before you can launch your boat (jetskis 300 MT) and there may be a slipway fee of around 50 MT.

Game-viewing At the moment, the chances of seeing great herds of game and the Big Five are pretty slim, but things are looking up. **Gorongosa National Park** has been demined and reopened. Chitengo camp has been cleaned up, and it is now possible to camp there or stay over in basic bungalows. The network of roads in the park is passable (sometimes only by 4x4) and there is now a team of dedicated rangers. It's amazing how wild animals survive by hiding out in pockets of bush all around the country and, with protection and grazing in the park, the animals will start returning. There is also a plan to reintroduce game and upgrade the camp.

Maputo Elephant Reserve is reasonably accessible and still has elephants and game rangers, so all is not lost there.

The **Niassa Reserve** up on the Tanzanian border probably has the most game as it slumbers in peaceful isolation, but getting there can be something of an expedition.

The recently declared **Great Limpopo Transfrontier Park**, linking South Africa's Kruger National park with others in Mozambique and Zimbabwe, has an optimistic future. (See page 22 for more details.)

Hiking and mountain climbing Although opportunities for these two activities do exist, they are not well catered for in Mozambique. But

Diving is one of the most popular drawcards to the Mozambican coastline.

Warm waters and trade winds are great for sailing, but conditions may change quickly.

knowing the hiking and climbing fraternity, this is just the sort of challenge they welcome. The granite domes, inselbergs and sheer rock faces that occur between Cuamba and Nampula will make any true rock climber drool, while the hills around Gurue offer great hiking opportunities. (There are, however, still a few landmines around and even fewer facilities, so beware.) It is also possible to hike along the beach between the resorts of Jangamo, Tofo and Barra, or between Morrungulo and Pomene, or even Vilankulo and Inhassoro.

Off-road driving and quadbiking While off-road opportunities may be hard to find in your home country – or you have to pay exorbitant fees just to drive on a commercial 4x4 track – you don't have to look far in Mozambique. In fact, it is sometimes quite difficult to avoid a good **4x4** challenge here. The sandy tracks down to the beach resorts in the south and the muddy trails in the north are true challenges, but remember, if something breaks you can't just phone the local garage to come tow you in, so you will need to be relatively self-sufficient in this regard.

Quadbikes are a completely different ballgame, however, and I can only condone them if used sensibly. In Mozambique you see too many irresponsible riders (sometimes unlicensed youngsters, but many adults too) tearing up the enviroment and disturbing others. Many holiday-makers tow them down and they are also for hire at a few resorts. Please use them with care and consideration.

Surfing Let's be honest, there're a lot of hungry sharks off Mozambique. But if you really must surf, the best breaks are 'Backdoor' and 'Monument' at Tofinho, just south of Tofo in the Inhambane district. Spoken of with awe in surfing circles around the world, the steep take-off over a shallow reef ledge will get the adrenalin pumping as you rush in at the rocky headland. Most beaches and points have something to surf, but there are not too many boards around, so bring your own.

Watersports Windsurfing, sailing, water-skiing and jet-skiing are all popular and, if you don't have your own equipment, it can be hired at most of the larger resorts. Renting a local dhow with captain and crew is a great way to access and explore the islands off the coast. Vilankulo to Bazaruto is your easiest option.

Car hire

If you need to hire a vehicle to tour around Mozambique, do so in South Africa if you can. South African operators offer 4x4 vehicles and campers, and complete all the documentation necessary to cross the border. Check the advertisers in *Getaway* magazine (see the website www.getawaytoafrica.com/magazine/allfeatureindex/ or contact:

Britz 4x4 Rentals, tel: +27-(0)11-396-1860, e-mail: britz@iafrica.com, website:
 www.britz.co.za
Kea Campers, tel: +27 (0)11-397-2435, fax: +27-(0)11-397-2679, e-mail: infoget@keacampers.co.za, website: www.keacampers.co.za
Hire-a-Landrover, tel: +27-(0)11-621-6352, e-mail: neil.kemp@smhgroup.co.za, website: www.hirealandrover.co.za
Bushlore Africa, tel: +27-(0)11-792-5300, e-mail: info@bushlore.com
AJC 4x4 Hire, tel: +27-(0)14-717-3631, fax: +27-(0)14-717-3061, e-mail:

andre@ajc4x4sa.co.za, website: www.ajc4x4sa.co.za

In Mozambique, car-hire firms tend to operate mostly from the large cities and towns like Maputo, Beira and Pemba. See the individual listings under those towns.

Credit cards

In general, hotels, garages, restaurants and shops do not accept credit cards, with the exception of some luxury establishments. But plastic is beginning to gain ground, and recently Bank Austral and Bank International de Moçambique (BIM) introduced ATMs that accept Both Visa and MasterCard.

Customs regulations

You may import, free of duty and tax, the following items:

◆ 1 litre spirits

◆ 2.5 litres wine

◆ 400 cigarettes

◆ other goods (such as groceries) to the value of $200.

Firearms are prohibited, and if you have items such as a laptop or expen-

---

PUBLIC HOLIDAYS

1 January – New Year's Day
3 February – Heroes' Day
7 April – Women's Day
1 May – Workers' Day
25 June – Independence Day
7 September – Victory Day
25 September – Armed Forces Day
4 October – Day of Peace
25 December – Christmas Day

sive camera equipment, it is advisable to declare them.

Electricity

Electricity is 220V and uses the two- or three-pinned round plugs (same as South Africa). Surges, 'brownouts' (when voltage drops quite drastically, with possible dire consequences for electricity-driven equipment) and blackouts (complete power cuts) are common, so protect sensitive electrical appliances. Some resorts that are not hooked up to mains electricity generate their own, but frown on guests using their own appliances.

E-mail and Internet

Most large towns have Internet cafés, and hotels and lodges sometimes offer Internet access for their guests. There is also a TDM (national telephone company) office in every town, sometimes with Internet access.

For tourist and other information on Mozambique, browse the following useful **websites**:

www.mozambique.mz
www.newafrica.com
www.mozguide.com
www.cia.gov
www.fco.gov.uk

Embassies

The following countries have embassies in Mozambique (all of which are based in Maputo):

Australia: 1st floor, 33 Story Building, corner Zedequias Manganhela and Vladimir Lenine, tel: 21-42-2780
Canada: 1128 Av Julius Nyerere, tel: 21-49-2623
France: 2361 Av Julius Nyerere, tel: 21-49-1603
Germany: 506 Rua Damiao de Gois, tel: 21-49-2714
Malawi: 75 Av Kenneth Kaunda, tel: 21-49-2676
Netherlands: 285 Rua de Mukunbura, tel: 21-49-0031

TIPPING AND BARGAINING

Tipping is not usually expected in the cheaper bars and restaurants, but between 5% and 10% is customary in up-market establishments (unless a service charge has already been added to the bill). Too much tipping spoils the delicate relationship between tipper and tippee, so rather show extra appreciation by personally thanking staff for good service. Bargaining is a necessary evil if you don't want to be ripped off. The further off the beaten track you go, the less you need to bargain; it's the smooth operators in the big towns that see a tourist coming and hike the price. The prices of curios and handicrafts (in fact, anything that a tourist may buy) are usually inflated – it's even acceptable to bargain down the price of accommodation. But don't be too mean – the service provider usually needs the money more than you do. And don't bargain just for the fun of it; only enter into negotiations if you truly are interested in buying.

Portugal: 720 Av Julius Nyerere,
tel: 21-49-0316
South Africa: 41 Av Eduardo Mondlane,
tel: 21-49-0059
Swaziland: Av Kwame Nkrumah,
tel: 21-49-2451
Tanzania: 852 Av Martires de Machava,
tel: 21-49-0110
United Kingdom: 310 Av Vladimir Lenine,
tel: 21-42-0111
USA: 193 Av Kenneth Kaunda,
tel: 21-49-2797
Zambia: 1286 Av Kenneth Kaunda,
tel: 21-49-2452

Maps

I like to use the *Road Atlas to Southern and East Africa* (scale 1:1 500 000) published by MapStudio, tel: +27-(0) 11-807-2292, fax: +27-(0)11-807-0409, e-mail: research@mapstudio.co.za, website: www.mapstudio.co.za

Another good map is *Michelin Map No. 955* of Africa south of the equator (scale 1:4 000 000)

Sunbird Publishing has also produced a number of good maps and atlases of southern Africa, tel: +27-(0)11-622-2900.

Office hours

Banks are open 08h00–15h00, Mondays to Fridays. **Shops and offices** generally open 08h00–12h00 and 14h00–18h00 on weekdays, and 08h00–12h00 on Saturdays.

Post, parcels and couriers

The postal system is probably too slow to be of much use to travellers making their way around Mozambique, but the DHL courier company is quite well represented (see the individual listings in towns).

Radio and TV

The local radio stations play some good African music, but television is pretty poor. Satellite TV is shown in many tourist bars, restaurants and hotels – great for keeping up to date with international news and sport.

Shopping

Every city, town and village has at least one market where you should find the basic necessities. In smaller towns, there are generally very few shops, but in the cities (Maputo, Beira and Chimoio), there are branches of Shoprite, the South African chain of supermarkets, where you can stock up with anything your heart desires. For souvenirs and mementoes of Mozambique look out for woodcarvings and masks by the Makonde tribe in the north, intricate silver jewellery from Ibo island and baskets and pottery from around Inhambane. *Capulanas*, the colourful cloth worn by women around their waists, can be bought at almost any market and make an easily transportable memento that can be used as a tablecloth, wrap or wall hanging. And that old Mozambican standby, cashew nuts, still makes a good gift for the guy who's been looking after your dog back home. A special plea to all visitors to Mozambique – don't buy shells, coral, ivory or turtle products. Not only is it illegal, but it will only encourage the harvesting of the 'commodities' and continue to do the country and the environment irreparable harm.

Telephones

Your best option in Mozambique is a cellular phone. You could have your existing cellphone linked to 'international roaming', which has the advantage of retaining your original phone number, but is not available to pay-as-you-go clients. A better option is to buy a local starter pack and sim card when you enter the country (about 120 MT and available everywhere, even at border posts). Airtime, known as *giro*, can be purchased anywhere. Operated by Vodacom and mCell, the network is amazingly widespread and still expanding. The service is not expensive, and SMSs are almost for nothing. Even some out-of-the-way lodges have obtained reception by erecting high antennas – ask them to hook up your phone if you must make a call. Please note that a Mozambican sim card and number is cancelled and becomes invalid if not used for 45 consecutive days.

The local fixed-line telephone service in Mozambique is poor but improving fast. Public phones are popping up all over, or look out for TDM's green offices in all the towns. Sometimes it is only a mobile container, but there will always be a connecting line and public phone from which you will be able to make all

To make an international call from Mozambique, dial 00 for the operator.

DIALLING CODES

Local area codes are as follows:

◆ Beira	23
◆ Chimoio	251
◆ Chokwe	281
◆ Inhambane	293
◆ Maputo	21
◆ Nacala and Nampula	26
◆ Pemba	272
◆ Quelimane	24
◆ Songo and Tete	252
◆ Vilankulo	293
◆ Xai-Xai	282

calls, including international. They also sometimes have an Internet connection and fax facilities. The international dialling code for Mozambique is 258. The area codes are used everytime you dial a number, even when you are calling from within that area.

Tourist information

The **National Tourist Organisation** (ENT) has an office at 1179 Av 25 de Setembro, Maputo, tel: 21-42-1794, fax: 21-42-1795, e-mail: entur@virconn.com

Visa extensions

If you are nearing the end of your visa, it can be extended at any immigration office (*migracao*). Obviously, they can be found at borders, but also at some ports and in all provincial capitals. But be warned – do not let your visa expire, or you will be in for a hefty fine.

> Various changes have been made recently to the dialling codes, fixed line and mobile phone numbers. This book reflects the latest information at time of going to press, but more changes are rumoured to be in the pipeline, so be sure to check before dialling.

11 South of Maputo

Your long journey through Mozambique begins by approaching the Ponta do Ouro border post (open 08h00–17h00) from Kosi Bay in the extreme north of KwaZulu-Natal in South Africa. Coming off the N2 from either Durban or Johannesburg, the road passes through Jozini and then Kangwanase (turn left where the road forks after the Spar supermarket) before reaching the border. Hopefully, you have a smooth passage through the formalities (see Chapter 5 for tips on crossing borders) and you find yourselves on Mozambican soil (S26° 51.841 E32° 49.761).

The bountiful coral reefs around Inhaca Island reward divers with extraordinary sights of colour.

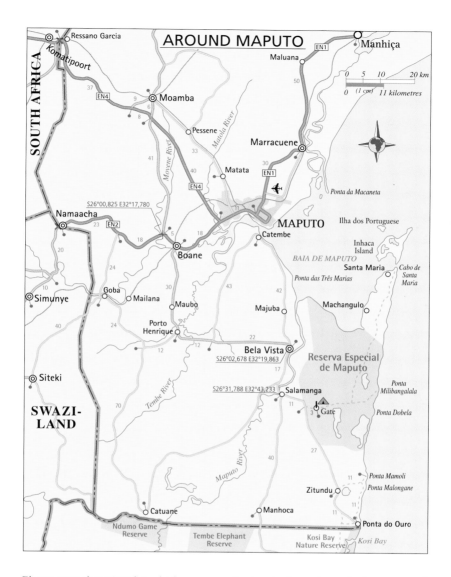

AROUND MAPUTO

Please note that visas bought here can only be used in the southern area and you may not exit through any other border post. Swing left and head north to take the sandy track to Bela Vista and on to Maputo (14 kilometres to Zitundu), or keep right and east along the border fence towards the coast and Ponta do Ouro. Tracks to Ponta veer off in all directions, but hold your heading and after 8.5 kilometres of sandy 4x4 tracks over the dunes you will reach the little marketplace in the centre of town (S26°50.385 E32°52.994).

Introducing Ponta do Ouro

Ponta do Ouro (meaning 'Point of Gold') saw its first small wave of adventurous visitors in 1995, when the border opened, and it's been increasing ever since. Mains electricity arrived in 2002 and by 2003 all landmines had been cleared. Houses are being renovated and wealthy Maputans visit over the weekends. But, other than the small stretch of tar near the market, the roads in town are all as sandy and churned up as they are on the way from the border – especially during the South African school-holiday season. This is also the time when quadbikes, jetskis and the South African rand dominate, English is widely understood, and you can't even get a decent hot peri-peri chicken in the crowded restaurants. But the holiday-makers don't come to have their palates burned, they're here for the great golden beach, good surf, diving, fishing and other watersports, such as kite surfing. A headland to the south forms a large protected bay, ideal for launching boats, and the packed dive-school boats attest to the fact that Ponta has been rated one of the top 10 dive sites in the world.

Over the hill and down towards the beach is the nucleus of a little town centre. Clustered around a parking area are a few shops, bars, restaurants, a petrol station and public access to the beach. Just above the beach is the beautifully positioned Florestinha do Indico restaurant and bar, ideal for sundowners, and where you can feel the sand between your toes. Behind it, on the square, is Babalaza, another laid-back eatery with a local flavour and wide veranda that serves good espresso. Next door, above the shops, is the spacious Fishmongers Baracas, serving tasty surf-and-turf specials, and popular with holiday-makers. Next door again is the Bula-Bula restaurant with indoor, patio or garden tables. Café del Mar overlooks all of this from the highest dune across the road and serves up the best view, cold draft beer and loud music. All menus in Ponta offer very similar options of omelettes, steak rolls, grilled chicken and a good selection of seafood, dominated by prawns. Prices range from 60 MT for light meals to 300 MT for a big plate of prawns.

On this same square are a couple of little grocery shops – don't expect too much, but at least you can buy ice, bread and booze – and over on the northern side is the Petromoc service station selling petrol and diesel (although, how they drag the tankers in here over the dunes remains a mystery to me). South of the square, at the entrance to the camp site, is the new bakery, Scandals, which sells delicious bread, rolls, pies and muffins, as well as light meals and good filter coffee. Back at the market, where we came in, is the new and neatly tiled Peixeria e Talho Tembo, selling fresh fish, cheese, eggs, chicken, bacon and vacuum-packed meat and sausage from South Africa – all at prices only slightly more than those across the border. The Peixeria can also organise game-fishing expeditions.

Accommodation in Ponta

As can be expected, there is a good selection of accommodation in Ponta, but you must book in advance if you are planning to visit during the South African school holidays or long weekends. The large **Tanje Beach Resort**, on the beach just south of the square, is the official camp site. The ablution blocks are adequate, the sites well shaded and partially grassed, and accommodation costs 195 MT per person per day midweek and 255 MT over weekends and holidays. They also have well-used two-bed chalets at 600 MT per chalet per night midweek and 870 MT on weekends and holidays. Two-roomed, four-bed chalets are 1560 MT and 2160 MT and six beds will cost you 2640 MT and 3450 MT. All chalets have a gas hotplate, cutlery and crockery. For bookings, tel: 21-40-3217 or 21-40-9617. Lifeguards are on duty during the busy holiday periods (although the beach is quite safe for swimming) and the resort is also home to a couple of dive operations, a dolphin research centre, small shop, bar and restaurant.

This is a very popular and busy place, and not for someone looking for a quiet, restful holiday.

The other large accommodation complex is the **Motel do Mar**, on a quieter section of the beach. They rent out double-storeyed apartments, which are serviced and kitted out for four people, with fridge, hotplate, cutlery and crockery. A complicated pricing structure ranges between 1370 MT, midweek out-of-season non-sea-facing and 3290 MT for a sea-facing apartment during high season. They also have a small bar and restaurant. For bookings and info, tel/fax: 21-65-0000.

Away from the busy beach is the compact, quiet and well-run **O Lar do Ouro Guest Lodge**. Neat-as-a-pin double or twin *en-suite* rooms (with mozzie nets and screens) are set in a small garden with pool and patio. Dinner, bed and breakfast per person per day costs 1200 MT to 1350 MT (off-peak to peak). Theresa is an excellent cook, and Janice makes sure everything runs smoothly. Contact them, tel/fax: 21-65-0038, local cell: 82-776-1280, South African cell: +27-(0)82-574-0213, e-mail: info@pontadoouro.com, website: www.pontadoouro.com

Other accommodation options in Ponta are the new reed huts with shared ablutions behind the **Café del Mar** – a great position, but noisy due to the late-night bar. Dinner, bed and breakfast here costs 1200 MT. Contact DC on tel: 21-65-0048, fax: 21-65-0049, e-mail: cafedelmarponta@tropical.co.moz. There is also **Coco Cabanas**, three streets back from the beach. A bit run-down, they offer self-catering cabanas that sleep four for 1050 MT to 1425 MT per night (off-peak to peak). Contact Jorge in South Africa, tel: +27-(0)11-478-3686, fax: +27-(0)11-478-3684, e-mail: gbastos@hixnet.co.za. Three doors down is **1023 Backpackers** (look out for the '1023') . They have dorms and double rooms, a kitted-out kitchen, linen and towels and charge 285 MT per person out of season, while in season they usually rent out the whole house for 2400 MT per day. Speak to Chris, who is the chef at Scandals.

Diving off Ponta

Because of the accessible tropical reefs (Pinnacles, Doodles and Bass City), variety of fish, lack of current and excellent visability (up to 30 metres), diving is hugely popular in Ponta. The best diving conditions are from November to May, but it gets very crowded during the South African school holidays. There are a couple of dive operations based at the camp site, with their own reed huts or tented accommodation. **Simply Scuba** is based in South Africa, tel: +27-(0)11-678-0972, fax: +27-(0)11-678-0970, e-mail: dive@simplyscuba.co.za, website: www.simplyscuba.co.za. The other operation, **Scuba Adventures**, also has South African contacts, tel: +27-(0)11-648-9648, fax: +27-(0)11-487-2605, e-mail: scubatravel@iafrica.com. Set back from the beach, with very comfortable accommodation in a beautiful and restful garden setting, is **Devocean Diving**. Speak to Kerry or Damien on the South African cell: +27-(0)82-332-9029, Moz cell: 82-905-6630, e-mail: devoceandiving@absamail.co.za, website: www.devoceandiving.com. All the above-mentioned operations offer gear hire (full gear per day 525 MT), individual dives (around 550 MT with own gear), a range of courses (four-day PADI open-water course 7200 MT) and accommodation packages (three nights, five dives, food and accommodation at 6000 MT).

Another exciting dive option is snorkelling with the dolphins. **The Dolphin Centre**, based at the camp site, is involved in research and the conservation of the approximately 200 bottlenose dolphins in the area. They offer four-day packages (7500 MT all inclusive) or individual dives (480 MT per hour), which take you into the realm of these mammals, with the bonus of possibly encountering humpback whales. Contact Angie in South Africa, tel: +27-(0)11-462 8103, or on the Moz cell: 82-271-6010, e-mail: addelphicent@mweb.co.za, website: www.dolphin-encounters.co.za.

Out and about in Ponta

There is no bank in Ponta do Ouro, but also no need to change money, as the locals will accept almost any currency, especially South African rands. For medical emergencies, first speak to your lodge owner or dive master, as there is no hospital or pharmacy in town. They will be able to assist or advise you whether to use the little local clinic (opposite the big radio tower down the Ponta Mamoli road) or evacuate down to the Manguzi hospital in KwaZulu-Natal.

For public transport, there are *chapas* (see page 53), which leave for Maputo daily from the border or Ponta; from Maputo, they depart from the Catembe Ferry. The town is quite safe, with very little crime or harrassment. There are public phones around town (the number for the one at the camp entrance is 21-65-0006), good Mozambique cellphone reception and, if you get up onto the highest hill in town, you can even get reception for a South African cellphone number. There is a well-stocked craft market down near the camp site and the police station is just off the main intersection in town. Finally, if you don't have a 4x4, you can still visit Ponta by driving to the nearby border and organising a transfer through the place where you are staying – your car will be safe and under guard till you return.

Beyond Ponta

Leaving Ponta do Ouro, you can head inland to join the 'main road' by leaving town the way you came in. But, instead of heading for the border, keep slightly north and follow the power lines to meet up with the road leading up from the border (all sandy, 4x4 driving). This passes through Zitunda and eventually Bela Vista on its way to Maputo. A more interesting alternative is the coastal track up past Ponta Malongane and Ponta Mamoli. Start at the main signposted intersection in Ponta do Ouro (S26°50.424 E32°53.070) and head north out of town through the residential part, passing the medical clinic on your left. After approximately 5 kilometres of sandy track, you will reach the turn-off right to the rustic little **Campismo Ninho** camp site, situated high on a ridge overlooking the ocean. There was no one around when we visited the place, but I did see some very basic ablution facilities.

A couple of kilometres further, you will reach a much smarter and well-organised place, the Ponta Malongane Holiday Resort. Like a secure, self-contained village, it offers all you need for a holiday by the sea: horse riding, fishing charters, diving, snorkelling, shop, bar and restaurant – and all are very conservation conscious (they ban quadbikes). Well-shaded camping is 120 MT to 240 MT per person (out-of-season midweek to in-season weekend), while rondavels with *en-suite* bathrooms cost 360 MT to 465 MT per person. The dive centre and fishing charter only seem to operate during the busier times of the year, so be sure to check with them first. Contact Malongane in South Africa, tel: +27-(0)13-741-1975, fax: +27-(0)13-741-3730, e-mail: reservations@malongane.co.za, website: www.malongane.co.za

The southern resort of Ponta Mamoli offers many activities, including horseriding.

The narrow, sandy track winds north through the coastal forest, skirting small lakes where busy pied kingfishers work the waters (the area offers a selection of pristine birding habitats). After 11 kilometres, you will reach an old, potholed tar road. Turn left and travel a further 3.5 kilometres to the **Ponta Mamoli Resort** (another 8 kilometres brings you to Zitundu and the 'main road' to Maputo). This resort offers a bar, restaurant, pool and air-conditioned conference facilities, and also suggests that you celebrate your wedding there. Accommodation is in modern timber chalets built amid the dunes on raised decks and linked by wooden walkways. With *en-suite* hot showers, overhead fans, mosquito nets and daily servicing, they cost between 1 800 MT and 2 520 MT per person per night, inclusive of dinner and breakfast. The resort boasts a watersport centre that offers turtle expeditions as well as the usual diving and fishing. For bookings contact the resort on tel: +27-(0)11-444-3260, fax: +27-(0)11-444-1920, e-mail: bookings@pontamamoli.com, website: www.pontamamoli.com

Head back to Zitundu via the incongruous old tar road and rejoin the sand road north to Salamanga. This road has some deep wallows that fill with water during the rainy season, but are quite easy to negotiate as the sand hardens when wet. After 27 kilometres, you will reach the turn-off to the **Reserva Especial de Maputo**, also known as **Maputo Elephant Reserve** (S26°31.788 E32°43.233), and 3 kilometres down this road is the gate and main camp. Entry fees are 210 MT per person and per vehicle. A daily fee of 105 MT is levied for camping, which is the only accommodation available. The main route is down to Ponta Milibangalala (what a great name!) on the coast, where there are also camping facilities. Halfway down this road is a signposted road north to Cabo de Santa Maria. Outside the reserve (so no camping fees) and at the northern tip of a peninsula, it is just a stone's throw away from the southern tip of Inhaca Island. There are reported to be at least 300 elephants in the reserve, but not much else other than similar flora and fauna to that on the road coming up. We saw fresh elephant dung and footprints, but the forest is dense and the ellies very skittish, so don't expect to see much.

Continuing north, the road improves a little after the reserve turn-off, and **Salamanga** town, with its bridge (watch out for the vicious speed bumps!) across the Maputo River, is reached after another 11 kilometres. It is here that the decent tar road starts, and buses run up and down from Maputo (actually from Catembe, across the bay by ferry). About 17 kilometres up the road is the short turn-off to the pretty little town of **Bela Vista**. There is no reason to turn in here, but if you do, you can eat and sleep at the neat little **Complexo Quinta Mila**, down an avenue of old flamboyant trees and overlooking the wide Maputo River. Prices are very reasonable: 500 MT for a double room and 700 MT for *en-suite*. A basic meat, fish and chicken menu with a selection of cold drinks makes it a pity that there's no real reason for stopping over here. Contact Emelia, tel: 21-62-0027, cell: 82-320-4500.

If you are heading for the Ressano Garcia border and South Africa, you could turn west to Boane just north of Bela Vista (S26°19.612 E32°39.646). Then it is 64 kilometres of sand and dirt (passable with a two-wheel-drive) to the tarred road at Boane (S26°02.678 E32°19.863). A right turn here would take you down to Maputo via Matola, but turn left to continue your drive to the South African border. About 5 kilometres up the road is the turn-off left (S26°00.825 E32°17.780) to the Swazi border at Namaacha, and another 41 kilometres will bring you to the main EN4 toll highway between Maputo and the Ressano Garcia border post into South Africa.

But from Bela Vista, you're on your way to Maputo, so head straight for 42 kilometres on a good gravel road until you reach **Catembe**. With its position across the bay from Maputo, Catembe offers an impressive view of the capital city's skyline. The ferry costs a mere 5 MT per person and an expensive 200 MT per vehicle. Smaller, cheaper, but way more dodgy passenger-only ferries ply this route more frequently, but check them out first.

Driving onto the ferry is pretty painless – to the end of a long jetty and then down a ramp – but you have to wait until there are at least eight vehicles on board before she will depart. If the ferry is still across on the Maputo side, the wait can be much longer, so be prepared. You will dock at the jetty the Inhaca Island ferry used to use opposite the Ministry of Finance, and there you are – you've arrived in downtown Maputo.

12 Maputo

Maputo is developing so fast that it is difficult to give it an accurate and up-to-date description. Visit it today and you will find a new 33-storey building, shopping malls selling international fashion brands, new state-of-the-art hotels with bluetooth Internet connections and lovingly restored old buildings. Residents are painting and improving their homes and street crime has diminished drastically. Business and industry is booming and it's becoming easier to get things done. And a whole new generation of residents and tourists has grown up not knowing who or what Lourenço Marques was. Yes, Maputo is striding ahead – but I wish they would fix the holes in their roads and sidewalks!

The rusty old ferry runs from Maputo across the bay to Catembe.

MAPUTO

Maputo Bay

Praia da Polana

Espirito Santo

to Holiday Inn and Costa do Sol

CENTRAL

POLANA

ALTO MAÉ

MAPUTO

0   200   400 m

0   240 metres
(1 cm)

Maputo has style – leafy avenues lined with jacaranda and flame trees, an accessible and popular seafront, an interesting variety of buildings and architecture, and seafood and sidewalk cafés. The people have style, too. They appreciate the good life – good food, good music, nice clothes and regular siestas. It's difficult not to fall under the city's spell.

The old city

But it hasn't always gone well for Maputo. The Portuguese navigator, Lourenço Marques, came ashore in 1545 to find a protected bay with potential for trade. Later Inhaca Island, just off-shore, was chosen by the Portuguese as a safe base for a small settlement. The Dutch and British tried to establish trading posts in the 17th and 18th centuries, but there was little profit to be made in this quiet outpost – it was simply too far outside the sphere of East Coast Swahili influence. What changed Lourenço Marques' (as Maputo was then known) fortunes was the discovery of diamonds and gold in what was then the Transvaal province of South Africa. The Witwatersrand developed, a railway line was built in 1894 and Lourenço Marques (or simply LM) and its port began to prosper. By the mid-20th century, the city had also become the playground of hordes of Transvaal holiday-makers. But independence, politics and civil war put an end to all that and it is only now that the city, with a new name and new attitude, is rising again.

Getting around Maputo

Maputo has a very easy-to-follow, rectangular shape with its streets laid out in a grid pattern. The old hub of the city was above the port and ranged up Av Samora Machel towards the botanical gardens and cathedral. But lack of renovation and restoration in this area (which has great potential) has meant that the main shopping, eating, drinking, staying and general strolling-around area has shifted to Av Julius Nyerere in the Polana district.

Inhaca Island is blessed with some of the most pristine beaches in Mozambique.

> ## A quick note on swimming
> in Maputo… Use your hotel's pool, if it has one. The beaches are tidal and shallow, and the water is murky from pollution and river inflow.

These two areas are linked by the city's main thoroughfare, Av 24 de Julho, which also houses many important and useful addresses for the tourist. None of the once-popular budget accommodation in the old downtown area can be recommended anymore as better, cleaner and safer establishments have sprung up elsewhere.

Rich history, pleasant location and a vibrant population have made Maputo a city well worth exploring. Coming from the South African border of Rossana Garcia or from the north of Mozambique, you would enter the city down the western end of Av 24 de Julho. Watch out for the traffic lights at all intersections, there's only one per corner and if you're in front of the queue, you might not see it. The roads are fairly well signposted, but badly potholed in places. To head downtown and to the port, turn right at Av Karl Marx or Av Vladimir Lenin (communism was big after independence). The main road out of this busy area is Av 25 de Setembro. Heading east, you will pass through what is becoming a new fast-food and shopping area with Nando's, Pizza Inn, Debonairs Pizza, Steers, Standard Bank (with an ATM and currency exchange) and Mobil service station all along the lefthand side of the road. On the right-hand side is the original fairground,

with small restaurants that used to be the best budget eats (still pretty good value and good fun, but getting a little tatty). The Av 25 de Setembro becomes the Marginal and swings left and north to follow the coast past the Naval Club. Families park along this pretty palm-lined promenade in the evenings and over weekends. Dads fish while mums stroll and the kids ride bikes.

A left turn swings off just after the presidential palace to bring you up into Av Julius Nyerere and you head back south into town past the magnificent old Polana Hotel, the ultra-modern Hotel Avenida, trendy bars and restaurants, and the all-new shopping mall on the corner of Av 24 de Julho. A right turn at this intersection will take you back into the centre of town.

Walking Maputo

The main tourist sights are all around the older part of town and can be seen on a walking tour. Start at the top of Av Samora Machel outside the imposing **Cathedral of Nossa Senhora da Conceicao** – if you have a car, park it safely outside the Hotel Rovuma next door. Take off down the road and you will pass the **Casa de Ferro** (Iron House). This prefabricated iron building was designed by Eiffel (of 'Tower' fame) as the governor's residence, but was too hot and stuffy to be of any use to him. Behind this folly is the **Jardim Tunduru** (botanical gardens). A little overgrown and in need of some pruning, but I think it's great that it survived Mozambique's recent turmoil. The buildings further down Av Samora Machel are also in need of some freshening up, especially the block on the right-hand side of the road, which is a real gem, just crying out for restoration. Down at the bottom, on the left, just above the harbour, is a fort built by the Portuguese in the mid 19th century and still in pretty good shape. And across the road is the **Praca 25 do Junho** where a regular Saturday craft market is held. Turn right here and wend your way through the narrow streets to the railway station on Praca Trabalhadores – its impressive dome was also designed by Eiffel. Head one block up and into Av 25 de Setembro where you'll find the **Central Market**. Curios, fruit, vegetables, almost anything can be found here, but watch your valuables – pickpockets rule! Back up Av Samora Machel brings you to the end of this little circuit and back to your car.

Around Maputo

There are other interesting excursions that can be made from Maputo. The **Hotel Costa do Sol** is at the far end of the Marginal (6 kilometres past the Holiday Inn) and is a great place for a meal or sundowner on the wide veranda overlooking the beach and curio sellers. As well as prawns, chicken and steak (all around 200 MT), they serve a mouth-watering selection of chilled desserts, fresh pastries and real coffee. They also offer accommodation upstairs – comfortable singles cost 600 MT and doubles 900 MT, including breakfast. Please note that it is not feasible to head further north up the coast from here, simply because the off-roading can be extremely dodgy for the casual traveller without sound 4x4 skills; rather head back into town and take the main road out of Maputo.

Another pleasant excursion is to **Inhaca Island** 35 kilometres offshore. Unfortunately, the old public ferry that used to run from the Catembe ferry jetty is no longer in operation. It was slow and cheap and gave you time to appreciate Maputo's skyline and get to know your fellow passengers. The new alternative is a luxury ferry that runs daily at 08h00 from the Porto de Pesca (the fishing harbour at the bottom of Av Samora Machel) and costs 540 MT. For bookings, tel: 21-49-7483 or 82-478-9270. There is a marine biological museum and research centre on the island where studies are made of the prolific marine life around the island. The coral reefs (some of the most southerly in the world) teem with colourful fish and are easily accessible from the shore – a paradise for snorkellers. Over 300 bird species have been recorded on Inhaca, including the crab plover, mangrove kingfisher and greater fregate bird. Accommodation is available at the **Inhaca Lodge**, tel: 21-30-5000.

Catembe, just across Maputo Bay, is also worth a visit, if only to get out across the water and view the city's skyline. It's dirt cheap (5 MT), takes just 15 minutes and leaves about every two hours (or when the vehicle deck is full). When you reach the other side, drop into one of the little restaurants for prawn and beer bargains. If you're in a real hurry or have a serious death wish, take one of the overcrowded bathtubs that run back and forth all the time – they're even cheaper!

The Holiday Inn in Maputo provides a welcome refuge.

Top-end accommodation in Maputo

As with any fast-developing city, places come and go. Maputo has seen the opening of some fine new hotels, the refurbishment of others and the downfall of an entire area. The following are worth considering.

At the top end of the market is **Hotel Polana**, 1380 Av Julius Nyerere, tel: 21-49-1001, fax: 21-49-1480, e-mail: res@polana-hotel.co.mz, website: www.polana-hotel.com. This elegant five-star hotel in a superb location overlooking the sea is like the Mount Nelson in Cape Town and the Old Cataract Hotel in Aswan – a magical mix of colonial and African charm with world-class comfort and service. Pool, tennis court, bowling green, gymnasium, restaurants, bars, business centre and casino, the Polana has it all. Double rooms in the elegant main building cost from 3690 MT and in the newer Polana Mar section from 3 330 MT and include breakfast in the price.

The **Hotel Avenida**, 627 Av Julius Nyerere, tel: 21-49-2000, fax: 21-49-9600, e-mail: bookings@hotelavenida. co.mz is modern, classy and sophisticated. This hotel has great facilities for the visiting businessman – conference centre, business rooms and health club. Standard rooms are 2340 MT single, 2700 MT for a double and breakfast is included.

The **Hotel Cardoso**, 707 Av Martires de Mueda, tel: 21-49-1071, fax: 21-49-1804, e-mail: hcardoso@zebra. uem.mz, website: www.hcardoso.com, is extremely well positioned, offering stunning views over the city, bay and beyond. Centrally situated, it also has a large pool and pleasant gardens. Prices start at 2070 MT single and 2610 MT double, including breakfast.

The **Holiday Inn**, Av Do Marginal, tel: 21-49-5050, fax: 21-49-7700, e-mail: himaputo@southernsun.com, website: www.southernsun.com is situated out of the town centre and right on the beach. It is a smart new hotel that has been tastefully decorated and has all the facilities a businessman or holiday-maker could need. The deluxe or standard rooms cost 2070 MT single and 2286 MT double, breakfast included.

Mid-range accommodation in Maputo

The most centrally situated of the hotels in the mid-range accommodation is the **Rovuma Hotel**, 114 Rua da Se, tel: 21-30-5000, fax: 21-30-3960, e-mail: cro@pestana.com, website: www.pestana.com. Opposite the cathedral, the Rovuma has 200 rooms, an outdoor pool, sauna, gymnasium and large conference and banqueting rooms. A standard room costs 1800 MT single and 1980 MT double, with breakfast.

The **Bahia Hotel**, 737 Rua Patrice Lumumba, tel: 21-36-0360, fax: 21-36-0330, e-mail: girassolbahiahotel@visabeiramoz.co.mz, is just down the road from the Hotel Cardoso and has similar great views, a pool and gardens. Comfortable singles cost 1620 MT and doubles 1800 MT.

The **Hotel Villa das Mangas**, 401 Av 24 de Julho, tel: 21-49-7507, fax: 21-49-7078, e-mail: villadasmangas@hotmail.com is conveniently situated and has well-appointed rooms around a central courtyard with pool. Singles cost 1450 MT and doubles 1790 MT.

The **Residencial Augustijn**, 204 Pereira Marinho, in the suburb of Sommershield, tel/fax: 21-49-3693, e-mail: t.theunissen@tvcabo.co.mz, website: www.augustijn.co.mz, is a small guesthouse is in the foreign embassy suburb of Sommershield and furnished with antiques and persian carpets.

Rates are 1170 MT single and 1530 MT double, negotiable for longer stays.

The **Hotel Terminus**, 587 Rua Francisco Orlando Magumbwe, tel: 21-49-1333, fax: 21-49-1284, e-mail: termhot@terminus-hotel.com, website: www.terminus-hotel.com, is just a few blocks back from busy Av Julius Nyerere in the Polana district. This quiet garden-set establishment offers free high-speed Internet access, with breakfast included in the prices of 1080 MT single and 1530 MT double.

The old Parque de Campismo (camp site) has been redeveloped into the **Kaya Kwanga**, Av Marginal, tel: 21-49-2706, fax: 21-49-2704, e-mail: kayakwanga@hotmail.com. This park resort has a hotel, residential accommodation and conference facilities, but no longer offers camping. Air-conditioned chalets cost 1080 MT single and 1350 MT double, while for longer stays you can rent a small house that sleeps four for 1800 MT per night.

Mozaika, 769 Av Agostinho Neto, tel: 21-30-3939, fax: 21-30-3965, e-mail: mozaika_guesthouse@hotmail.com, website: www.mozaika.co.mz has been billed as Maputo's best-kept secret. This small luxury guesthouse is also set in a garden suburb and is popular with NGO workers for longer stays. With a pool, bar and good security, they charge from 1080 MT to 1260 MT single/double.

The **Monte Carlo**, 620 Av Patrice Lumumba, tel: 21-30-4048, fax: 21-30-8959, e-mail: res@montecarlo-hotel.net, website: www.montecarlo-hotel.net is another hotel in the conveniently situated Av Patrice Lumumba. This one offers value for money at rates from 900 MT double.

Budget accommodation in Maputo

The **Pensão Martins**, 1098 Av 24 de Julho, tel: 21-32-4926, fax: 21-42-9645, e-mail: morgest@tvcabo.co.mz is a clean, safe, well-run hotel with a pool, bar, restaurant and off-street parking – and in this price range, it is a real find in Maputo. *En-suite* single rooms cost 720 MT and doubles 810 MT, and include a continental breakfast.

Maputo Backpackers, Quarta Avanida, Costa do Sol, tel: 82-467-2230, is a little way out of town along the Marginal at Costa do Sol, but is situated in a clean, uncluttered house down a quiet side street. Dorm beds start at 180 MT and a double room will cost you 660 MT.

Fatima's Backpacker, 1339 Av Mao Tse Tung, tel: 21-30-2994, 82-414-5730, fax: 21-49-4462, e-mail: fatima@virconn.com, website: www.mozambiqueback-packers.com was the original budget accommodation in Maputo and is now resting on its laurels. It's clean enough, laid-back, and has a communal kitchen and full notice board, but I didn't feel the vibe. Dorms cost 150 MT, singles 350 MT and doubles 600 MT.

The **Pensão Alegre**, 1371 Av 24 de Julho, tel: 21-30-7742, is pretty basic, but at least it has safe off-street parking,

and only charges 300 MT for a single and 550 MT for a double, with shared ablutions facilities.

Pensão Central, Av 24 de Julho (between Vladimir Lenin and Olaf Palme), tel: 21 424476, is a little dingy, but safe and clean, with guarded street parking. Rooms with shared facilities cost 250 MT single and 350 MT double.

The Base Backpackers, 545 Av Patrice Lumumba, tel: 21-30-2723, 82-452-6860, fax: 21-31-3750, e-mail: thebasebp@tvcabo.co.mz is a newish place run by husband-and-wife team Luis and Francisca. It is conveniently situated in Av Patrice Lumumba, with a fabulous view of the bay from the deck. Internet, laundry and off-street parking – a nice place. Dorm beds cost 150 MT and double rooms 450 MT.

Eating out in Maputo

There are so many restaurants catering to all tastes and budgets in Maputo that I cannot even attempt a list of recommendations. What I can do is highlight certain streets or areas that are worth checking out. The best street for cafés and restaurants is **Av Julius Nyerere**, south of the Polana Hotel. Here you will find peri-peri chicken, spicy Thai food, Indian cuisine, seafood restaurants, coffee shops, pizzerias, as well as ice-cream and pastry shops. A right turn down Av 24 de Julho will take you past more restaurants and several fast-food outlets selling pizzas and pies.

Fiera Popular, the old fairground on Av 25 de Setembro, is getting a little frayed around the edges, but the kiddie rides are still whizzing around and the little local restaurants still serve up value-for-money seafood and chicken. The dodgems spit blue sparks, the swings fly horizontally and the whip elicits screams from the girls in the old-style fun of a fair, while you guzzle prawns and suck on a 2M beer. It is well worth the 10 MT entrance fee, so be sure to visit before the developers bulldoze it to build yet another mall!

The malls are already across the street and this is where many South African fast-food outlets have set up shop. Nando's, Pizza Inn, Debonairs Pizza and Steers are all on hand to satisfy your wildest fast-food fantasies. And if that's not enough South African fast food for you, there is also a Spur Steak Ranch on the Marginal, out past the Holiday Inn.

All the large hotels have excellent restaurants, but those on a very tight budget should drop into any of the open-air markets for cheap and tasty plates of food.

Nightlife

The Bar Africa on Av 24 de Julho has live music and the **Maritimo Club** plays cool jazz. A good pub is **Sinatra's** on Av Julius Nyerere, and you could also try **Zozo Sanzala** in the Fiera Popular and **Mini-Golf** along the Marginal. If it's disco, dancing and action you crave, then check out **Coconuts** on Av 25 de Setembro, **Mambos** on the Marginal, **Lusos** on Bagamoyo Avenue, and **Cinema** in Av Julius Nyerere.

Shopping in Maputo

There are two interesting and useful shopping malls. The first is the **Shoprite Centre** (S25°57.120 E32°34.751) on Av

Acordos de Lusaka, the road to the airport. Fully fenced and secure, with lots of free parking, the centre offers a Shoprite supermarket that stocks all the food and drink you can think of, as well as hardware, camping gear, motor oils and magazines. You can pay in meticais, dollars or rands (but at a poor exchange rate). There is also a pharmacy, bank, ATM, photographic studio, sports shop, fast-food outlet, Woolworths, CNA stationers, cellphone operator and Total petrol station.

The other shopping complex is the **Polana Mall**, which has just opened on the corner of Av Julius Nyerere and Av 24 de Julho. A smart up-market place, it has an ice-cream parlour, bank and exchange bureau, delicatessen and cellphone shop on the ground floor. On the first floor you will find a modern Internet café, hairdresser, tobacconist, pharmacy, optician, bookshop (with a small selction of English books), a small superette and clothing shops. The second floor contains a café, DVD rental shop, curio outlet and a mouthwatering chocolate emporium.

Just across the road from the Polana Mall in Av 24 de Julho, and next to the Piri Piri Chicken Restaurant, is a very clean and well-stocked butchery, delicatessen and fish shop. And for larger items and appliances, a big new Game Store has opened along the Marginal on the way to Costa do Sol.

The markets of Maputo deserve special mention. The main **Mercado Municipal** on Av 25 de Setembro stocks just about everything in the fresh food line, while the **Janeta Market**, at the intersection of Av Mao Tse Tung and

Vladimir Lenine, stocks more in the line of household goods and second-hand clothing. The most entertaining, though, is the huge and chaotic **Xipamanine Market** out west on the Rua dos Imaos Roby. Hardware, spare parts and furniture crowd around the scary-looking stalls of dismembered animal parts, herbs and medicinal plants, all for *muti* (traditional medicines). The **Saturday Craft Market** on Praca 25 do Junho, at the bottom of Av Samora Machel, is another interesting place to visit for its wide selection of handcrafts from all over Mozambique. All these markets have a criminal element, so don't visit them wearing expensive jewellery or accessories, don't flash your money, and don't be tempted to change money or buy illegal substances.

Public transport

Instead of one large sprawling bus station, long-distance buses in Maputo leave from the companies' separate depots. Here is a list of the main ones:

Transportes Oliveiras, tel: 21-40-5108, is out on Av 24 de Julho, just past the big traffic circle (Praca 16 Junho), and can be reached by *chapas* heading west out of the city along the main thoroughfare. They have an extensive network in southern and central Mozambique and run express or local buses. Tickets are sold on the premises on Av 24 de Julho.

Transportes Virginia, tel: 21-42-1271, operates mainly in southern Mozambique and leaves from the Hotel Universo on the corner of Av Eduardo Mondlane and Karl Marx.

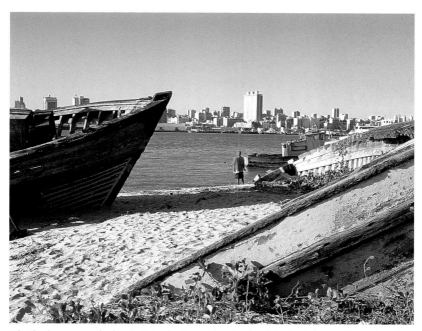

Take the ferry across the bay to Catembe for great seafood and the best view of Maputo's skyline.

◆ Fresh rolls (rather than loaves of bread) are found at bakeries all over town. A couple of the more prominent ones are: **Nautilus** (corner Julius Nyerere and 24 de Julho), **Aziz** (Av Samora Machel) and the in-store one at **Shoprite**.

◆ You will probably be able to have laundry done where you are staying but if this is not possible, use the centrally situated **EcoSec Lavandarias**, at 413 Av 24 de Julho, tel: 21-49-5574. They charge 65 MT for a kilogram of washing and also do dry-cleaning.

◆ Curios can be bought at all Maputo's markets, but also outside hotels Cardoso, Polana and Costa do Sol, and on the traffic island at the corner of Av Julius Nyerere and Av 24 de Julho – where everything seems to happen!

◆ Most of the accommodation establishments, from budget to top end, offer **Internet** access and facilities. Otherwise, there are a couple of Internet cafés along Av 24 de Julho and Av Julius Nyrere and the latest, most up-to-date one is in the new Polana Shopping Centre on the corner of the two above-mentioned avenues.

◆ **DHL** is on the corner of Samora Machel and 25 de Setembro.

◆ The **Public Information Bureau** (BIP) is on the corner of Av Eduardo Mondlane and Av Francisco Magumbwe, tel: 21-49-0200, fax: 21-49-2622, e-mail: bip@teledata. mz. They sell city maps and books, some in English, but are closed 12h30–14h00.

TSL goes as far as Tete and Nampula and leaves from the Praca dos Combatantes at the end of Av das FPLM (accessible by *chapas* heading out of town along Av Vladimir Lenin).

The closest thing to a bus station in Maputo is **Junta**, the sprawling stretch of Av de Mozambique heading north out of the city. All buses on their way north must pass through this area, and it is indeed possible to board here, although you are better off catching them at their depots.

Even though there is a very inexpensive city bus service (no rides cost more than 2 MT), most residents use *chapas*, which seem to go everywhere (and cost 3 MT). Routes are called out by the conductor and you hop on and off when you like. Taxis stand outside all the bigger hotels and also up and down the length of the busy avenues 24 de Julho and Julius Nyerere (choose one with a meter and make sure that it's turned on).

The Laurentina Brewery has moved from the corner of Av 25 de Setembro and Albert Luthuli, but this is still the area to head for to pick up a minibus taxi to Swaziland or South Africa. **Intercape** luxury buses travel daily between Johannesburg Station and the offices of Tropical Travel in Av 24 de Julho, and **Translux** runs a similar service that turns around at Simana Travel in the same street. The Mozambique-based service, **Panthera Azul**, is at 273 Av Zedequias Maganhela and runs to Johannesburg every day and Durban on Tuesdays, Thursdays and Sundays. Prices are all around 650 MT one way.

Driving in and around the capital

There are many service stations at which to fill up with fuel. The Mobil garage next to the Polana Hotel also has a car wash, and another Mobil opposite the Hotel Cardoso can repair punctures and pump tyres. The newest one is down in Av 25 de Setembro next to the fast-food outlets (petrol costs 17,5 MT a litre, unleaded 17,27 MT and diesel 14,94 MT). For vehicle spares, try one of the many small shops down Av Karl Marx, and for tyres, shocks, bearings and batteries try Bandauto Continental at the unfashionable end of Av 25 de Setembro, between Said Barre Av and Fernandos Farinha. Camping gas can be refilled at Mocacor in Av Karl Marx, just below Av 24 de Julho. The Toyota dealer is at 141 Rua do Logo Amaramba, tel 21-40-0405, fax: 21-40-0471, e-mail: sales@toyota.virconn. com. For help with your Nissan, contact Motorcare Mozambique, Rua Paulinho dos Santos; tel: 21-31-2931, fax: 21-31-2930, e-mail: info@moz.motorcare. com, website: www.motorcare.com. Mitsubishi is represented by Tecnica Industrial, 2803 Av 24 Julho, tel: 21-42-8078 and Ford is at 47 Av Samora Machel, tel: 21-32-0123.

For car hire, visit **Hertz**, tel: 21-49-4982, fax: 21-42-6077, at the Polana Hotel, or **Avis** at the corner of Julius Nyerere and Mao Tse Tung, tel: 21-46-5498, fax: 21-46-5493. They also both have offices at the airport.

Banking

For best rates and complete safety, change money at a *cambios*, which you will find dotted all over town. SA Cambios is at 118 Av 24 de Julho and No's Cambios is in the same street, between Pensão Alegro and Hotel Santa Cruz. Halfway down Av Samora Machel, just below the bakery, is the Maputo Cambios, and there are others in Av Julius Nyerere. Banks change money, but take a long time doing it, and hotels do so at a lower rate. Don't use the street – you could be ripped off.

Health and safety

For medical emergencies, head straight for the **Sommershield Clinic** (S25°57.576 E32°35.769), 52 Rua Pereira do Lago, just off Av Kim 2 Sung, tel: 21-49-3924. It is open 24 hours a day and always has doctors and specialists on call. Expect to be charged upfront, but credit cards are acceptable. Just down from the Santa Cruz Hotel, in Av 24 de Julho, is a large yellow building that houses the **Clinica Bathesda**. You might have difficulty communicating without some Portuguese, but they are equipped for most emergencies. Alternatively, they will be able to refer you.

Pharmacies are dotted around town, with the old favourites, 24 de Julho, Julius Nyerere, Shoprite Centre and the Polana Shopping Mall the best.

There is a dentist on Av Julius Nyerere, above the Spicy Thai Restaurant, and another at the top end of Av Patrice Lumumba – check their supplies of Novocaine first!

Travellers should be able to get by speaking English, but for helpful Portugese words and phrases see page 186–189.

13 North to Inhambane

To get to the EN1 and places north, head out of Maputo on Av 24 de Julho, across Praca 16 de Junho (this is like a history lesson), and to the highway intersection (S25°56.535 E32°32.353) with the EN4 road that extends from the South African border. This intersection is well signposted (to Xai-Xai). Turn right into Av de Mozambique (EN1) and fight your way through the chaos of taxis, trucks and trollies that crowd this busy part of town. If you were coming down from the South African border and bypassing Maputo, you would turn left here.

Lagoons, protected bays and sailing dhows epitomise the coastline north of Inhambane.

Please note that it is not feasible to leave Maputo via the Marginal out north, past Costa do Sol, as the route is simply too precarious for anyone with less-than-expert off-roading skills. Fuel is available at large Petromoc and Mobil service stations, and on your right as you leave this area, a large branch of Trentyre will be able repair punctures and sell you new tyres.

A feature of the road north is that it's always just inland from the coast, so to reach any of the country's many seaside resorts, you have to turn off and head down to the coast. The bigger resorts have better roads leading to them, while others can only be reached with a 4x4 vehicle.

The EN1 north

The first turn-off is reached after only 30 kilometres and is to the **Marracuene Lodge**. Four-wheel-drive is necessary to travel the sandy 4.5 kilometres down to this camp (follow the signposts). A small bar and restaurant overlooks the Incomati River and visitors can launch boats here to fish or birdwatch in the river's delta. Neat, comfortable, self-catering chalets have bedding, mosquito nets, hot and cold water and fully equipped kitchens. The four-person or two-person accommodation costs 450 MT per person (dinner, bed and breakfast 650 MT). A large camp site offers shady, but sandy, sites at 150 MT per person. To book, tel: 84-484-9230, e-mail: marracuene@advisor.co.mz, website: www.marracuene.co.za

A good overnight option when travelling north is **Casa Lisa**, 46 kilometres from Maputo. Just 1 kilometre off the highway, the turn-off to the left is well signposted at a small road-side snack bar called Ultra City (S25°35.024 E32°40.029). Expertly run by Bruce and Michelle Buckland, Casa Lisa has a comfortable bar, good food and a swimming pool. It offers camping in a well-grassed area (each with its own thatched lapa) for 120 MT per person, and attractively decorated, self-contained chalets with mozzie nets at between 400 MT and 525 MT per person per night. For bookings, tel: 82-304-1990, e-mail: buckland@teledata.mz

The EN1 north continues in fairly good condition through **Manhica**, where you will find a bank, pharmacy, small shops and a garage for fuel and minor repairs. There is also the **Laurentina Hotel** in the main street. Clean *en-suite* double rooms cost 400 MT per person and 300 MT for rooms with shared facilities (the rooms facing the street could be noisy). This is a busy and popular spot for a drink on the patio, doughnut or samoosa in the café, or good local specialities in the air-conditioned restaurant, where the menu boasts 'Steak Poll' and 'Suckling Ping'.

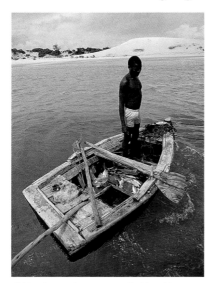

Fishing in Moz is not generally hi-tech!

Roadworks on the EN1 start from here, so be careful and adhere to the speed limits and stop/go signals. Passing over the Incomati floodplain, you travel through sugar-cane fields to the town of **Macia** (144 kilometres from Maputo). Macia has a Petromoc service station/mini-market on the left as you come into town, and in the centre are a market and restaurants. You will also find the turn-off (S25°01.626 E33°05.776) to the seaside resort of **Bilene**. Turn right here to travel the 32 kilometres of good tar down to the coast, but be warned that it can be quite depressing to see the road-side stalls selling wood, charcoal and illegally harvested indigenous plants, all dying in the harsh sun.

Bilene

Bilene is situated on the **Uembje Lagoon**, which is separated from the sea by a narrow line of sand dunes. Only sometimes open to the sea, the lagoon is not great for swimming, but fine for most forms of boating and watersports. Known as Sao Martinho during colonial times, it has always been a popular holiday destination and therefore has a good selection of accommodation. Bilene is entered at a traffic circle, where you will also find the Bilene Hotel – a bit far from the beach, but solid and modern, with a large, airy bar and restaurant. A suite for two persons costs 800 MT, a four-person self-contained bungalow 1500 MT, and for six it costs 2000 MT. For bookings, tel: 282-59014, fax: 282-59012. Drive the 1.5 kilometres down to the lagoon and turn left, continuing to beyond the little circle at the Complexo Palmeiras until you reach the Park Floris Camp. We'll start here and work our way back.

Park Floris is a basic, unpretentious little outfit with a small bar and an even smaller store. The sandy, but neatly raked and shaded camp sites cost 120 MT per person (some have electrical points). There are also small rondavels that contain only two beds for 400 MT and larger four-bed rondavels with equipped kitchens for 700 MT. All ablutions are shared. Back at the circle on the Marginal is the smarter **Complexo Palmeiras**. Spread out under shady trees along the waterfront are neat little brick-built chalets with verandas right on the sand. The chalets sleep four people, with linen and daily servicing, but are not self-catering, with no cutlery or crockery. They do, however, each have fans, a fridge and braai facilities and cost 1200 MT out of season and 1620 MT in. The rondavels are similar to the chalets, but sleep two people and cost 900 MT and 1350 MT (in and out of season). Camping facilities are available under shade above the beach (some electrical points) at 135 MT per site, plus 90 MT per person per day in season. Out of season, they charge the per-person rate, but not for the site. There is a comfortable bar, restaurant with a pool table, standard menu and even an espresso machine. For more information, tel/fax: 282-59019, Moz cell: 82-304-3720, e-mail: palmeira@bilene.virconn.com

Working our way back still further, we pass the extremely dodgy **Municipal Camp Site** opposite the Petromoc service station. Stuck between the main

---

THE TAX MAN

Remember that a general marine tax is applicable throughout Mozambique:

* boat in a lagoon   500 MT
* boat in the sea   650 MT
* jetski   350 MT

There is also a diver's tax of 150 MT.

---

road and the lagoon, this camp has no fences, even less security, and ablutions that are shared with the public. On the corner opposite the camp site is a small market where you can catch public transport back to Macia or Maputo. Just up this side street are two small hotels that face each other. On the far side of the road is the recently restored **Pousada Sao Martinho** where a house for four people, with fridge, hotplate, microwave, kettle, all utensils, fans and a comfortable veranda, will cost you 1500 MT per day, or a squeaky-clean double room in the main block 500 MT. Set in pretty gardens, there is a swimming pool and bar/restaurant with pool table. For details, tel: 82-490-1440. Across the road, the **Complexo Acapital** has neatly tiled double rooms with air-con and TV, but no *en-suite* bathrooms, for 650 MT. For information, tel: 82-404-8700.

Working still further south down the main road, there are the Estrela do Mar, Carioca and Complexo Aquarias restaurants. A little further down, on the inland side of the road, is the large, refurbished and very secure **Sao Martinho Resort**. It consists of a group of brick-built bungalows that cost from 1050 MT for a three-bed, non-self-catering unit, to 2100 MT for a six-bed, self-contained one. It is run together with the beach pavilion bar and restaurant across the road, where you have to book in and pay. For bookings and further information, tel: 282-59001 or 82-880-2900. Just past the pavilion, up a side street away from the beach, is the **Lagoa Azu** complex. Small chalets sleeping four, with a small kitchen, cost 1500 MT and a larger two-bedroomed house with elegant lounge and dining room, plus fully-kitted kitchen costs 2400 MT. For details, tel: 282-59006.

To get to the more up-market **Praia do Sol Resor**t (S25°17.500 E33°13.855), we have to keep heading south along the Marginal and then follow the signs through the houses. There are two options: one for 4x4s and the other for standard vehicles. Both bring you to an attractive group of wooden chalets dotted across the dunes, all with stunning views of the lagoon. A restaurant,

bar, watersports centre and swimming pool are linked by wooden walkways, and chalets sleep two, four or six people. Rates vary between 1275 MT and 1950 MT per person in and out of season and include dinner, bed and breakfast. Contact Leo Rogers, e-mail: leo@pdsol.co.za or in South Africa on tel: +27-(0)82-570-4300 and in Moz on tel: 82-319-3040, website: www.pdsol.co.za

Away from the beach, off the road back to the traffic circle, is the exclusive **Humula Complexo**. Accommodation is in large, comfortable two-bedroomed houses furnished with the latest in fridges, stoves and furniture. Each house has a private garden and carport and costs 3576 MT a night for four people. Motel-style double rooms with air-con, TV and fridge are 1430 MT a night. This is an attractive and secure complex set in beautiful gardens. For more information, tel: 282-59020, fax: 282-59022.

Boating and watersports are the things to do here and all resorts offer launching facilities at a fee of around 30 MT for a jetski and 50 MT for a single-engined boat.

Another exciting activity in Bilene is a scenic flight in a microlight plane. Flying from the aerodrome just outside of town, you can spot turtles, manta rays, whale sharks and dolphins as you slowly cruise up and down the picturesque coastline. The cost is 1050 MT for a 20-minute flight. Contact Louis or Lee-Ann in Mozambique, tel: 82-234-2460, or in South Africa, tel: +27-(0)82-825-1034.

Head back up to the EN1 at Macia and turn northeast. As you leave town, opposite the new Mobil petrol station, you will pass the turn-off left (S25°01.511 E33°06.099) to Chokwe, Massingir and the South African border at Pafuri in the north of the Kruger National Park. Hopefully this will soon become a popular route as the Transfrontier Park develops around Massingir and a new border post opens west of there. Before leaving town, stop to buy some delicious cashew nuts from the street vendors (the average price is 100 MT a kilogram). The road surface deteriorates (contractors are working on it) from about here. Just before the town of Xai-Xai, you cross the bridge over the Limpopo River. No toll is charged when heading north, but coming the other way motorists are charged 5 MT for a car and 10 MT for a pick-up.

Xai-Xai and surrounds

Xai-Xai (pronounced *shy-shy*) is a fairly large town with most amenities – bank, pharmacy, general dealers, fast food, transport depots and a reasonable hotel on the main street opposite the central square and gardens. The **Hotel Kaya Ka Hirva** has clean, large, airy rooms upstairs, with TV and air-con, for 375 MT single and 600 MT double. With your own bathroom, it costs 700 MT for a double. There is a restaurant at street level. For details, tel: 282-22391.

On the other side of town, up on the hill, is a hospital and, just past it, the turn-off right to Xai-Xai beach (S25°03.374 E33°40.296). It is a short 10 kilometres down to the rather forlorn and neglected resort. Although Xai-Xai suffered heavy damage during the 2000 floods, it is still inexplicable that, with so much development up and down Mozambique's coast, this beautiful spot has been passed over by promoters and tourists. A large, old derelict hotel dominates the main beach, but accommodation is available next door (northeast) at the newly renovated and refurbished **Nyala Guest House**. An *en-suite* double room with TV and air-con costs 850 MT and there is a communal kitchen for the use of all guests. For information, tel: 282-23043 or 82-301-4640, fax: 282-22658, e-mail: saminvestment@teledata.mz. Fish and ice are sold from the small house situated between the derelict hotel and Nyala.

Northeast, off the ring road that runs around Xai-Xai beach, is the **Complexo Touristico Halley**. The hotel is set back slightly from the beach and hosts a disco in season. Not new, but still clean and neat, they have *en-suite* sea-facing double rooms for 900 MT or back-facing for 750 MT, including breakfast. For information, tel: 282-35014, fax: 282-35003. On the ground floor, there is also a general dealer (Estrela do Mar)

that sells basic foodstuffs, and across the road, on the beach, is a restaurant that is also part of the complex.

Just past Halley's is the **Xai-Xai Camping and Caravan Park** with a variety of accommodation options. Camping is 135 MT per person, basic reed huts cost 480 MT for two people and 780 MT for four, and a rustic, self-catering bungalow with fridge, stove and accommodation for four is 1 260 MT. There is a bar and restaurant, but security in the camp is poor. For further details, tel: 282-35022 or 82-712-6520, fax: 282-35016.

On to Inhambane

Back on the EN1, and approximately 65 kilometres from Xai-Xai town, you will reach Chidenguele village. To reach the beach at **Paraiso de Chidenguele**, turn right here and follow the signs. The road skirts a huge inland lake (see page 87) and ends high above the beach, where solid thatch-roofed bungalows dot the well-wooded dunes. The bungalows have fridges, stoves and even Weber braais and are linked by wooden walkways. They cost between 2 720 MT for a four-sleeper out of season to 5 280 MT for an eight-sleeper in season. Overnight *en-suite* accommodation is also available at between 640 MT and 736 MT per person. This is a pristine stretch of coast where the fishing is unmatched (rock, surf, fly, paddle-ski or deep-sea) and regular competitions are held here. The walls of the bar are covered with photographs to prove how good the fishing really is, and the restaurant serves delicious (surprise!) seafood meals. For enquiries, tel: 282-67001 or 82-398-7450, e-mail: pariasodechid@teledata.mz, website: www.chidbeachresort.com

Following the EN1, the potholes are bad around Zandamela as we head north again. Just on the other side of Quissico there is a turn-off (S24°42.920 E34°44.916) to the **Praia Mar e Sol 4x4 Bushcamp**. A well-signposted, but very sandy track winds down through thousands of coconut palms and crosses the enormous lake (look out for the interesting fish traps at the bridge) to climb up the dunes again to a well-laid-out 4x4 bushcamp. Flushing toilets, showers and thatch-shaded sites offer some luxury, but it is still very isolated. Camping is the only option and it costs 180 MT per person. For information, tel: 82-272-7530.

Back on the EN1, beware speed traps when passing through the small towns. The local *transitos* have an old, well-used, hand-held radar that is used with devastating – and profitable – effect.

Inharrime and north

Inharrime is not the most attractive of places to stop, but it does have a decent Galp service station and a dingy-looking hotel. About 10 kilometres out of town is the turn-off left down to Zavora Beach. This is a reasonable 17-kilometre road through rows of coconut palms with only the last section a bit sandy – just passable with two-wheel-drive. You will spot the lighthouse in the distance as you get closer. The beach is pleasant and there is good snorkelling, but most visitors come for the fishing. Zavora Lodge is the only tourist accommodation, but it is a little run-down.

Self-catering bungalows that sleep four cost 450 MT per person and the larger six-sleeper houses are 510 MT per person. Camping with rough amenities is charged at 180 MT a person (charged for a minimum of six in season) and a thatched shelter with electrical plug is another 60 MT per night (300 MT in season). Mosquitoes are a big problem, as is poor security. For details, tel: 82-301-9330 or, in South Afruca, +27-(0)13-750-0431.

About 57 kilometres north of Inharrime, at Lindela, the road forks. Keep left and stay on the EN1, continuing up through Maxixe to Vilankulo, then swing right for Inhambane and all its surrounding beaches and resorts.

THE VERSATILE COCONUT

The coastal strip of Inhambane province is blanketed by about two million coconut palms. Each *cocos nucifera* plant produces over 20 kilograms of coconuts annually, from which oil is extracted for soap, hair products, perfumes, cosmetics and confectionery. The trunk is also tapped for its sap, which is used for the production of palm wine, while the fronds are used for roofing material or woven into mats. When no longer productive, the palms are chopped down and the trunk used for valuable building timber. Look out for home-made coconut-ice sweets sold in markets and on the street. Made with desiccated coconut and raw brown sugar, it's delicious.

---

14 Inhambane & surrounds

The district of Inhambane, including the beaches of Jangamo, Tofo and Barra, is the most popular destination for tourists in the entire Mozambique. But it wasn't tourism that brought Arab trading dhows to this large protected bay at Inhambane as early as the 10th century. These traders brought beads, salt, cloth and ceramics in exchange for gold and ivory.

With its uninterrupted views and balmy climate, Inhambane is a prime holiday destination.

INHAMBANE REGION

0   5   10 km

0 (1 cm) 3.15 kilometres

Morrumbene

4x4 Track

Baia de Inhambane

Linga-Linga

*Ponta da
Linga-Linga*

EN1

26

White Sands Camp

Praia da Barra
Barra Lodge

Ponta da Barra
Lighthouse Campsite

Bamboozi's
Dino's Beach Bar
Fatima's Nest
Nordin's Lodge
Hotel Marinho

7

Tofo

Tofinho

6

S23°50,698 E35°30,069

Maxixe

Inhambane

18

Praia da Rocha

9

20

11

15

EN101

S24°00,195 E35°28,508

3

Coconut Bay

7

5,5

EN1

Seabound Charters

11

9

Jeff's Resort
Jangamo Beach Resort
Grunjata Bay Resort
Paindane Beach Resort
Casa de Mar
Ilha da Rochas

3,5

S24°16,699 E35°14,206

26   4x4 Route

Lindela

S24°06,068 E35°29,839

Trade increased with the arrival of the Portuguese and the town prospered. Gold dwindled, ivory soared and in the mid-18th century Inhambane was one of the first Mozambican ports to establish a trade in slaves. It developed into the third-largest town in the country after Maputo and Beira, and the beautiful colonial buildings, which can still be seen today, were built. Now a bit of a backwater – even the main EN1 highway bypasses it – it slumbers in faded glory.

Beach resorts of Jangamo

Before we reach Inhambane itself, we will explore the beach resorts the area has to offer. The first turn-off (S24°16.699 E35°14.206), to Praia de Jangamo, is just 3.5 kilometres past the EN1 fork and is signposted to Sol de Ligogo, Ilha de Rochas and Paindane Resort. This is very definitely a 4x4 route and not easy to follow, but saves going the long way around via Inhambane. The sandy track winds through the bush, passing villages, huts and fields of manioc. It is signposted, but because the signs are generally high in trees and there are so many forks in the track, it is difficult to follow. You are, however, rewarded with one of the best bits of off-roading you're likely to do in Mozambique – a 4x4 route you'd pay good money to drive if it was in South Africa and a good test of you and your vehicle.

Follow the signs for Paindane and, after about 26 kilometres, you will reach the gates (S24°06.068 E35°29.839) of this large, well-run resort. Spread over an attractive palm- and bush-covered slope, **Paindane Beach Resort** can accommodate up to 500 people at the height of season. The lively bar and restaurant, high on the hill, overlooks a beautiful beach. Protected by an offshore reef, the beach is perfect for swimming and snorkelling, and launching boats, too. There is a variety of accommodation options. Self-catering chalets come in four-, six-, seven- and eight-bed versions and include all linen and a fully equipped kichen. Their verandas offer great views of the sea, and the cost is about 420 MT per person per day. Basic camping is 195 MT per person per day with bright, clean ablution blocks. For more comfortable camping, hire a *baracca* – thatched, open-sided structures with a cement floor, wash-up sink and tap. These can be used as camping kitchens, living rooms or a protected place to pitch your tent under. They cost an extra 540 MT a day. The ultimate in camping, though, must be the *casitas*. These are similar to the *baraccas*, but have their own toilet, hot shower, kitchenette with gas cooker and electric plug, and cost an extra 975 MT a day. The above rates are all for in-season – there is a 40% discount for out-of-season. There is also a watersports centre on the premises. For reservations and more info, contact Marian van Wyk in South Africa, tel: +27-(0)82-569-3436, fax: +27-(0)13-750-3202, e-mail: paindane.sa@mweb.co.za, website: www.paindane.co.za

South of Paindane are a couple of low-key, difficult-to-reach resorts. Some naughty people ride along the beach at low tide, but this is illegal and you are liable to be fined 5 000 MT if caught by the *maritimos*. About 5 kilometres down, as the seagull flies, is the small, ecologically friendly **Casa de Mar**. Des Dandridge has reed huts in the dunes overlooking the beach and can be contacted in South Africa, tel: +27-(0)83-789-5522 or +27-(0)31-266-4716. A couple of kilometres further down the beach is a larger, sprawling collection of reed huts and camp sites that is **Ilha de Rochas**. Set among the bushes on the dunes overlooking a small offshore rock island, they can be reached on tel: 82-410-5460, or contact Michelle in South Africa on +27-(0)11-893-3110 or +27-(0)83-272-2224, e-mail: islandrock@hotmail.com

Back in **Praia de Jangamo**, there are three more popular resorts. The first, just 3.5 kilometres north of Paindane, is **Guinjata Bay**. This large, attractive, up-market complex overlooks a bay and small headland and has a beautiful beach and protected boat-launching area. The restaurant is one of the most attractive I've seen in a lodge in Moz, and there is a nautically themed bar and surprisingly well-stocked little shop (booze, batteries, toiletries, fishing and snorkelling gear, as well as basic foodstuffs). They offer fly-in packages to Inhambane and diving and fishing excursions from their on-site watersports centre. Catered accommodation costs from 1 300 MT a person for dinner, bed and breakfast in low season to 1 830 MT a person for full board in high season. Self-catering is available in chalets that sleep between four and 16 people. The four-bedder costs 2 475 MT in low season and 2 805 MT in high. Camping is available under protective *baraccas* equipped with water and electricity for 150 MT per person per night. Contact Nicole, in South Africa, for bookings and more info, tel: +27-(0)13-741-2795 or +27-(0)83-283-6918, fax: +27-(0)13-741-3149, e-mail: reservations@guinjata.com, website: www.guinjata.com. They have a very useful document that you can download from their website. It's a letter in both English and Portuguese that can be presented to any traffic official who harasses you. In it is a request for fair and courteous treatment and a form for the official to fill in, requiring his name and details, the amount of the fine and receipt number.

Next door to Guinjata is the **Jangamo Beach Holiday Resort**. Although it was once a top spot, it was experiencing management problems and going downhill fast when I last visited. Backpacker-type accommodation was available in the main building at 300 MT a person, while four-bed cabanas cost about 1 800 MT. Contact Jangamo Beach in South Africa, tel: +27-(0)15-516-0229 or +27-(0)82-895-3626, e-mail: info@jangamobeach.com, website: www.jangamobeach.com

While most resorts have on-site dive centres, special mention should be made of the **Mozambican Manta Research Project**. Presently based at Jangamo Beach, but soon to move to Paindane Beach, it is run by Andrea Marshall, who is doing her PhD on these magnificent creatures. The project aims to study and protect manta rays along this stretch of coast and, in conjunction with the local Marine Dynamics Dive Centre, offers a full range of dive

The coastline stretching from Inhambane boasts many picturesque resorts.

courses. As many as 30 mantas have been spotted on a single dive, as well as the only recorded observations of their mating and birth in the world. Contact Andrea in Moz, tel: 82-352-1030 or in South Africa, tel: +27-(0)82-478-9251, e-mail: andrea.marshall@uq.edu.au. The **Marine Dynamics Dive Centre** can be contacted in South Africa, tel: +27-(0)83-657-1751 or +27-(0)82-384-1005, e-mail: jpb@iafrica.com, website: www.dive.co.za

Colin Jefferies has been involved with both Paindane and Guinjata, but has now developed his own place next door called **Jeff's Resort**. Brand new, solidly built villas sleep eight people in four *en-suite* bedrooms around a central open-plan living room. Prices per villa range from 3600 MT in low season to 6000 MT in season. Smaller cabanas sleep four in two bedrooms for between

1620 MT and 2400 MT. All villas and cabanas are fully equipped with bedding, cooking utensils, deep freezer and gas cooker. Here, one can camp in style, too, under a thatched roof with private bathroom, electrical plug, lights and a kitchen sink with hot and cold water – 500 MT a night plus 150 MT a person. For bookings or more info, contact Hantie in South Africa, tel: +27-(0)83-254-4685, tel/fax: +27-(0)13-932-1263, e-mail: jeffsmoz@mweb.co.za, or in Moz, tel: 82-714-0220.

Another newish operation at Guinjata Bay is **Seabound Charters**, run by Ralph and Celeste Jones (the first place on your left if you are arriving from Inhambane). They offer exclusive and personalised fishing charters and are always available, unlike so many advertised fishing concerns that only operate in the height of season. Ralph has good local knowledge and supplies everything you need – rods, tackle, bait and licences. Barracuda and dorado are plentiful, and he charges 6 000 MT a day to fish for marlin, 4 800 MT to fly-fish, and 2 400 MT for a two-hour introduction to fishing. They also have a well-appointed self-catering guest flat that sleeps six in luxury and comfort. It costs 3 900 MT a night, but only 3 000 MT if you are fishing with them. Contact the Jones' in Mozambique, tel: 82-814-8730 or in South Africa, tel: +27-(0)83-665-2104.

On to Inhambane Town

Heading back to Inhambane, the sandy track becomes a harder surface after about 7 kilometres, at the turn-off (S24°00.195 E35°28.508) to **Baia dos Cocos** (Coconut Bay). A sandy 3 kilometres down through palms and casava fields brings us to the only Mozambican-owned resort in the area. I liked the atmosphere at this low-key resort. The layout is neat and orderly, with grassed terraces and surfaced roads. A small bar and restaurant serves genuine local dishes, cooked by Rosa the chef/man-

> ## The Museum of Inhambane
> is in Av da Vigilancia, off the Av da Independencia. It has a good collection of old photographs dating back to the early colonial period and a full range of artefacts, including farming implements and musical instruments.

ager; the beach has good surf, and it doesn't look like another Jo'burg-let-your-hair-down kind of resort. Prices are reasonable too – with camping costing 60 MT per site and 90 MT per person in low season (double in season), reed-hut *casitas* for two at 750 MT to 1 200 MT, rondavels for four at 1 140 MT to 2 040 MT, and chalets that sleep six at 1 800 MT out of season and 3 000 MT in season. Chalets and rondavels are neat, brick-built units, fully equipped with hot water, fridge, hotplate and all kitchen utensils. For information, tel: 82-311-7250, 293-20882 or 82-712-2420, e-mail: coconutbay@teledata.mz

The main road to Inhambane is intersected (S23°56.693 E35°23.894) just 11 kilometres from the Coconut Bay turn-off and Inhambane town is just 9 kilometres further on. Av Eduardo Mondlane ushers you in along the waterfront, past the hospital, and to the jetty in the centre of town. Here you can catch the regular passenger ferry (every 20 minutes or so) across the bay to Maxixe on the mainland (3.5 kilometres and it takes about 40 minutes by sailing dhow). Dhows will also ferry you to Linga Linga or the two small uninhabited islands in the bay, Ratos and Porcos. The town is looking a lot

smarter since the governor of the region granted the residents a year to paint and renovate their properties without having to apply and pay for a special permit! Just past the jetty, on the waterfront in Rua 3 de Fevereiro, is **Pensão Pachica**, a clean, quiet house offering double rooms with mozzie nets and immaculate linen for 600 MT or dorm accommodation for 210 MT. Safe parking is available in the backyard, there is a fully-equipped kitchen, and info and help with local excursions is available too. For details, tel: 293-20565, e-mail: inhambane@africamail.com

Up the wide Av de Independencia, which runs from the jetty, you will find a general dealer, bank for changing money and an ATM, petrol station and the old train station at the top. Turn right at the traffic circle here and you will head out of town towards Tofo and Barra. But further right around the circle brings you into Av de Revolucao. This street has all the action, with an Internet office, bakery, restaurants and a bustling market – stock up here before you head out to the beaches again. *Chapas* also leave from here to Barra, Tofo and the main EN1 highway at Lindela (to connect with the intercity buses). If you plan on staying over and want to rave it up, try the **Discoteca Zoom**, Rua da Chimoio (behind the Casa da Cultura), which is open from 18h00 till late. They offer a bar, pool table, snacks and a night club, so for the lowdown, tel: 82-424-9140.

Tofo

The road passes the airport (Charlan Air flies here directly from Lanseria

Airport in Johannesburg every Monday and Friday) on its way out of Inhambane, and after about 18 kilometres (S23°50.698 E35°30.069) you will reach the Bar Babalaza. Turn off right here to Tofo, or carry on straight to Barra. This popular crossroads spot can become quite crowded as expats and holiday-makers pop in for sundowners or a bite to eat (they also sell ice, but no longer offer accommodation). The tarred road continues for another 6 kilometres down to Tofo and ends at the market and *chapas* stand, opposite the main beach. Because of its easy access, this beautiful spot is visited by local Inhambane residents over the weekends to picnic and play soccer on the sands. The laid-back lifestyle at the camp sites, resorts and hotels of the area draws foreign visitors from far and wide too, particularly backpackers, but Tofo is spread out enough to handle them all.

Left of the market is the neat little double-storeyed **Hotel Marinho**. With secure and shaded parking in the street (where they will also wash your car for you), they offer sea-facing double rooms for 1 880 MT (single 1 060 MT). A kettle with tea and coffee is supplied, and breakfast is included. They also have cheaper non-sea-facing rooms or more expensive air-conditioned suites. For bookings, tel/fax: 293-29043.

Just across the road, on the corner, is the **Centro Turistico de Tofo**, a motel-styled establishment offering air-conditioned *en-suite* rooms with three beds and kitchenette (not equipped) for 800 MT a night. Excellent security, shaded parking and a spacious bar/restaurant makes this a good, simple, value-for-money option. Just up the side street is the newish **Casa de Comer** restaurant. They not only offer delicious Mozambican and French cuisine, but serve the best espresso in town.

Beach driving is strictly forbidden, except at certain boat-launching sites.

Heading north along the coast brings us to more places to stay. The first is **Nordin's Lodge**. Although a little run-down, with poor security, they do have a great position right on the beach and only charge 1000 MT for a four-bed chalet. **Fatima's Nest** is next. This well-known place has seen better days and is now looking a bit tatty. With a bar/restaurant on the beach, communal kitchen and very basic ablutions, they charge 100 MT for camping, 150 MT for a dorm bed, and 300 MT single, 450 MT double in small reed huts. Book through Fatima's in Maputo.

Next along is **Dino's Beach Bar**, a great, multilevelled, vibey spot with cool music, cold beer and hot pizzas. There is also a shop selling hand-made shirts, skirts, trousers and bikinis made from the colourful local cloth – the resident tailor will make anything to order while you take refreshments at the bar. At the end of this sandy track (1.5 kilometres from Fatima's) is **Bamboozi's**. They don't offer camping, but do have a small swimming pool and nice A-frame chalets with equipped kitchens. A very large, airy rondavel serves as a dorm and they also have small reed huts. The funky ablution block has hot water and the big open-air communal kitchen is well equipped. Huts cost 150 MT a person, dorms 180 MT and the three-sleeper chalets are 900 MT. For information, tel: 293-29004 or 82-459-0560, e-mail: bamboozi@teledata. mz, website: www.bamboozi.com

Near to Bamboozi's is a horse-riding stable, run by Volker. He has 10 horses and offers lessons and rides along the beach or through the coconut planta-tions. Your first ride will cost 500 MT, but decreases with subsequent bookings or if you are in a group. Contact Volker, tel: 82-308-0300 or 82-391-5680, e-mail: gvhorst@gmx.net. There are also two dive operations in Tofo. **Diversity Scuba** is situated in the village behind the market and near to the Casa de Camer restaurant, tel: 293-29002 or 82-468-5310, e-mail: info@diversityscuba. com, website: www.diversityscuba.com. The other dive shop operates from the Casa Barry Resort and is called **Tofo Scuba**, tel: 293-29030 or 82-826-0140, e-mail: tofoscuba@teledata.mz, website: www.tofoscuba.com. Both offer PADI courses, have equipment to hire and will show you the area's wide variety of marine life, including mantas, whale sharks, dolphins, humpback whales and turtles.

If you were to turn right (south) on arrival at Tofo Beach, you would negotiate the short, sandy track just above the beach past Casa Azul (which was closed at the time of writing) to reach **Casa Barry**. This well-run and organised resort is situated right on the beach, where self-catering chalets shelter under whispering casuarina trees. The costs are 1800 MT for four people, and 2700 MT for six. Basic four-bed reed bungalows with shared facilities cost 180 MT a person. The restaurant has a spacious wooden deck overlooking the beach and serves tasty snacks, food and drinks all day. It is a large, professionally run resort in a good position. Contact them, tel: 293-29007 or, in South Africa, +27-(0)31-762-3469, fax: 293-29029, website: www.casabarry.com

Behind them on the hill is **Paradise Dunes**, a collection of solidly built holiday homes that sleep four, six or eight in comfort and style. The kitchens are particularly well equipped, with both fridge and freezer. Two-bedroomed houses cost 1 680 MT a night out of season and 2 400 MT in season, three bedrooms 2 520 MT to 3 600 MT, and four bedrooms 3 360 MT to 4 800 MT. Contact Louis locally, tel: 82-864-1440 or, in South Africa, tel: +27-(0)82-894-6581, e-mail:ivoryguesthouse@webmail.co.za

The small residential area of **Tofinho** has a Frelimo monument to fallen heroes on the headland, near to where unfortunate victims of the colonial era were thrown into a sea cave to be drowned by the rising tide. The waves off the point here make this Mozambique's best surfing spot, and the breaks known as 'Backdoor' and 'Monument' are spoken of around the world. **Turtle Cove Guest House** is a couple of blocks back from the beach (signposted) and was being renovated in Moorish style when I visited. But it still offers dorm beds at 180 MT and accommodation in reed chalets for 360 MT a person. Lazy hammocks and a star-gazing platform make this a great chilling spot. Contact Charles, tel: 82-430-2880 or Nic at Mozambique Connections in South Africa, tel: +27-(0)11-803-4185, website: www.mozcon.com. Other accommodation at the **Blue Roof**. Nice double-bedded, self-contained cottages (with fridge, hotplate and utensils) overlook the best surfing spots and are a bargain at 500 MT a night per cottage. Contact Blue Roof, tel: 82-818-2470 or book through Fatima's in Maputo.

Barra

Back at Bar Babalaza, turn right onto a good dirt road and head for Barra. After 5 kilometres there is a turn-off to the right that will take you to the lighthouse at **Ponta da Barra** (signposted to Farol da Barro 4x4 Campsite). You will need a 4x4 for this 2.3-kilometre track, but you'll be rewarded with one of the most beautiful sights along this coast. The lighthouse is situated on a high bluff with a fantastic view back along the beach towards Barra Lodge. There is also a picturesque camp site here, which shares the spot and the view. **Lighthouse Campsite** is run by Dennis Adams and, although it is a bit rustic at the moment, there are plans to renovate the old governor's weekend retreat into a more permanent bar/restaurant. The ablutions are fine and the security good. Dennis is an imaginative cook and only serves filter coffee, no instant. He allows no quadbikes, no jetskis and no loud music. In season, he charges 90 MT per site and 210 MT per person, while out of season it is 60 MT and 120 MT. His son Derrick organises occasional one-week student packages from Johannesburg (check the website for more details). For more information, tel: 82-355-9590, or in South Africa, +27-(0)76-105-8517, fax: +27-(0)13-744-9848, e-mail: pontadabarra@absamail.co.za, website: www.barralighthouse.com

Back on the main road to Barra Beach, it is only another 1 kilometre to the signposted left turn that takes you on to Barra Lodge, Barra Reef Resort and Flamingo Bay (all about 1 kilometre apart). **Barra Lodge** (S23°47.509

E35°30.646) is the largest of the three and the first along this road. Built right on the beach, the lodge nestles among coconut groves, and all the accommodation has sea views. There is also a beach bar, large exotically shaped and landscaped swimming pool, games room, activities centre and a 60-seater restaurant. They offer sailing trips on a 33-foot catamaran, snorkelling and scuba diving, quadbike trails, fishing and horse-riding. This is a big professional operation that can tailor-make your holiday, wedding or honeymoon, depending on your needs.

Twin-bedded *casitas* with *en-suite* shower and toilet are 1 620 MT per person, dinner, bed and breakfast in low season, and 2 025 MT in high season; self-catering two-bedroomed cottages that sleep six have big verandas and cost 2 990 MT and 3 350 MT, and there is even a clean, comfortable bunkhouse that offers dorm beds at 195 MT to 225 MT. The lodge has constructed a wooden walkway over a nearby mangrove swamp, which gives an interesting glimpse of life in the tidal zone. They also offer fly-in packages and good dive packages. For reservations in South Africa, tel: +27-(0)11-314-3355, fax: +27-(0)11-314-3239, e-mail: reservations@barralodge.co.za, website: www.barralodge.co.za. Alternatively, you could contact Barra Lodge locally, tel/fax: 293-20561, e-mail: barralodge@teledata.mz

Next along is the **Barra Reef Resort**, smaller and less slick but nice and laid-back all the same. The beach and sea views are the same and there is also a dive centre offering diving, fishing and cruises. The bar/restaurant is on the beach, as is some of the accommodation. *En-suite casitas* that sleep two in a single bedroom and, possibly, another two on the large veranda cost 1 140 MT a person for dinner, bed and breakfast in low season, going up to 1 350 MT in season. The larger self-catering chalets are well equipped and cost 450 MT a person, going up to 750 MT in season, while their bunkhouse offers double rooms with shared facilities that cost from 330 MT to 450 MT. For more info, tel: 293-56020 or 82-367-8490, e-mail: mozbarrareef@hotmail.com, website: www.barrareef.co.za

The newest and best lodge along this stretch (or any other stretch, for that matter) is the magnificent and exotic **Flamingo Bay Resort**. Conceived and constructed by Dave Law of Barra Lodge, it consists of 20 luxury chalets built on stilts over the waters of a protected bay. The spacious main building is built on a small island and the whole complex is interconnected by wooden bridges and walkways. Chauffeur-driven golf carts ferry you around. Guests can go diving off the porch of their chalets or swim in the pool that gave Dave so many headaches while he was building it. Contact Barra Lodge for bookings and more information on what Flamingo Bay has to offer.

Finally, right out on the tip of the Barra peninsula, in an unbeatable location, is **White Sands**. The self-contained chalets and camp sites shelter under palms, and diving and fishing can be arranged. For the lowdown, tel: 82-490-9280, or in South Africa, +27-(0)14-533-0210.

North to Vilankulo 15

From Inhambane, you have to retrace your steps to rejoin the main road north (EN1). This can be done by driving down to the main intersection at Lindela or by turning right 24 kilometres south of Inhambane. This 5.5-kilometre short cut is a good dirt road that joins the EN1 about 20 kilometres south of Maxixe and saves about 12 kilometres on the road.

Murals are a fairly common form of artistic expression, and you will see them on many walls in Mozambique, especially in and around the towns.

Maxixe

Maxixe (pronounced *masheesh*) is a pretty little waterfront town situated just across the bay from Inhambane. The Shell service station on the south side of town has a small shop, air for pumping your tyres and sometimes even unleaded petrol.

The **Campismo de Maxixe** is in the centre of town, on the right just before the ferry jetty. This pleasantly situated camp site is on the water's edge and has good security. Brick-built bungalows for two with *en-suite* facilities cost 500 MT per night, cottages that also sleep two but have shared ablutions cost 400 MT a night, while camp sites (most have electric plugs) are 70 MT a person. For further information and enquiries, tel: 293-30351.

Just past the jetty, in a welcoming cool garden under huge flamboyant trees, is the Stop Restaurant. This is a good spot to break your journey for a bite to eat or something cool to drink, and they also do takeaways. Across the road from the jetty is another petrol station, bank, cellphone shop and closed-down hotel. A few blocks north on the left-hand side of the road is the **Residencial Tania**, which offers bright and clean accommodation on the second floor of a rather dirty and dingy building. *En-suite* rooms cost 350 MT single and 400 MT double. Contact the Residencial Tania, tel: 293-30059

The road north of Maxixe is very badly potholed, but they are working on it. After about 30 kilometres, you reach the little town of Morrumbene; turn right here to visit fascinating Linga Linga.

Linga Linga

Situated at the end of the peninsula jutting into the northern side of Inhambane Bay, Linga Linga is the site of an old whaling station. Accessible only with 4x4 or by boat from Inhambane, Maxixe or Morrumbene, there is good birding and fishing in the area, and if you're lucky, you might even spot a dugong. White sandy beaches to relax on and the popular Funky Monkey backpackers' lodge for accommodation and food – what more do you want for a few days of chilling?

Massinga

Just before reaching Massinga, you will cross the Tropic of Capricorn – you are now officially in the tropics. For food and accommodation in Massinga, you only need one name – **Dalilo's** The restaurant of that name is in the centre of town and the hotel is on the left-hand side of the main street a few blocks up. Plain double rooms with shared facilities cost 250 MT, *en-suite* with bedroom and a little veranda is 400 MT and, for 750 MT, they'll throw in a TV, air-con and fridge. For details, tel: 293-71043.

Morrungulo

About 8 kilometres north of the centre of Massinga is the turn-off right to Morrungulo, and 13 kilometres down a good dirt road brings you to the gates and reception of **Morrungulo Beach Resort** (S23°14.047 E35°29.401). This is a well-established and well-run place with neat lawns under large shade trees. A small wetland area has good birdlife and tame crested guinea fowl roam the camp. The beach is at your chalet's doorstep and the whole place is spacious enough to not get too crowded. Four-sleeper, fully-equipped chalets cost 2100 MT out of season and 1875 MT in, while two-sleeper bungalows are 900 MT and 1500 MT. Camping is 210 MT a person and another 450 MT if you want the comfort of a *barraca*. For more information, e-mail: mg10@bushmail.net, website: www.morrungulo.co.za.

There are two other establishments in this area. Just before you reach the Morrungulo Resort, there is a turn-off on the left that leads to **Baobab Lodge**. This is the backpacker's alternative for the budget-conscious traveller. High on a hill overlooking the bay, this rustic, locally run spot offers camping at 150 MT in season and 100 MT out of, and two-bed reed huts with shared ablutions cost 900 MT and 600 MT. The other camp is much smarter and expertly run by Les Ryan. **Sylvia Shoal Resort and Adventure Divers** is signposted off the road down to Morrungulo and is set among grassed dunes just above the beach. They offer bungalows with bathrooms and kitchenettes that sleep two, but are equipped for six so that extra family and friends can camp next to the bungalow and share with you. Bungalows range between 1440 MT and 1830 MT (seasons) and camping is between 150 MT to 210 MT a person. *Baraccas* cost an extra 390 MT to 630 MT. The dive operation offers all the usual scuba courses, as well as snorkelling and fishing. For more info and bookings, contact Stephanie Teale in South Africa, tel: +27-(0)82-900-4886, tel/fax: +27-(0)11-884-6055, e-mail: stephanie.teale@iafrica.com, website: www.mozambique.za.com, or contact Les in Moz, tel: 82-394-8960.

Pomene

Resisting the kids' cries of 'Sweeeeets!' on the drive back up to the EN1, continue for only a quarter of a kilometre up the main road, and turn off again (S23°15.281 E35°22.280) for the drive down to Pomene. The kids along this road are far more discerning than those down the Morrongula road, for instead of begging for sweets, the cry is for 'Chocolaaaate!'. This is also a rougher road, especially the last 9 kilometres, which are very narrow and sandy. Beautiful coastal dune forest gives way to a mangrove swamp and you end up dodging rather large land crabs as you wind your way down to this gloriously isolated spot. The sea breaks gently onto an endless sandy beach, while birds feed in the lagoon just behind you. A river forms a mangrove-ringed estuary and it's a birder's paradise. Sparsely populated and unspoilt, this is also a good spot to look for the illusive dugongs. Fortunately, 20 000 hectares of the surrounding area was declared the **Pomene Reserve** in 1972 and this wonderful ecosystem of mangroves, dunes and lagoon with its birds and marine life is protected.

The road runs all the way to the headland at the end of the bay where the empty shell of what was once the Pomene Hotel stands, begging to be renovated. The view from here is magnificent and when it is once more made habitable, I would love to be one of the first guests. But back along the beach (more 4x4 driving) is the very comfortable **Pomene Lodge**, which was badly hit by the storms of 2000. Recovering nicely now, the resort offers all the amenities such as restaurant, bar and curio shop, as well as organising diving and fishing activities. Self-catering cottages have their own toilet and shower with hot and cold water, as well as cutlery, crockery, a two-plate gas cooker, freezer, mosquito nets and bedding. Costs range from 1500 MT for a three-sleeper out of season to 4500 MT a day for a six-sleeper in season. Camping costs 250 MT per person per day. Pomene Lodge is owned and operated by the folks at Barra Lodge, so for bookings and info, contact their South African office, tel: +27-(0)11-314-3355, e-mail: reservations@barralodge. co.za or bookings@pomene.co.za, website: www.barralodge.co.za or www. pomene.co.za

Slightly inland, near to the airstrip (850 metres long and a great way to visit the area if you are lucky enough to own a plane) is the new **Pomene View Lodge** (S22°56.945 E35°35.145). Solidly built with bricks and mortar (one gets a little tired of all the quaint rustic bamboo huts sometimes), it sits high on a hill and overlooks one of the best views in Mozambique. Created by the friendly father-and-son team of Clint and Dave Krause, Pomene View has big shade trees (the grass is still struggling), large braai boma, wooden deck with the famous view and a swimming pool. They offer walks through various habitats where the birding is outstanding (fish eagles, flamingoes and kingfishers, to name a few of the common ones).

The spacious accommodation is fully equipped to sleep five and costs 1800 MT to 2700 MT, depending on season) They can be contacted directly on e-mail: 2pomview@bushmail.net or book through Cathy, e-mail: garry@lantic.net.

On the drive back to the main EN1 highway, stop at a little marshy lake along the way (S23°12.003 E35°23.043). This lily-covered waterway is another fine birding spot.

Yet another accommodation option in the Pomene Bay area is **Casa Rei** on the north bank of the estuary. Ray Preen is an experienced Springbok fisherman with two world and 18 South African records to his name and is passionate about conserving his little piece of paradise. It's difficult to reach, as the road is not the same as for the south-bank resorts (Ray's very detailed instructions for the three-hour, 65-kilometre route take up no less than two foolscap pages).

Accommodation is in five self-contained camps on the water's edge, each equipped to cater for up to eight people. Each camp has four two-bed reed huts, a living-room lapa, kitchen, shower and toilet. Cooking is over an open fire and lighting is by paraffin lamp, but you are allocated two trained staff to do everything for you. Bring all you need, and relax, relax, relax. For info and bookings, contact Mellery in South Africa, tel: +27-(0)21-790-0104 or +27-(0)82-338-9639, or Ray himself at e-mail prarn@mweb.co.za

The road on up to Vilankulo is badly potholed, but work is in progress. No reliable fuel is available until you get into the town of Vilankulo itself.

Vilankulo and the Bazaruto Archipelago 16

About 146 kilometres from the Pomene turn-off, you will reach the poorly sign-posted road down to Vilankulo – you will recognise it by the large radio towers and small market that has sprung up (S21°59.825 E35°08.710). The countyside around here is pockmarked with small, round lakes' the origin of which, some believe, is a meteorite shower. Just before reaching Vilankulo, you will pass the turn-off (on the right) to the airport (fly-in options are available, so see Chapter 9) and, about 18.5 kilometres down, you will reach the main T-junction in Vilankulo town. Turn right for the market, village shops and fuel, or left to reach the harbour and most of the accommodation and restaurants. It is not a large town, but is quite spread out.

Trek-net fishing keeps the markets of Vilankulo well stocked with fresh fish.

Introducing Vilankulo

If you start your tour of Vilankulo by turning right, you will run straight into the municipal market a couple of blocks down, passing small restaurants and a bakery on your right and a bank and pharmacy on your left. This is not only the hub of most commercial activity, but also where to go for public transport. Buses to Maputo and Beira leave in the early morning, but make local enquiries for the latest info. Turn left at the market and head down to the town's one-and-only fuel station (unleaded is 22,5 MT/litre, leaded 20,1 MT/litre and diesel 17,5 MT/litre). This is also the part of town where you can stock up with supplies if you are going across to the islands or heading further north up the coast. Drive back around the block and stop at the Mozambicano bakery for fresh bread, pastries and coffee before making your way back to the central intersection.

Heading down the main street away from the market area, we pass Oliveiras bus terminus on our left and then the shore-based office of Gabriel's Resort on Benguerra Island (turn right opposite here, if you need the hospital). A little further down, on the right, is the turn-off down to Complexo Bimbi, then Café Edson and Motel Darcia, the Deli and Talho Butchery (closed at time of writing). The popular Na Sombra restaurant and rooms is next on your left, and then there's the bank (with ATM) and an auto-repair yard across the road. Curios and fresh fish are sold at the T-junction, from the old converted blue bus, where this road runs up against the bayside beach.

Turn left here. The road follows the beach, with its boatbuilders, until we reach the smart, upmarket Casa Rex restaurant and accommodation. Across the road is the Ka Massingue Snackbar and the Maritime Office (the place to go for boat-launching licences). Next is the Vilankulo Conference Centre, shortly followed by the Aguia Negra Resort and finally, the Vilankulo Beach Lodge. Back at the blue bus junction, you could turn right to pass Smugglers bar, restaurant and accommodation and then carry on to the (still closed) Hotel Dona Ana. It beats me why so many hotels in the best and most beautiful positions in Mozambique stand empty and derelict. The Dona Ana is on the headland of the little Vilankulo harbour, with boats bobbing in the bay on one side and a palm-fringed beach on the other – and it's closed! Dhows and ferries to the islands leave from the little jetty here. Swing right and continue down the beach front, which was partially washed away by the storms in 2000. You will pass Sail Away and then reach Vilankulo camping on your right. A little further on is the Tropical Restaurant on your left and Casa Josef on your right. Look carefully to spot the little lane that leads off right to the Zombie Cucumber (all will be revealed later…). This beachfront road will lead you to Margie at Tourist Services and eventually Baobab Beach Backpackers.

Overnight in Vilankulo

There is a lot of accommodation on offer in Vilankulo – in fact, it starts 15 kilometres from the EN1, before you even reach the town. A turn-off to the

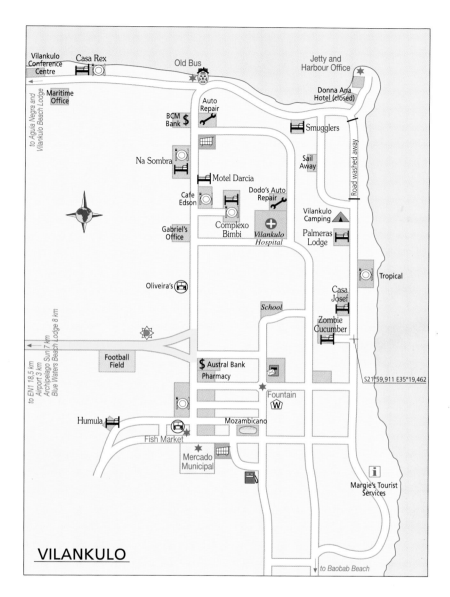

VILANKULO

Vilankulo Conference Centre · Casa Rex · Old Bus · Jetty and Harbour Office

Maritime Office · to Aguia Negra and Vilankulo Beach Lodge · Auto Repair · Donna Ana Hotel (closed) · Road washed away

BCM Bank · Smugglers

Na Sombra · Sail Away

Motel Darcia

Cafe Edson · Dodo's Auto Repair · Vilankulo Camping

Gabriel's Office · Complexo Bimbi · Vilankulo Hospital · Palmeras Lodge

Oliveira's · Tropical

School · Casa Josef

Zombie Cucumber

to EN1 18.5 km · Airport 3 km · Archipelago Sun 7 km · Blue Waters Beach Lodge 8 km · Football Field · Austral Bank · Pharmacy · S21°59,911 E35°19,462

Humula · Fountain · Mozambicano

Fish Market

Mercado Municipal · Margie's Tourist Services

to Baobab Beach

left (S21°59.971 E35°17.072) is sign-posted to the Archipelago Sun and the Blue Water Beach Resort, both about 7 kilometres down this dirt road and nicely isolated from the hustle and bus-tle of Vilankulo town. **Blue Waters** is a well-tended, secure spot with grass and shade just above the beach. Compact *en-suite*, self-catering bungalows that sleep two cost 900 MT a person, larger four-sleeper bungalows are 2520 MT, and six-sleepers cost 2880 MT. There is also camping at 180 MT a person. Contact: Brian in Mozambique, tel: 82-807-5750, South Africa, tel: +27-(0)82-330-6252, or in Zimbabwe, tel: +263-(0)4-77-6498; website: www.vilankulo-resorts.com

The nearby **Archipelago Sun** used to be called Baia do Paraiso, but has been considerably upgraded and now has 18 large houses, each one fully equipped for eight people. Sea-facing units cost 3780 MT and others are 3240 MT a night. There is a watersports centre on site, and they also sell timeshare. For bookings, tel: 82-767-0900, e-mail: isadoretsatsa@hotmail.com

The two accommodation areas are the main beach and town centre (for value-for-money options), and the smarter up-market resorts north of town. We start down at the southern end of the beach at the run-down **Baobab Camp**. Well past its sell-by date and with really bad security, I can't in all honesty recommend this place, but list it only in the hope that it might one day be renovated. Camping is 120 MT, dorm beds 150 MT, small reed huts with a double bed 400 MT – and the ablutions are completely inadequate. Contact Mandy, tel: 82-731-5420 or 82-865-0210. Still on the beachfront, but more central, is the totally different **Zombie Cucumber** – now this is how a backpackers' lodge should be run! Set in a pretty garden, down a narrow lane (S21°59.911 E35°19.462), there is both privacy and good security. John and Stephanie run this clean and compact little camp very well and offer dorm beds at 200 MT, and two-bed A-frame chalets at 550 MT. The shared ablutions are spotless, a washing service is offered and Stephanie cooks a delicious special daily meal. Info and assistance are offered for all local activities – contact them on tel: 82-804-9410, e-mail: steph@zombiecucumber.com

The islands and reefs of the Bazaruto Archipelago are protected as a national park.

Just up the road, also opposite the beach, is the old-established **Casa de Josef e Tina**. Situated on a large grassed property, it has *en-suite* reed rondavels for two people at 500 MT, and 800 MT for four people. Communal cooking is available in an open-air kitchen. There is also a large, self-catering house that offers accommodation for up to eight in well-equipped luxury for 1 620 MT. For information, tel: 293-82140.

The next place along this beachfront road is a bit out of place as it is just so posh. **Palmeiras Lodge** is set in exotic tropical gardens with a pool. Bed and breakfast in free-standing, *en-suite* chalets costs 900 MT single and 1 440 MT double. There is also a large, self-catering and serviced villa for six people, and this costs 2 700 MT. Contact the Palmeiras Lodge in Mozambique, tel: 293-82388, fax: 293-82314, or in South Africa, tel: +27-(0)21-706-0517, fax: +27-(0)21-706-0515, e-mail: palmeiras@vilankulo.co.za

Next door is **Vilankulo Camping**. With well-grassed sites under whispering casuarina trees, this spot is also a little past its prime, with poor security and scruffy ablutions. Camping is 210 MT a person (270 MT in peak season) and they also have rooms that share facilities for 390 MT double (280 MT peak). For bookings, tel: 293-82043, or in South Africa, tel: +27-(0)15-516-1427, website: www.vilankulocamping.co.za. (There is a very interesting craft and plant market here on the first Sunday of each month.)

Continuing to the end of the beachfront, you will reach the **Hotel Dona Ana**. This well-positioned place just can't stay closed forever, so watch the space… Following the road around the harbour brings you to **Smugglers**, popular with overland tour groups. There is a clean, casual and reasonably priced restaurant, vibey bar with darts, a pool table and international dance music. A secure, residents-only back garden with neatly trimmed lawns contains the accommodation. This consists of rows of rooms each with two beds, a table and fan, and leads out onto a veranda overlooking a swimming pool. The costs are 450 MT a person in season and 300 MT out. Two double *en-suite* rooms are also available at 540 MT and 360 MT per person. Laundry can be organised as well as just about anything else going on in Vilankulo. Contact Smugglers, tel: 293-82118.

At the old blue bus, swing left and away from the harbour to take the main road through town. Pass the bank on your right and you will spot **Na Sombra**, one of the nicest locally flavoured restaurants in town. From continental breakfasts to evening grills and everything in between, this is the place in which to linger. There are also rooms – a bit basic and old, but jolly and clean. All have a fan and share facilities at a cost of 280 MT single, 350 MT double and 530 MT for a four-bedder. There can be some noise from the bar at night. For the lowdown, tel: 293-82090, or Oliver on tel: 82-762-4350. Further down the road, on the left, is the **Motel Dercia**, behind Café Edson. A little garden, secure off-street parking, small *en-suite* A-frame chalets for 450 MT and plain double rooms for 350 MT make this a good budget option. For bookings, tel: 293-82070. The final in-town accommodation is signposted off left further down the street. **Complex Bimbi** is like a small village with two-bedroom and three-bedroom houses, each with air-con and TV in a quiet, secluded garden compound. Four-bedders cost 1 440 MT and six-bedders 1 800 MT. Contact the complex, tel: 293-82105.

The resorts of Vilankulo

Heading back to the old blue bus, take a sharp left to follow the harbour road around to reach the up-market resorts of Vilankulo. First up on the right is the classy **Casa Rex**. Recommended for a good, well-served meal in gracious surroundings, Casa Rex also has limited accommodation. Charmingly decorated with custom-crafted wood furniture, the rooms have views of the bay. The *en-suite* rooms with double bed cost 1 200 MT, twin bed 1 400 MT and a luxury suite with double bed is 1 600 MT – all per person, with a single supplement of 400 MT. For bookings, tel: 293-82048, e-mail: casarex@teledata. mz, website: www.casarex.co.zw.

Aguia Negra is next up and also on your right. Twelve thatched A-frame chalets offer bed and breakfast from 1 050 MT single to 3 510 MT for six people. There is also a solid, hotel-like block of luxury rooms with air-con, TV and fridge for 1 650 MT single and 1 350 MT double, all set in an exotic garden with views of the bay. For the South African booking office, tel: +27-(0)21-847-1160, fax: +27-(0)21-847-1169, e-mail: hotel@erinvale.co.za, website: www.aguianegra.co.za, or contact

Aguia Negra direct, tel: 293-82387, e-mail: aguianegra@teledata.mz

Last, but definitely not least, is the delightful **Vilankulo Beach Lodge**, 5 kilometres from the town centre. From the shaded and secure parking down to the main building with bar and restaurant and on through the gardens, past the pool and out onto the beach, this lodge feels welcoming and comfortable. The *en-suite* chalets all have great views from their own private balconies, and non-motorised watersports are free. Prices are for bed and breakfast, per person sharing, and range from 1 650 MT for a standard chalet out of season to the deluxe suite in season at 2 550 MT. Contact the reservations centre in South Africa, tel: +27-(0)21-691-1763, fax: +27-(0)21-691-1764, e-mail: beachlodge@vilankulo.co.za, website: www.vilankulo.co.za, or contact the lodge, tel: 293-82388, fax: 293-82314, e-mail: beachlodge@teledata.mz

Finally, for bookings of all accommodation and activities, and info on transport and health issues, contact Margie at Tourist Services, tel: 293-82228, e-mail: margie@teledata.mz. Another local booking agent you could try is Malibu, tel: 293-82291 or 82-807-6170, fax: 293-82091, e-mail: malibutlagency@teledata.mz

Eating out in Vilankulo

With all the restaurants already mentioned at the lodges and camps, you really don't have to look any further to find a place to eat. One very up-market place, however, does deserve special mention, the **Vilankulo Conference Centre** between Casa Rex and Aguia

Negra. Decorated with stone and wooden out-of-Africa furniture, their **Boa Vista Restaurant**, as its name applies does indeed have a beautiful view as well as good food expertly served in pleasant surroundings.

On the road in Vilankulo

If you have been unfortunate and had a mechanical breakdown, you will have to call Kinito who runs a tow-in service and workshop at **Auto Muçoque**. He is based opposite the BCM Bank near the old blue bus junction and can be contacted on tel: 82-842-3000. At the time of writing, Dirk was about to open a service centre across the road on the corner (tel: 82-764-4400), and the old established **Dodo's** (tel: 82-891-4050) down near the hospital has a big workshop, a yard full of donor vehicles and enough oil soaked into the ground to make Red Adair nervous.

Off to the archipelago

Vilankulo has always been a jumping-off point for the Bazaruto Archipelago and has struggled to keep tourists interested in staying in the town. The larger resorts to the north and south of town are making it very tempting with their watersports and one, the Vilankulo Beach Resort, has plans to build a bird hide over a nearby wetland. There is also a cinema close to the entrance to Complexo Bimbi, with performances every night at 20h30, except Mondays, and on Fridays and Saturdays they host a disco after the movie (tel: 82-861-2540).

But, of course, most visitors want to get to the islands, or at least onto the water. **Sailaway Dhow Safaris** is situated one street back from the beach, near to Hotel Dona Ana, and offers day trips as well as two-, three-, and four-day dhow safaris. The day trips can be to either Magaruque or Benguerua Island, where you are free to snorkel the reef or wander the beaches. The cost per person of 720 MT includes dhow transport, park entry fees and use of snorkelling equipment (take your own picnic lunch). Overnight safaris visit Bazaruto, Benguerua and Magaruque, where you snorkel the reefs and hike the islands. The cost of 1 260 MT per person per day includes accommodation at Gabriel's Lodge on Benguerua, park entry fees, all meals, use of snorkelling equipment, and dhow transport. Each sailing dhow has a crew of three – captain, cook and translator/guide – and also has life jackets and a stand-by motor. For further details, contact Sailaway tel: 293-82385 or 82-387-6350, e-mail: sailawaymoz@hotmail.com

The world-renowned **Bazaruto National Park** consists of five pristine islands – Bazaruto, Benguerua, Magaruque, Bangue and Santa Carolina – all situated 10–15 kilometres offshore between Vilankulo in the south and Inhassoro in the north. The park is managed by the National Directorate for Conservation Areas in the Ministry of Tourism, in collaboration with the WWF and the Endangered Wildlife Trust. Bazaruto is the largest island, Bangue the smallest, and uninhabited. Santa Carolina, previously the most popular and known as Paradise Island, currently has no tourist facilities. Famous for the rich marine life around

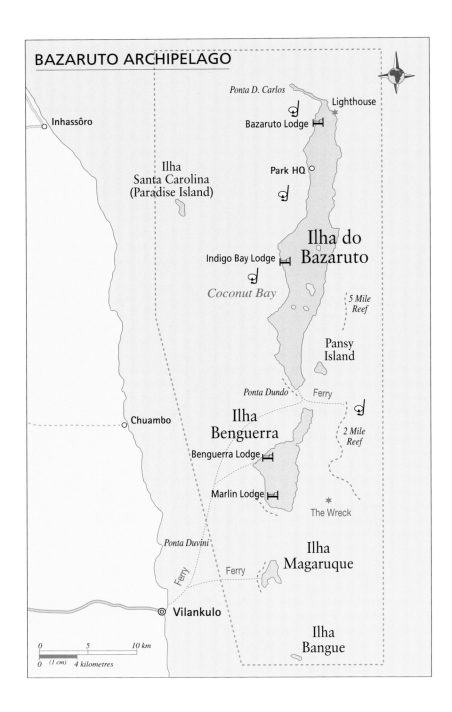

BAZARUTO ARCHIPELAGO

Ponta D. Carlos

Lighthouse

Inhassôro

Bazaruto Lodge

Ilha
Santa Carolina
(Paradise Island)

Park HQ

Ilha do
Bazaruto

Indigo Bay Lodge

Coconut Bay

5 Mile
Reef

Pansy
Island

Ponta Dundo   Ferry

Chuambo   Ilha
Benguerra

2 Mile
Reef

Benguerra Lodge

Marlin Lodge

The Wreck

Ponta Duvini   Ilha
Magaruque

Ferry   Ferry

Vilankulo

Ilha
Bangue

0   5   10 km

0   (1 cm)   4 kilometres

the islands – dugongs, whales, turtles and 2000 fish species – there is also a list of over 180 birds to be spotted here, including the crab plover and olive bee-eater, which tunnels its nest into the sand dunes. Add to all this the fresh-water crocodiles that inhabit the lakes on two of the islands and you have a truly unique fauna. Camping is prohibit-ed in the park, and there is only accom-modation on Bazaruto and Benguerra. Park entry tickets (200 MT per entry per person) must be bought prior to visiting, and are available at the Vilankulo WWF office or from registered tour operators. If visiting with your own boat, there is an additional fee of 150 MT.

Accommodation in the Bazaruto Archipelago

The accommodation on the islands is understandably rather exclusive and expensive. **Indigo Bay** on Bazaruto Island is a large resort offering watersports, cultural tours, sandboarding, island drives and horse-riding. Full-board rates (in-cluding transfers from Vilankulo) start from 5500 MT per per-son a night sharing. For reservations, tel: +27-(0)11-467-1277, fax: +27-(0)11-465-9623, e-mail: reservations@raniafrica.co.za, website: www.ran-iafrica.com

Marlin Lodge, on Benguerra Island, is a pretty lodge constructed from Mozambican hardwoods and elevated on stilts. There are excellent fishing and diving facilities, and full-board rates start at 4350 MT a person a night sharing. For details, tel: +27-(0)12-543-2134, fax: +27-(0)12-543-2135, e-mail: reservations@marlinlodge.co.za, web-site: www.marlinlodge.co.za

Another up-market option on the island is **Benguerra Lodge**; tel: +27-(0)11-483-2734, fax: +27-(0)11-728-3767, e-mail: benguerra@icon.co.za, website: www.benguerra.co.za. Fortunately for budget travellers, there is also **Gabriel's Lodge** on Benguerra Island. The standard and condition of this backpacker-type establishment had been going down for a while, but is now reported to be improving. They offer camping at 400 MT, dorm beds at 400 MT, *cabanas* at 600 MT and dinner, bed and breakfast in an *en-suite* chalet for 1000 MT (all per person, per night). They have a shore-based office in Vilankulo, tel: 293-82230 or 82-389-4250.

On to Inhassoro and beyond

The EN1 continues north from the Vilankulo turn-off through the Tamane gas fields (which are not especially conspicuous) until, after approximately 49 kilometres, you reach the Inhassoro turn-off (S21°34.370 E35°04.266). There is an impressive little tyre shop here, in case you need to have a puncture repaired. It is another 14 kilometres down a single-lane tar road to the coast and Inhassoro. On the way down, at S21°33.970 E35°06.074, the road cross-es a shallow river and wetlands (which are actually navigable from Vilankulo by canoe), which is a good spot for aquatic birds – we spotted openbilled stork and African jacana. A T-junction as you enter Inhassoro gives you the choice of turning either left into the Seta Estancia Turistica, or right into town.

Seta Estancia Turistica has 12 neat and newly renovated self-contained chalets in leafy, park-like surroundings. With new linen, tiled bathrooms and fully-equipped kitchens, the two-sleepers cost 1000 MT, four-sleepers 1600 MT and six-sleepers 2500 MT. A large airy bar/restaurant overlooks the beach, and boat launching as well as trips to the islands can be arranged. Contact Seta on tel: 293-91000 or 82-302-0990, fax: 293-91002, e-mail: hotelseta@hotmail.com. A separately run camp site is entered through the Seta complex. It is well situated above the beach, with trees and grass, but has ablutions that must date back to colonial days. Cost is 100 MT per site per day, plus 100 MT per person.

A right turn at the T-junction brings you into the small village with basic shops and a bakery. The old **Inhassoro Beach Lodge** on the left is being renovated and might reopen soon.

Back at the EN1, there is a large Total service station just north of the Inhassoro turn-off (no unleaded petrol). This is the last fuel for the next 200 kilometres. The 62 kilometres to the bridge across the Save River is reasonably well tarred and runs through more gas fields. There is a small toll payable when crossing the Save bridge, and be careful of the checkpoint there – the officials can be evil. The BP garage at Mushungu is reached after another 140 kilometres, where you can buy all fuels (including unleaded). The road has some bad potholes beyond the Buzi River, but after another 95 kilometres you reach Inchope and the big cross-roads (S19°12.477 E33°55.983) of the EN1 and the EN6, the highway down from Mutare in Zimbabwe to Beira.

ROUGH RIDE TO KRUGER

An interesting alternative route back to South Africa from Vilankulo is the rough two-day ride that heads west from the Vilankulo area to Pafuri in the northeastern tip of the Kruger National Park. With no fuel available along the way and at least 700 kilometres to Pafuri, make sure you fill up with enough fuel in Vilankulo before tackling this route. A good dirt road turns off west from the EN1, about 32 kilometres south of the Vilankulo turn-off and goes to Mabote, your last chance to buy any supplies. From there, it is a sandy track (don't deviate, as the area has not yet been cleared of all landmines) as far as Machaila, and it then improves again as it heads southwest to cross the railway line at S Gorge de Limpopo and reach the Limpopo river at Mapai. There is no bridge at Mapai, just a drift through the river, so this route is best travelled in the dry season. During the wet season, the river is too deep and the crossing is dangerous or impossible. A reasonable dirt road runs up along the Limpopo from the crossing through beautiful countryside to the Mozambique-South Africa border at Pafuri. On entering South Africa, you are in the Kruger National Park and can then choose your route south through the park or straight out to Makhado (the town previously known as Louis Trichardt) via Thohoyandou.

Beira 17

Pretend you are coming down from Zimbabwe. Whether driving from South Africa via Masvinga and Birchenough Bridge or from Harare, you would have to travel through Mutare. Mozambique's second largest city is like a neglected stepchild. Rundown and economically stagnant now, it will hopefully surge ahead when (and if) Zimbabwe sorts itself out.

The landmark Moulin Rouge restaurant is a popular and inexpensive eatery in Beira.

BEIRA

INDIAN OCEAN

MACÚTI

PALMEIRAS

MUNHAVA

MAQUINO

BEIRA

Rio Púngue

to Airport

Estrada Carlos Pereira

Lighthouse

Estoril (disused)

Macúti

Macúti Housing Compound

Av. FPLM

Biques

Club Nautico

Antonio José de Almeida

Complexo Gumo

Av. Exterior

Av. FPLM

Sports Club

Market

Rua Roberto Ivens

Rua Vasco da Gama

Capitaes Sofala

Rua dos Capitaes

Praça da Independencia

Miramar

Club Oceana

Rua Krusse Gomes

to Dondo and Chimoio

Av. 24 de Julho

Av. 24 de Julho

Rua Fernão Veloso

Rua Alfredo Lawley

Rua Fernão Lopes de Castanheda

Rua Cap. Pereira do Lago

Rua do João Madeira

Rua Frei João Veloso

Rua Fernão Veloso

Correia Monteiro

Rua Victor Gordon

Rua de Lourenço Marques

Av. Samora Machel

R. General Teixeira de Aragao

Pio Filho

Rua da Rocha

Viera da Rocha

Rua Baltazar de Aragao

Rua General

Rua do Algarve

Rua da Estremadura

Rua do Dr. Guilherme Aragia

Av. do Alentejo

Rua do Dr. Guilherme Aragia

Av. Pero do Canto Resende

Artur do Canto Resende

Av. Alfredo Lawley

Rua de Cabo Verde

Av. Armando Tivane

Market

Shoprite

Bus stop

Savoy

Observatory

Correia de Brito

Rua Moyznio de Albuquerque

Av. Eduardo Mondlane

Rua D. Francisco Barreto

Com. Galvão

Rua D. Francisco de Almeida

Av. M.S. Mutemba

Travessa da Igreja

Grand (disused)

Rua do Gen. Machado

Palace of Weddings

City Hall

Av. Paiva de Andrade

Embaixador

Market

Hotel Tivoli

Predio Infante de Sagres

Praça dos Trabalhadores

Av. Alves Rocadas

0   500   1 000 m

0   (1 cm)   440 metres

From Mutare

If you decide to stay over in Mutare, I would suggest you look up Anne Bruce on the corner of 6th Ave and 4th St (S18°58.257 E32°40463), the best budget accommodation left in town – a friendly house with a homely atmosphere in a quiet street, and within walking distance of everything. The exchange rate makes prices fluctuate madly in Zim, so don't laugh when I say it cost $4.50 (US$ not Zim$!) for a bed in a dorm or private room and only $6 in a suite. Contact Ann, tel: +263-(0)20-63569. Comparatively speaking, the nearby Holiday Inn is ridiculously expensive at $117 for a standard room with two beds. The Spur Steakhouse is located on the hotel's premises, too, and charges $7.50 for a fillet steak with all the trimmings.

When leaving Mutare, head down Herbert Chitepo Street to the corner of Robert Mugabe Avenue (last-minute shopping can be done at the OK Bazaars there), turn east and go down, past the offices of the Automobile Association of Zimbabwe, across the little river and refuel at the petrol station on the left (with the current shortage of fuel in Zimbabwe, probably not!). Turn right into Park Road and at Number 52 you will pass the only other budget accommodation option in town, the **Homestead Guesthouse**. A historical old building that was the first school in the area, it is set in large grounds with lots of safe parking. A standard double room costs $12.75, *en-suite* double $14.25, and breakfast $4. Keep on Park Road, driving through the industrial area and take the left turn

signposted to Beira. The road winds down the valley past the **Valley Lodge**, Mutare's luxury accommodation. The birdlife alone is worth the stay – the comfortable rooms and good food are a bonus, and a bargain at $42–75 for a double and $55 for a family room. For information, tel: +263-(0)20-62868.

Machipanda border post, 10 kilometres from Mutare, is a breeze – usually not very busy and mostly free of the hustlers that make so many border posts a chaotic nightmare. Leaving the Zimbabwean side should be quick and painless, and the Mozambique side is clean and orderly, with polite and honest officials (see page 49 for details on crossing the border into Moz). A good new road leads away from the border, and 75 kilometres from Mutare (S19°03.515 E33°17.340) you will pass the turn-off that leads north to Tete (see page 179). Chimoio is a further 22 kilometres.

Chimoio and Inchope

It's hard to believe that this town is actually the fifth largest in Moz, but it does have all the amenities, such as banks, fuel, general dealers, bars, restaurants and hotels – you'll spot them when driving through. And do drive through, as all you will need (except accommodation) is on the other side of town, on your way out. That is where you will find the big, new Shoprite Centre. The supermarket stocks everything, the Hungry Lion serves takeaways, and there is also a bank and pharmacy. The parking area is fenced off and patrolled by guards and next door is a smart new Total service station.

The fine new EN6 highway continues east following the railway line and clusters of big, old mango trees (they say you can trace the ancient slave routes by following the concentrations of these trees), and after 63 kilometres you will reach the intersection with the EN1 at Inchope. There is no fuel here, nor is there accommodation or much of anything else, just the inevitable sprawl of an informal market and *chapas* blocking the road. North leads to the Gorongosa National Park, Zambezi River and Nampula, and south takes you down to Maputo. Let's carry on straight to Beira…

On to Beira

It's only another 135 kilometres to Beira, but the road deteriorates slightly and there is a bad stretch of potholed gravel between Tica and Dondo across the Pungue Flats. We finally enter Beira down the long Av Samora Machel, which will take you right into the heart of town. To get to the seafront, turn off left into Av Armando Tivane at the circle with the BP garage and Shoprite Centre, and then right at the next circle.

Beira owes its existence to the riches of Monomatapa, the early gold-mining civilisation based in what is now Zimbabwe. But originally it was through Sofala, 40 kilometres to the south, that the gold was traded. The Portuguese built a fort there, but Sofala and the gold didn't last, and so the region languished until Joaquim Carlos Paiva de Antrada set up shop at the mouth of the Pungue River, on the site of present-day Beira. He controlled vast estates inland and also benefited from the growth of Rhodesia, as Beira was this British colony's closest harbour link. This grew to be Mozambique's second-largest city and a harbour of importance as it also served Zambia and Malawi. In more modern times, it suffered as independence wars and civil strife strangled trade and industry. Unfortunately for Beira, it was a Renamo stronghold, and when Frelimo came out tops after the civil war, the city was ignored by the new government, a problem it still has today, as Beira has a Renamo mayor. By all accounts, though, the city is fairly well run and has great potential, especially if Zimbabwe can sort out its problems and help the entire region to forge ahead.

Beira's somewhat tatty appearance also stems from the fact that a good chunk of the city lies below sea level

One of the fine tiled murals in the Predio Infante de Sagres.

and is a little marshy (their tallest building, 10 floors, is cracking as its foundations sink away). Another reason for the rather down-at-heel appearance is the fact that you may not paint your building without special permission from the authorities – you pay per colour! I'm also told that the very large and lucrative prawn industry is slowly but surely being overtaken in importance by drug trafficking (from Nacala to Johannesburg). But other than that, there is no serious crime, just the petty, opportunistic stuff like muggings and pickpockets (on deserted beaches and in crowded markets).

Introducing Beira

The circle on the seafront (Praca da Independencia) is a good place to start your orientation tour. Take Av das FPLM (street nameboards are printed in blue and attached to the walls of buildings on the corners) along the seafront, which is similar to the Marginal in Maputo. After a kilometre or two, you will pass the hospital on your left and then a BP petrol station. **Clube Nautico** is just across the road on your right. For a daily charge of 10 MT you can use their facilities, which include a big swimming pool and good bar/restaurant. There is a good selection of curios out front in the street (also in front of Biques). The road becomes a sandy track here and a 4x4 might be necessary – most cars turn away from the seafront just before the hospital and continue out to Macuti on Av Martires da Revolucao. Staying on the sandy Av das FPLM, just past the Clube Nautico, at Number 2080 is the house of Marion and Davey Rowell. This pleasant, helpful couple have a couple of spare rooms, which they let out at

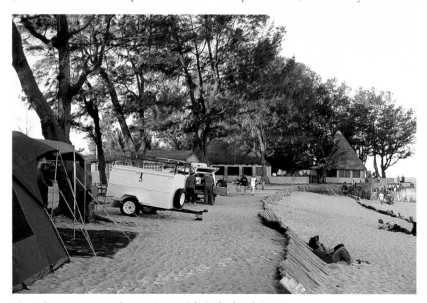

Biques bar, restaurant and camp site are right in the beach in Beira.

225 MT per person sharing. Contact the Rowells, tel: 23-31-1915 or 82-571-6480, e-mail: kapensis@mango.zw

Ploughing on through the increasingly thick sand, you will reach the popular **Biques** (from Mozam*biques*). This is the place to go for beer, pizza, seafood, beer, sport on TV, playing pool, beer, camping, swimming at the beach and beer. Owner Ross Muir is a mine of information and can put you in touch with expats who rent out reasonably priced rooms in their private homes. Across the road is the **Complexo Gama** restaurant, which has a local menu that is excitingly different from the usual flat chicken or prawns. Further up the sandy track is the very up-market **Macuti Housing Compound**. Keep going until you reach the lighthouse and the wreck of the *Macuti* that gave its name to this part of Beira. Two archi-tectural wrecks in this area are those of the Estoril and Dom Carlos hotels – more shells of once-beautiful hotels in the most sought-after positions, crying out for restoration. This stretch of coast is extremely photogenic and there is a good beach, but watch yourself and your belongings, especially in isolated spots.

If you had decided to head straight through the circle back at Shoprite, you would reach **Continuadores Square**. This is a busy area with small restaurants, cheap hotels and long-distance buses coming and going. Carry on straight across a bridge and small river to reach **QJM Square** where you will find the Hotel Savoy and a Mobil service station. Keep straight until you reach Av Eduardo Mondlane. A left-hand turn down Eduardo Mondlane will bring you back to Independencia Square and the road out to Macuti.

In the northern coastal areas a white face mask, known as *musira*, is used to protect and beautify the skin.

A right into Mondlane will plunge you into the confusingly laid-out city centre. You will recognise the **Praca de Municipalia** by the imposing buildings around it, one of which is the city's jail. The inmates of this fortress-like structure stretch their arms out between the bars to receive food from friends and relatives – the only sustenance available to them. Head on through the Praca do Metical to the dockyard area. Clustered here are the wildly aerodynamic-styled railway station, Moulin Rouge restaurant – complete with windmill on the roof – and the **Predio Infante de Sagres** (Manhica Freight building). Try to talk your way into Predio Infante as the building contains some outstandingly beautiful old murals on hand-painted tiles of the early Portuguese seafarers and their ships.

To head back to Independencia Square, try to follow Av Mateus Sansao Mutemba, for at the town end there is a spectacular monument going to waste. The unfinished **Grand Hotel** was abandoned by its builders and annexed by hundreds of squatter families. This huge, multistoreyed building has no water, electricity or sanitation, which means that everything is thrown out over unprotected balconies or through windowless openings in the walls – generations are growing up in this squalor and chaos. Just across the road is another fascinating monument, this one to life. The **Palace of Weddings** is the official registration office for births, weddings and deaths, and is fronted by a long futuristic mural depicting life, from the womb to the grave. Av Mateus Sansao Mutemba now follows the sea-front back to Independencia Square via Club Oceana and Hotel Miramar, with a slight deviation around a section that has been washed away by heavy wave action.

If you are staying awhile in Beira, there are a couple of recommended excursions you could try. The closest is a leafy picnic and birding spot called '**6 Miles**'. When leaving Beira on the EN6, turn off at the Hindu cemetery and drive down for about 1 kilometre. The other spot, **Rio Savane**, is 40–50 kilometres away on a bad road. Leave your car in the guarded park and take the ferry across the river to a small resort where there are overnight *baraccas*, a bar and restaurant.

Overnight in Beira

There are not many hotels from which to choose in Beira, especially in the luxury class. Here are some of the best, in diminishing order of price and comfort…

It is difficult to believe that the rather plain and basic **Hotel Tivoli**, 363 Av de Bagamoyo, tel: 23-32-0300, fax: 23-32-0301, e-mail: h.tivoli_beira@teledata.mz, website: www.tdhotels.pt, is the best Mozambique's second-largest city can offer. This centrally situated, recently renovated establishment also offers conference facilities and charges 1500 MT to 1800 MT (single and double) for rooms and 2230 MT to 2460 MT for a suite (all inclusive of a buffet breakfast). Not very central, but extremely comfortable and excellent value for money, is the **Macuti Housing Complex**, Av dos Martires da Revolucao, tel: 23-31-1988 or 82-

509-2810, fax: 23-31-1804, e-mail: mhcadms@teledata.mz (S19°50.861 E34°53.375). Like a small village, it is set in the walled security of a large garden compound out in the suburb of the same name. The complex offers tennis courts, swimming pool and a sauna to complement its flats and houses (the kitchens have three taps – hot, cold and drinking water!). One-bedroomed flats cost 1 260 MT per night and three-bedroomed houses are 2 700 MT (discounts for longer stays).

The **Hotel Ambassador**, Rua Major Serpa Pinto, tel: 23-32-3785, fax: 23-32-8561, used to be the top hotel in town until the revamping of Hotel Tivoli. A typical downtown establishment, it is central, quite smart and offers parking in a garage. *En-suite* singles cost 950 MT a night and doubles 1 160 MT, including breakfast. **Hotel Infante** is a nice little multistoreyed hotel on Rua Jaime Ferreira, tel: 23-32-6603, in the heart of town. *En-suite*, air-con and breakfast costs 590 MT single and 640 MT double. Take away the air-con, and you'll be charged 540 MT and 590 MT. If you want to sample some of Beira's night life, the Aquarius Club and Africa Bar is just across the road.

Just off the traffic circle at the intersection of Rua Major Serpa Pinto and Samora Machel is the basic, but clean **Hotel Savoy**. A double with your own bathroom costs 550 MT, and if you're prepared to share facilities, a single will cost 200 MT and a double 400 MT. For reservations, tel: 23-32-9302. The **Hotel Miramar**, tel: 23-32-2283, is just of Praca da Independencia in Dom Francisco Goriao (no access from the front as the sea has washed the road away). A little dingy, it has double rooms with air-con for 400 MT and without for 300 MT. **Pensão Messe** is in Av Daniel Mapatina, where the inter-city buses rev and hoot. A bit dirty and rough, they charge 250 MT for a room with a double bed (it's one of those hotels) and 300 MT for a triple (kinky!). Just around the corner is the low-down, dirty, but very cheap **Pensão Sofala**. If you can make it past the drunks in the front bar, the rooms are 180 MT single and 190 double MT (no phone, no pool, no pets).

The only camp site in Beira is at **Biques** (S19°51.043 E34°53.094), where a sandy spot with poor ablutions and dodgy security will cost you 85 MT per person, but you do have a great beach and pub on your doorstep to compensate. For info, tel: 23-313051, fax: 23-31-2451, e-mail: biques@teledata.mz

Eating out in Beira

Eating in Beira can be a pleasant experience. Of course you will find good-ol' chicken and prawns on most menus, but there seems to be a far greater variety of restaurants here than anywhere else in Moz. My favourite is the **Moulin Rouge**, 10 Rua do Bagamoyo (down near the harbour between the station and the Casa Infante de Sagres/ Manhica Freight), tel: 23-32-2130. A wild and infamous night club in the 'bad old colonial days', this one-time haunt of debauched sailors and tourists is now a popular lunch-time venue for the locals. The old club is still firmly boarded up downstairs and the restaurant is situated upstairs in what was

Fresh fish is always on the menu in Beira.

And if you are still hungry after a big plate of this, they bring you seconds – all for 60 MT!

Rua Costa Serra boasts two more top restaurants. The **Pique Nique** (tel: 23-32-6518), with good food and service, is a classy establishment that is regarded as one of Beira's best. The restaurant across the road at the disused **National Cinema** serves authentic Goanese curries. In Av Poder Popular is another favourite, the **Arcadia Restaurant**, and out at the **Clube Nautico** they serve great seafood and chips. **Biques** is the place for a draught beer and good food while watching the beach, playing pool or enjoying rugby on TV. Across from Biques is the restaurant at the Complexo Gama (see page 120), which serves great Lebanese tapas and further down at the Macuti Housing Complex (see page 121) is **Wings**, where you can savour Macau-style Chinese food. As I said, a great variety of flavours and cuisines in Beira – enjoy!

once the club's billiard room. Under a stern portrait of Senhor Beira, the city's citizens roll up to eat at long communal tables or fill their plastic containers to take away. The busy buzz of families enjoying an outing, the TV playing soccer in the corner and an occasional tinny tune from a cellphone combine with the clatter of cutlery on crockery in this popular 'peoples' restaurant'. The speciality of the house is Cozida a Portuguese, a wholesome stew of beef, pork, chicken, blood sausage, dumplings, cabbage, carrot, potatoes and rice.

Out and about in Beira

Club Oceana is Beira's nightclub – a bit tatty, but it has all the main ingredients: a bar, restaurant, dance floor and stripper. You'll find Club Oceana on the seafront near to the Hotel Miramar, but don't arrive before 22h30. **The Africa Bar** and **Aquarius Club** are good, lively nightspots in Rua Jaime Ferreira and don't forget **Biques**, where there's always a good crowd.

For shopping, the best place to start is the **Shoprite Centre** at the intersection of Samora Machel and Armando Tivane. This supermarket is the best stocked in Beira, with groceries, meat, bakery, dairy products, fruit and veg, hardware, some camping gear and even simcards and airtime for your cellphone. Some of the other services in the complex include a takeaway, pharmacy, photo-lab and an ATM. Next door is a large BP service station where petrol costs 18,35 MT a litre and diesel 14,57 MT. There is also a small supermarket out in Macuti near the Housing Complex and other small general dealers dotted around the city.

Beira has a few good money changers. **Cambio 786** (they can also arrange money transfers) is at 31 Rua Machado dos Santos, next door to the big Mozauto Nissan dealership off Av Armando Tivane. Just around the corner, in Rua Acores, is another, called **Multi Cambios**. The great thing about *cambios* is that they always give the best rate, are fast, safe and efficient and don't charge commission. Internet cafés are few and far between in Beira, the best being in the TDM building, opposite the jail in Praca da Municipalia.

Clinic Avicena, 326 Av Poder Popular, tel: 23-32-7990, fax: 23-32-7988, e-mail: avicena.clinic@teledata.mz, is best for medical emergencies, as they have an ambulance, doctors, x-rays and a laboratory for malaria tests.

On the road in Beira

The airport is contactable on tel: 23-30-1071, and **LAM**, the Mozambican airline, has an office there, tel: 23-30-1024. The car-hire firms are also out at the airport. **Avis** is on tel: 23-30-1263, e-mail: avis@teledata.mz, and **Imperial Car Renta** may be contacted on tel: 23-30-2650. *Chapas* run along most

main routes in town and only cost 5 MT a ride. Marcello runs the traditional sort of taxi service and can be summoned on tel: 23-32-2921 or 82-324-9130. Intercity buses have their depots between Avs Daniel Napatina and Bagamoyo. The TSL and Oliveiras lines have daily buses to and from Maputo in the south, and Nampula in the north. There is also a bus to Tete.

Beira is well endowed with motor dealerships. Landrovers are supplied by **Setec Auto**, 539 Av Eduardo Mondlane, tel: 23-35-2257, e-mail: setecauto@teledata.mz, while Toyota is represented by **Toyota de Mozambique**, 2575 Av Base N'Tchinga, tel: 23-32-4329, fax: 23-32-3794, e-mail: toyotabeira@teledata.mz, and Nissan by **MozAuto**, 72 Rua Machado Santos, tel: 23-32-3739, fax: 23-32-3734. **CALS Motors** in Av Base N'tchinga fix suspensions, shocks and springs as well as doing general mechanical repairs, Contact Luis Teixeira, tel: 82-556-2390. **Shakrani Motors** – at the roundabout that boasts the giant plastic Coke bottle – stocks general spares, filters, lubricants and tyres, as does **Sena Centro** in Rua Antonio Enes, tel: 23-32-4430. For used nuts, bolts and anything else, try the sprawling market on Armando Tivane, and for tyres and puncture repairs, the BP garage at Shoprite.

And finally, if you are heading up to **Gorongosa National Park**, drop in at their offices in the Predio Infante de Sagres (Manhica Freight Building), 1 Av Poder Popular. They have the latest info and you can make bookings there. For information, tel/fax: 23-32-0346, e-mail: gorongosa@teledata.mz

Gorongosa National Park and on to Quelimane 18

Av Samora Machel is the way out of Beira and onto the EN6. It is 33 kilometres to Dondo, where there is a customs checkpoint (S19°34.599 E34°43.356) and the turn-off onto the old road north (the EN213 is signposted to Cheringoma). The road that runs up to Muanza is very bad, but at Muanza you can turn left for a novel, back-door entry to Chitengo Camp in Gorongosa National Park. It continues up to Inhaminga (turn left here for Mount Gorongosa) and eventually joins the EN1 just south of Caia on the Zambezi – a rough, tough road that is now only used by keen birders looking for those elusive 'mega-ticks'.

On the road in Gorongosa National Park…

Chickens for sale at Caia on the banks of the mighty Zambezi north of Gorongosa.

On to Gorongosa National Park

Staying on the EN6, the following 41 kilometres to Tica is badly potholed and even deteriorates to poor gravel as it crosses the marshy area around the Pungue River. About 135 kilometres from Beira, you will reach the intersection (S19°12.477 E33°55.983) at Inchope where the EN1 crosses the EN6. Turn north here onto a gloriously wide and smooth tarred road. The road markings and signage are all new and correct, but the speed limit is a low 100 kph, with long stretches of 80 kph.

After another 44 kilometres you will reach the turn-off right (S18°56.041 E34°07.980) to the Parque Nacional da Gorongosa. A good, single-lane gravel road, with solid little bridges that date back to 1936, runs down 11.3 kilometres to the main gate. The smart and efficient staff will book you in, and 17 kilometres further is Gorongosa's only camp, Chitengo (S18°58.740 E34°21.084).

Chitengo Camp

Make your way to the office and pay the entrance fee of 200 MT per adult plus 100 MT per day for camping. Some renovation work has already been done at Chitengo. The main focus is the lecture room, which has new desks, TV, screen and posters, and is where recruits are being trained and educated as game rangers. The ruins of a once-smart, but now bullet-riddled restaurant and swimming pool, bear testimony to the long civil war and the role Chitengo played as Renamo's headquarters. September–October is a popular time to visit, while January and February are bad because of the rain. Contact the head office in Beira, Predio Infante de Sagres (Manhica Freight Building), 1 Av Poder Popular, tel/fax: 23-320346, e-mail: gorongosa@teledata.mz

GORONGOSA NATIONAL PARK

An attempt has been made by a private concessionaire, Rui Valadares, to repair the bungalows, and a small bar and restaurant are up and running. The basic little bungalows sleep two and have a shower and toilet, but they have no self-catering facilities (you may use your own equipment) and cost 480 MT a night. The camp site is well shaded, and the partially restored ablution block has cold showers, washbasins and flush toilets. Chitengo has a power generator running from 06h00–21h00, and clearing up and repairs are ongoing. The chief administrator, José Paulo Capece, wants to expand the camp site, provide new ablutions and build more bungalows. He is working with the American Carr Foundation to restock the park, and some private concessions on the outskirts of the park are being considered.

At the moment, the game in Gorongosa is scarce and you are only likely to see warthog, impala, waterbuck and duiker; the birdlife, however, is varied and plentiful. The network of rough, narrow tracks in the park is okay in the dry season, but will require 4x4 in wet conditions. A map is available from the office and routes are numbered and signposted. The drives are punctuated by two old ruins. **Casa de Leos** (S18°54.256 E34°22.607) used to be a kiosk where you could stop and view the dozens of lazing lions on the surrounding grasslands, but it is now just a ruined shell on a barren plain. **Mira Hipo** (S18°54.812 E34°31.032) was a much grander, double-storeyed place with bar and restaurant overlooking Hippo Lake. The hippos have survived, as have the fish eagles, but I look forward to visiting this grand old viewing platform again one day, when it has been restored.

Beyond Gorongosa

Back on the EN1, continue north through the town of Gorongosa (not to be confused with the national park of the same name). Local buses and minibus taxis travel this route, so stay alert – especially for the dopey goats that graze along the sides of the road. The region is hilly and to the east you will see the impressive **Mount Gorongosa** (turn right in Gorongosa town). These mountains are definitely worth exploring, particularly if you're a keen birder – the green oriole is endemic here.

About 280 kilometres from Inchope (S18°02.361 E35°11.684), turn off right to James White's camp, the only accommodation along this stretch of road. James owns the Catapu Sawmill and adjoining **Mphingwe Camp** and just loves the company of visitors. He has a 25 000-hectare forestry concession and conscientiously plants three trees for every one he cuts down. The camp consists of five rustic cabins built of solid local hardwood and fitted with furniture made at James' own factory. There are also camp sites with cement slabs for your tent, and all accommodation shares the same immaculate ablutions. Clara oversees it all expertly and graciously, including a kitchen that is available for all to use. Beers and minerals are on sale and electricity comes on between 17h00 and 22h00. James is also very proud of the 75 species of birds and the 200 indigenous plants on his property. Camping costs 120 MT per person and the cabins are 320 MT single and 480 MT double. Contact James on tel/fax: 23-30-2161, e-mail: tct.dalmann@teledata.mz, website: www.dalmann.com

From the turn-off to Mphingwe Camp, it is about 30 kilometres to the town of **Caia**. This is a good, tarred road with little traffic, no roadblocks and a pleasure to drive. At Caia (S17°50.030 E 35°20.561), the road branches off north

> ## Before you leave the
> relative comfort of Beira and head up into the unspoilt splendour of northern Mozambique, make sure you fill all your fuel tanks as the next fuel stop is 600 kilometres away in Nicuadala, and you will probably want to explore Gorongosa as well. There are plans to build a fuel station at Inhaminga – check if it's opened yet. Otherwise, if you are desperate, blackmarket fuel is sold at the roadside around Caia in yellow 20-litre containers.

up to the old railway bridge across the Zambezi at Sena. Built in 1934, it is – at 3.7 kilometres – the longest rail bridge in Africa. Trestles have been laid across the tracks to enable vehicles to cross and you can carry on north into Malawi. Were you to turn off south here, you would pass the lonely site of Mary Moffat-Livingstone's grave on your way to **Marromeu**, the Zambezi estuary's best birding site (contact Bridget Gibson at the offices of the sugar mill in Marromeu for info on bed-and-breakfast or camping, tel: 23-960014). The only fuel available around here is from roadside sellers. They offer 20 litres of diesel for 350 MT and petrol for 600 MT – look out for the yellow plastic containers (these guys can also repair punctures). The ferry across the Zambezi is another 7 kilometres from the town, along a dirt road. They have not yet built a bridge here, but a couple of new ferries have replaced the tired old ones that kept breaking down and causing long delays.

Caia Ferry

What a spot – I just love ferries in Africa! Muddy banks crowded with little stalls offering the traveller food, drink, accommodation and other more dubious pleasures. Buses, trucks and 4x4s revving and jostling for position in the queues. Fat mamas carrying chickens and skinny men pushing overloaded bicycles. Women washing clothes in the shallows, dugout canoes drifting serenely by, and always that one vehicle stuck on the ferry ramp, holding up the loading process. People shout advice, the ferry churns up mud and somehow everything sorts itself out. I have learned that the only way to handle these sorts of situations is to hang back, not be in a hurry, take some photos and enjoy the show – it's a precious tableau that won't always

A number of rusty ferries ply the waters from Caia across the Zambezi River.

be around. One day there'll be bridges over all these rivers and we will miss the adventures and theatrics of ferry crossings. The car ferry carries about six vehicles and another larger one takes four long articulated trucks. They run from 06h30 to 17h00 every day and cost 100 MT for a normal-sized vehicle and occupants. Stock up with fresh bread (2 MT), juicy red tomatoes (2 MT) and home-made coconut ice while waiting.

More reed huts cluster on the other side, one of which is the **Pousada Malawian** run by the wide-awake (or just plain wide) Mrs Joao. She will rustle up chicken and rice for 25 MT, tea for 5 MT and even a double room with sheets and mozzie net for 50 MT. You're back on the tar now as you drive the 165 kilometres to **Nicuadala** and – thankfully – the chance to refuel. The stop sign and intersection here gives you the choice of turning right (south) to the coast at Quelimane or left (north) to continue up to Nampula and beyond. There is really no reason to visit Quelimane, especially as the Complexo Turistico Kassi Kassi at Zalala Beach is now closed for renovations, but let's go anyway.

On to Quelimane

The 37-kilometre road to Quelimane is good tar, but the swarms of cyclists transporting heavy loads of charcoal are a menace. Coconut-palm plantations stretch as far as the eye can see, but go largely unharvested. Quelimane is the capital of Zambezia province and quite busy, but I can't help thinking that, as the roads improve inland, so the reason for its existence as a small port will

> ## It's horrifying to think that
> during the the 17-plus years of the civil war, 14 000 buffalo and 3 000 elephants were eradicated from Gorongoza – and that's not counting the many other species that were brought to the brink of extermination here.

diminish. Its history is similar to that of Beira – gold, ivory and slaves – but with the added importance of a river and canal that once connected this town to the Zambezi River. David Livingstone was appointed the British Honorary Consul to Quelimane in 1858, and later started his exploration of the Zambezi from here.

The town is entered down yet another Av Eduardo Mondlane. Passing the Sacrada Familia Church, carry on straight to reach a BP garage and bus depot (to all routes south and north of Quelimane) on your left. The tyre-repair shop across the road does well as the roads are so badly potholed. At the Coke factory further down on your right is the turn-off (left) to **Zalala Beach**. This is a pleasant 33-kilometre run down to the beach on a tarred road through palm plantations, but find out if the **Complexo Turistico Kassi Kassi** has reopened before trekking all that way for nothing.

Further down on your right, oppo-site MozAuto Nissan, is the Pensão Quelimane and a couple of blocks further you run into Av Samora Machel. Turn left and cruise through town, passing the furniture craft market on your left, then the Hotel Chuabo, and

Intricately carved kists on offer at the woodcarvers' market in Quelimane.

the Riviera restaurant across the road. The Marginal along the waterfront is one block to the right and the rest of town is up to the left. At the end of Samora Machel, you will run into Av Julius Nyerere where a left turn will get you going in the direction of Zalala Beach again.

Out and about in Quelimane

The top place to stay in town is the **Hotel Chuabo**, tel: 24-213181, fax: 24-213812, a smart eight-storeyed building in Av Samora Machel. Comfortable air-conditioned rooms with TV cost 1 530 MT single and 2 520 MT for a double. There is a grand restaurant on the top floor with a terrific view, but it was sad to see a staff of eight waiters standing around 20 tables decked with starched linen and polished silver and not a patron in sight.

Pensão Quelimane is on the way into town in Av Eduardo Mondlane. It is near the bus depot, but probably a bit out of the public-transporter's price range, with singles costing 250 MT, doubles 300 MT and twin beds 350 MT. Clean *en-suite* rooms with fridge and air-con cost 750 MT single, 850 MT double and 1 050 MT for twin beds. The **Hotel Zambeze** on Av Acordos de Lusaka has a nice garden, courtyard and off-street parking. *En-suite* singles cost 250 MT and doubles 350 MT. **Pensão Ideal** (S17°52.603 E36°53.196) is difficult to find as it is not signposted, but it gets my vote as Quelimane's best value-for-money establishment. It is on Av Samuel Magaia, just below the big 'new' cathedral. Neat, well run and down a quiet side street, they have a small bar/restaurant, which serves the locals in the neighbourhood.

Singles cost 160 MT, doubles 200 MT and a large double with bathroom is 295 MT. For bookings and information, tel: 24-21-2731. But be warned, there are often water shortages in and around Quelimane, so your *en-suite* bathroom isn't always much use to you, no matter where you are staying.

Don't eat anywhere other than **Café Riviera**. This old-style, pre-independence-type restaurant has an extensive menu, a good selection of wines, pastries and cakes, and the choice of inside or pavement dining. Pizzas, ice cream and espresso coffee – pinch me, am I in the sticks of northern Mozambique? Other places to eat are at the above-mentioned hotels, with the Chuabo definitely the best of the bunch. Also look out for **Café Nicole** on Av 1 de Julho and **Pica-Pica Takeaway** opposite Chuabo Hotel.

To change money in Quelimane, try **Meizel Cambios** in Av 1 de Julho or the **Standard Bank** on the corner of Josina Machel and Samuel Magaia (look out for the huge bats that roost in the palm trees across the road!). **MozAuto Nissan** is on Eduardo Mondlane, opposite Pensão Quelimane, and the Toyota dealership is one block west on Rua da Residencia (this street also has other spares and tyre shops). General motor spares can be found at **Zambeze Pecas** in Samora Machel (tel: 24-214623). The hospital is in the block between Acordos de Lusaka and Julius Nyerere and for beautiful handcrafted wooden kists and furniture go to the corner opposite the Café Riviera.

North to Nampula

19

If you are leaving Quelimane in the early morning, look out for weaving bicycles in the mist. And if you're headed for Nampula (about 520 kilometres) then prepare yourself for a bumpy and difficult ride – the road is bad and the navigation tricky. From Nicuadala, the road comprises 30 kilometres of good tar to **Namacurra**, a pleasant enough town but no sign of fuel or accommodation.

The Makonde people are famous for their carved masks, like this one in Nampula.

Mocuba and beyond

We continue on for another 77 kilometres to **Mocuba**, first on a good, wide gravel road, then back onto new tar, with lots of work being done on this section of the road. Both diesel and petrol are available as you enter town. Also at the entrance to Mocuba, just before the fuel station, is the difficult-to-detect turn-off left (S16°51.356 E36°57.901) that doubles back and eventually takes you through to Milange in Malawi.

Passing the aerodrome, carry on straight to a fork, keep left, carry on through the traffic circle with the monument with a large metal star in the centre and take the double-laned Av 25 de Setembro to a large church on the right (getting through Mocuba can be very confusing!). With the police station opposite, swing left and drive across the traffic circle with the fountain in the middle (S16°50.420 E36°59.116).

This is the main street, and if you carry on through town you will cross a long bridge over the Lugela River and, thankfully, say goodbye to this confounding place.

But maybe you need food or accommodation. The **Pensão Cruzeiro**, tel: 24-81-0184, couldn't be more central as it is situated in the main street just below the fountain circle. It's the main bar and restaurant in town and has clean two-bed rooms with bathroom for 450 MT.

If you have the courage to navigate your way back to the southern entrance to town, you could try the grandly named **Pensão Estralagem Pariaso 2000 Mocuba**, a simple, clean and secure little motel-style establishment off left at the star monument traffic circle. There is a bar/restaurant and the double rooms cost 180 MT, and 250 MT with bathroom.

Shops are few and far between and often closed, so be fairly self-sufficient.

The road north from here to Alto Molocue starts out as reasonable tar, but soon deteriorates with signs of imminent repair work. There are some bad potholes as you approach the turn-off (at 66 kilometres) to Gurue.

Keep straight on, and about 100 kilometres from Mocuba, the road becomes a single dirt track to cross the bridge at Nipiodi. From here it is back onto tar again, but a similar dirt track bridge crossing awaits you at Naiopue. More deviations occur where new bridges have been built, but I would avoid this road in the wet.

If you thought it was tricky getting through Mocuba, then you're in for a hard time in Alto Molocue. On approaching the town, turn left off the tar and drive into the centre. The rather scruffy **Pensão Santa Antonio** is on your right. They offer safe parking and double rooms for 200 MT, or 300 MT with *en-suite* bathroom. Across the square is the neater **Pensão Fambo Uone** with a cool veranda that faces the dusty square and rooms that cost about the same as Santa Antonio. The compact little town centre has basic foodstuffs, bar and restaurant, but not much else (and no fuel when I was there). To get out of town, cross the river and wind your way up the other side, past the hospital and head for a big church and a house that looks like a fort. Keep right when approaching the church (left would take you to Gurue and Cuamba) and head out of town through the administrative centre and past the communications tower.

Two roads run parallel between Alto Molocue and Alto Ligonha and, depending on how the rebuilding of the northern route is progressing, you might be directed onto the southern one. This is a wide dirt road in reasonable condition, but don't look at a compass while on this road, because it will just scare you. At times you are heading directly south, when you know you should be heading north – but have faith and spare fuel! About 20 kilometres past Alto Ligonha you will cross the narrow bridge over the Ligonha River and enter Nampula province. A very courteous police roadblock will check your papers and you're off on a good tarred road to Nampula town. But there is still no fuel available along this stretch, and you start eyeing the 20-litre yellow drums filled with blackmarket fuel with new appreciation. Hopefully, you won't need them as you make your way through the fantastically shaped granite hills and kopjes. The ruins of a classic old colonial church on a hill heralds the approach to Nampula.

Introducing Nampula

Nampula is the capital of the north and Mozambique's third-largest city. Its position at the intersection of the main south–north highway and the railway line from Nacala to Malawi gives it commercial and administrative importance. With a pleasant climate, it is surrounded by impressive inselbergs, mountainous plugs of volcanic granite that soar up to 1 000 metres above the plains. Approaching from the southwest (the Quelimane side), you will spot Toyota and other motor-vehicle workshops as you pass the big water tower and enter town along Av de Trabalhio. Keep the railway line on your left until you reach the station, and then turn right into Av Paulo Samuel Kankhomba, Nampula's main street, which runs all the way down to a traffic circle at the bottom. The city is quite easy to figure out as it is laid out on a grid pattern, with a main intersection about halfway down where it crosses with Av Eduardo Mondlane.

Nampula's top hotel is undoubtedly the **Hotel Tropical**, 1 Rua Macombre, tel: 26-21-2232, fax: 26-21-6359, which is situated in a quiet, leafy street behind the National Ethnography Museum. Secure parking, a cool, shaded patio for dining out on, and comfortable rooms make this the preferred accommodation for visiting businessmen and NGO workers. They will also change money at a reasonable rate. Single *en-suite* rooms cost 1320 MT and doubles 1920 MT. Down Av Paulo Samuel Kankhomba, on the right-hand side, just before Eduardo Mondlane is your next best bet for accommodation – **Residencial Farhana**, tel: 26-21-2527. Newly renovated, this establishment is quiet and secure, but it has neither a bar nor restaurant. The rooms all have a bathroom, air-con, TV and fridge and cost 702 MT single, 994 MT with double bed and 1287 MT with two single beds. There is secure parking in a back yard. A block down on the same side of Av PS Kankhomba is the **Residencial a Marisqueira**. Very similar in rooms and price to Farhana, they too have been newly renovated and offer *en-suite* rooms with TV, air-con and fridge for 750 MT single, 850 MT double bed, and 1100 MT for two single beds.

GURUE
The highland town of Gurue is a good opportunity to get away from the coastal heat. Set among rolling hills and tea plantations, it has a high rainfall and a fresh and invigorating climate. Walking and climbing are worthwhile pastimes and there are waterfalls and caves to visit. The best place to stay is the newly restored Pensão Gurue, which also has a restaurant. Singles cost 250 MT, *en-suite* doubles 600 MT and camping 50 MT. Guides are available at 40 MT per day to take you for walks through the tea plantations, into the mountains and to the waterfalls.

The best value-for-money place in the budget range is further down SP Kankhomba, also on the right, near the circle at the bottom. **Pensão Parque**, tel: 26-21-2307, charges only 200 MT single and 400 MT double for shared facilities, but is nearly always full. That is because this is a neat and tidy little 'cheapy' in a good position. It also has a small bar/restaurant, patio and rooftop with a view.

There is quite a selection of accommodation in this area. **Pensão Residencial Estrela**, tel: 26-21-4902, is just above Pensão Parque and has reasonable rooms with bathroom, TV, fridge and air-con for 595 MT single and 795 MT double. Rooms without fridge and air-con are a litle cheaper. Across the road and down the side street next to the market, is the **Residencial Monte**

Carlo, tel: 26-21-2769. Large, airy rooms with a bathroom (cold water only) and balcony overlooking the market cost 300 MT single and 450 MT double. If you were to go around the circle at the bottom of Av PS Kankhomba and turn off right, you would reach the **Residencial Brasilia**, tel: 26-21-2126. A little pricier and more up-market than the last few places mentioned, they have rooms with air-conditioning, TV and bathrooms (with hot water) for 680 MT single and 750 MT double.

But for the seriously budget-conscious there is always the **Pensão Central**. The Central is not signposted, but you will find it a block down from the station on Av PS Kankhomba, above the Central Bar and Restaurant. Situated on the first floor, it also serves the cheapest food in Nampula. Rooms are rather scruffy and the shared bathrooms rather well used, but its rates of 125 MT single and 250 MT double and proximity to public transport (the train station and long-distance bus stops are close by) make it very popular with local travellers.

There are two good alternatives to staying in town. The first is the reasonably priced **Complexo Quinta Nasa**, tel: 82-32-31-340, fax: 26-21-6994, on the road out of town, going towards Nacala. Take the Av de Trabalio east out of Nampula to the traffic circle (S15°06.743 E39°17.012) and turn right to Nacala, Pemba and Ilha de Moçambique. About 3.7 kilometres further, there is a signpost on the right (S15°06.957 E39°19.019) that points you across the railway line and down through small fields and houses. Follow the signposts for 3 kilometres to the gates of Quinta Nasa (S15°07.746 E39°20.014). The complex is quite isolated, quiet and secure and is popular with local conferences and weekenders. Neat, double *en-suite* rooms cost 500 MT, and larger self-contained bungalows that can sleep up to six cost 600 MT double.

The other out-of-town option is much more up-market and on the other side of Nampula. Take the Quelimane road out along Av de Trabalio for about 40 kilometres and then turn off right (S15°06.685 E39°13.661) towards Ribaue and Cuamba – the **Apart Hotel** is just along on the left. With modern motel-styled accommodation, swimming pool, resort-styled bar and restaurant all set in well-kept gardens, this is very good value for money at 1 130 MT single and 1 500 MT double. Most suites are newly built and have air-con and satellite TV. For reservations, tel: 26-21-6595, fax: 26-21-6468.

Out and about in Nampula

The best eating in town is probably at the **Copacabana**, opposite the Hotel Tropical in Rua Macombre. Authentic pizzas and pastas are a speciality, along with great omelettes (try the prawn special). Shaded patios overlook a fish pond, and there is often live music. They also have a good selection of wine, a car guard on duty, and spotless toilets. The **Clube Tenis** is in Av PS Kankhomba and is reached via a short alley next to Protea Furnishers. A somewhat faded and jaded old place, it is nevertheless very central and the food is hot and the beers cold. Cool and comfortable during the day, it has a disco at night. For late-night pubbing, try the **Bagdade Café** on Av Eduardo Mondlane, two blocks down, east off SP Kankhomba and close to the Standard Bank.

A pleasant little sidewalk café for delicious cakes, pastries and coffee is the **Café Primavera**, a block west of Av PS Kankhomba on the corner of Av Eduardo Mondlane and Francisco Manyanga. Three doors down is the **Frango King** for grilled chicken and chips takeaways. Bread and pastries are available at the bakery on the traffic circle at the bottom of Av PS Kankhomba or from another *pastelaria* just off the circle next door to the Hotel Brasilia. One of the best-stocked supermarkets is **Mercado Ideal** situated just below the Bagdade Café in Eduardo Mondlane.

There are two groupings of interesting shops and services in town. The first is on **Av Eduardo Mondlane**, two blocks east of Av PS Kankhomba, where you will find – in a row – a travel agency, Bagdade Café, a pharmacy, photocopies, Standard Bank with an ATM and the Mercado Ideal supermarket. The wonderful Ethnography Museum is in the next block down. The other grouping is situated west of Av PS Kankhomba on the corner of **Av Francico Manyanga**. Clustered around this corner is Frango King takeaways, Gett Ida Internet services (20 MT for 30 minutes), SkyNet Couriers and business centre, Café Primavera, and Fotocopiodora for photocopies, photographic processing (digital, too) and even number plates. A big new shopping mall is being built just up the road, opposite the cathedral, which promises to have a supermarket, cinemas, hotel and restaurants, so watch that space.

Fuel is available from BP near the bottom of Av PS Kankhomba or the brand-new Petromoc 5 kilometres out of town on the road to Nacala (petrol 19,45 MT per litre and diesel 15,31 MT, air for your tyres, and a small but well-stocked minimarket). We saw the Toyota workshops as we come into town from the Quelimane side. For info, tel: 26-21-2125, fax: 26-21-3128, e-mail: toyotanpl@teledata.mz. The Nissan dealers, **MozAuto**, tel: 26-21-7144, are also out that way. **Tecnica Industrial** on Av Eduardo Mondlane is the agent for Mitsubishi; contact them on tel: 26-21-3153, e-mail: contjfs@teledata. mz, while the place to go for help with your Landrover is **Setec Auto**, Rua

Small towns have big churches in Mozambique although not all are in use.

Industrial, tel: 26-21-7172. You can rent a car from **Imperial** (tel: 26-21-6312) or **Moti** (tel: 26-21-7144), both of which are out at the airport. If you need to contact the airport (out east across the traffic circle at the bottom of Av PS Kankhomba), tel: 26-21-3138.

Transport east to Ilha de Moçambique and north to Pemba leaves from Av de Trabalho, outside the train station. For transport west towards Cuamba and south to Quelimane, head west along Av de Trabalho for about two kilometres to the junction where the road turns off to Ribaue and Cumba. The railways have a daily passenger service to Cuamba and a slow, unreliable goods train that runs on into Malawi – a great rail adventure (see page 51 for details)

But we can't leave Nampula without visiting one of the best museums in Mozambique, the **National Ethnography Museum**. Situated in Av Eduardo Mondlane, just below the Standard Bank, it is crammed full of articles and artefacts depicting the past and present cultures of this northern region. On display are weapons, pottery, fishing traps and gear, a small dhow, a great selection of musical instruments and Makonde masks. The Makonde, an important local tribe, are well represented with ceremonial drums and costumes, traditional medicine and jewellery. The exhibits are well captioned, and a guide is also available to show you around – and it's all for free, donations gladly accepted. Behind the museum is a very interesting craft workshop and market where you can watch carvers at work and then buy curios at very reasonable prices.

20 Ilha de Moçambique

To get to the fabulous Ilha de Moçambique, you take Av de Trabalho east out of Nampula to the traffic circle (S15°06.743 E39°17.012) and turn right towards Nacala and Pemba. About 5 kilometres past the turn-off to Complexo Quinta Nasa, you can refuel at the big new Petromoc service station. There is a police roadblock fairly close by, but they should simply wave you through.

Boat-building at the little fishing harbour of Santo Antonia, Ilha de Moçambique.

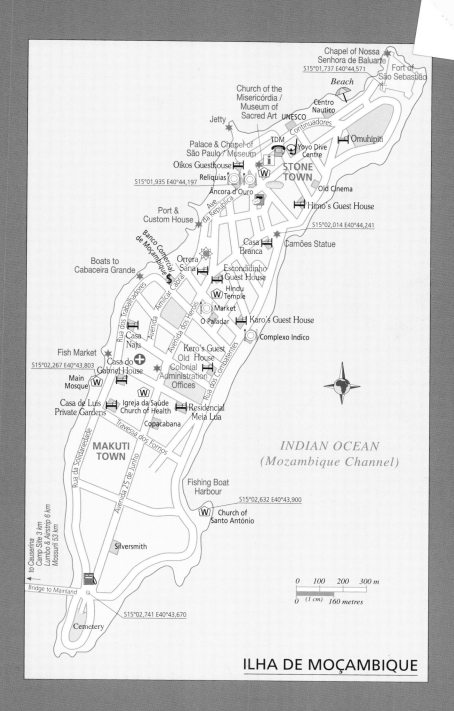

Chapel of Nossa
Senhora de Baluarte
S15°01,737 E40°44,571

Fort of
São Sebastião

Beach

Church of the
Misericórdia /
Museum of
Sacred Art

Jetty

Centro
Nautico

UNESCO

Continuadores

Palace & Chapel of
São Paulo / Museum

TDM

Yoyo Dive
Centre

Omuhipiti

Oikos Guesthouse

STONE
TOWN

Relíquias

S15°01,935 E40°44,197

Ancora d'Ouro

Old Cinema

Port &
Custom House

Himo's Guest House

S15°02,014 E40°44,241

Casa
Branca

Camões Statue

Boats to
Cabaceira Grande

Banco Comercial
de Moçambique

Orrera
Sana

Escondidinho
Guest House

Hindu
Temple

Market

O Paladar

Karo's Guest House

Complexo Indico

Rua dos Trabalhadores

Avenida Amilcar Cabral

Avenida dos Heróis

Rua dos Combatentes

Casa
Naju

Kero's Guest
Old House

Fish Market

S15°02,267 E40°43,803

Casa do
Gabriel House

Colonial
Administration
Offices

Main
Mosque

Casa de Luis
Private Gardens

Igreja da Saúde
Church of Health

Residencial
Meia Lúa

Copacabana

Travessa dos Fornos

Rua da Solidariedade

Avenida 25 de Junho

MAKUTI
TOWN

INDIAN OCEAN
(Mozambique Channel)

Fishing Boat
Harbour

S15°02,632 E40°43,900

Church of
Santo António

to Causerina
Camp Site 3 km
Lumbo & Airstrip 6 km
Mossuril 53 km

Silversmith

Bridge to Mainland

S15°02,741 E40°43,670

Cemetery

0   100   200   300 m

0   (1 cm)   160 metres

ILHA DE MOÇAMBIQUE

The grand entrance to the impenetrable Fort of São Sebastião.

En route to Ilha

A granite hill shaped like a Makonde mask looms on the left as you travel down this newly upgraded section of the EN8. This is cashew-nut country and young boys offer this delicacy at 100 MT (negotiable) for half a basinful. You will reach the junction town of **Namialo** after 86 kilometres. A left turn here takes you north to Pemba, but we first have to visit Ilha, so continue straight on. You'll reach the roadside town of **Monapo** after 39 kilometres where there is fuel available at a Galp service station (there is no fuel on Ilha de Moçambique). Carrying on straight would take you another 50-odd kilometres to **Nacala**. This large natural

harbour is northern Mozambique's most important port, but offers little for the tourist, so rather turn right here (S14°53.533 E40°19.117) and continue on a good tar road through pleasant countryside where baobabs make way for palms again. After another 43 kilometres, you will reach the **Complexo Continental**. Although it offers bar, restaurant, rooms and camping, it is expensive and too far from Ilha to be of any interest other than being at the turn-off to the 1918 British War Cemetery. Turn left here (the aero-drome is across the road) and a short way down you will see a neatly kept walled enclosure (S15°00.980 E40°40.137) on your left. Although it is called the British cemetery, I noticed that most of the graves were of South Africans with names such as Smith, Delport and Geldenhuys from the South African Medical Corp, Supply Corp and Labour Corp. The ride back to the main road passes the old Portuguese Maritime Offices and offers beautiful views across the bay to Ilha de Moçambique.

Another 3.6 kilometres brings you to the causeway to Ilha, but before you cross, have a look at the camp site down on the beach to the left. **Causarinha Camp**, tel: 82-446-9900, was popular when accommodation was hard to find on Ilha and it is still the only feasible place to camp. But now that there is such a wide choice of reasonably priced rooms on the island, I don't know why you would want to stay here and not immerse yourself in the history and culture of Ilha (the off-handed attitude of the staff doesn't help either). Camping is right on the beach and costs 75 MT a person plus 100 MT a car per night. Small rustic bungalows are also available at 200 MT single and 350 MT double. All share the same basic ablutions.

Ilha's past and present

Ilha de Moçambique was already well established as a trading post, and linked to others on the East African coast such as Kilwa and Zanzibar, by the time Vasco da Gama landed there in 1498. Trade with Madagascar, Oman and Persia to the north, and Sofala to the south, was flourishing. By 1507 the Portuguese had established a permanent settlement on the island and usurped most of the trade. Ilha also served as a valuable replenishment station for the ships and crews sailing between Portugal and their eastern bases in Macau and Goa. The mighty Fort of São Sebastião was constructed in the late 16th century and the island became the capital of Portuguese East Africa. Attacks by the Dutch and later the Omanis were repulsed and the island prospered. As it did, so Stone Town grew in beauty and stature, and the magnificent buildings we still see today were constructed during this time. Various factors contributed to the decline of Ilha de Moçambique around the turn of the 20th century – the abolition of the slave trade, the rise in importance of Delagoa Bay (Maputo) after the discovery of gold in the Transvaal and even the opening of the Suez Canal, which diverted much of the sea traffic north. So began the slow but inexorable decline and destruction of the island's economy and, with it, its buildings. The population shrunk towards the mid-

1900s, only to receive an unwelcome influx during the civil war as many refugees fled to the relative safety of this island. Firewood was scarce, and many irreplaceable carved doors and even furniture were burned. The declaration of a World Heritage Site by Unesco in 1992 has now focused attention on the island, but problems still plague restoration efforts. Ownership issues make it difficult to assign or accept responsibility for individual buildings, the ultimate usage of restored properties is undecided, and of course, there's always a shortage of money. But despite these problems, there is hope. There is a general consensus that the island's architecture and heritage are too important to ignore. The island is threatened only by decay – at least it doesn't have rampant development to contend with, and tourists are showing interest. I think that the slow but steady increase in tourism will make the islanders realise the value of what they have and encourage the restoration of more and more on the island.

Introducing Ilha de Moçambique

Although Ilha de Moçambique is an island, it is linked to the mainland by a 3.5-kilometre causeway, which means that – for a toll of 10 MT (pay on the island side) – you can drive a light vehicle across. The bridge is only a single lane, but passing bays are spaced at regular intervals for two-way traffic. Bollards at both ends limit the width of vehicles, keeping trucks and buses off the island (but no problem for cars, bakkies and 4x4s).

Once on the island you will encounter a traffic circle, but follow the road down the centre of the island and set off along Av 25 de Junho through the reed huts of **Makuti Town**. This southern end of the island is the poorer neighbourhood and contrasts sharply with the faded glory of the rest of the island. The first sign of the island's colonial past is the Ingreja da Saude Church on your left and then the once-magnificent hospital. It's difficult to believe that anyone would have built such a grand porticoed structure – it looks like it was once a five-star hotel – just to serve as a hospital. But, we must remember that Ilha was the hub of, not only the Mozambique colony, but the entire sea route between Portugal and the East. The hospital is now no longer operational, except for a small clinic at the back in one of the old wards. The withered gardens of the park across the road show the same neglect. But don't despair – it's gratifying to find that these historical buildings are still standing, and what is standing can still be restored.

Stone Town

You now enter the old Stone Town, so called because coral blocks were used as building material. The architecture is a mixture of Portuguese and African East Coast, the culture is Swahili and the predominent religion is Muslim. Narrow streets wind between double-storeyed, shuttered buildings, some perfectly restored, painted in pretty pastel shades and sporting rooftop patios, while others are only shells, held together by the roots and vines of wild fig trees. The road forks at a shaded little square where we find the beautifully restored **Escondidinho Guest House** (S15°02.066 E40°44.084). Bear left and continue past more houses and a few poorly stocked shops to the **Central Square**. On the left is the police station and on the seaward side the old customs house and disused boatyard, entered through impressive cannon-flanked gates.

Keeping left, pass the inviting Reliquias restaurant. Most streets are one-ways, so keep a sharp look out for them, and if you get caught going the wrong way, use me as an excuse! You now run straight into the historic core of the island, the Governor's Palace, the Chapel of Sao Paulo (both restored, and now a fascinating museum) and the Church of Misericordia. Still on your left, the old jetty juts far out into the bay. Then there's the island's secondary school. Centro Nautico overlooks the island's only clean, sandy beach and then, totally dominating the entire northern end of the island, the huge **Fort of São Sebastião.** Swing off to the right and you can continue your trip around Ilha de Moçambique by heading back to the causeway via the eastern (seaward) side.

Right up near the fort is the newly renovated, upmarket **Hotel Omuhipiti** followed by the old, boarded-up cinema. **Casa Branca** guesthouse, with the statue of writer Louis Camoes in front, slips by, as does **Karo's Guest House** and **Indigo** restaurant. The fishing boat moorings are always busy and beg for a photo, with palm trees and the Church of Santo Antonio in the background.

You're now back at the causeway, but a quick loop around the Hindu cemetery gives you a good view of the little fort on the island of São Lourenco, just south of Ilha.

Exploring Ilha de Moçambique

Ilha de Moçambique really doesn't need a museum – the whole island is one – but the **Governor's Palace** (S15°01.882 E40°44.219) has been renovated and furnished in the opulent 18th-century style of the island's heyday. Or maybe it always looked like this – it certainly looks and feels like the governor just stepped out to inspect the plantations or meet with his mistress. Built in 1610 and last used by Samora Machel on an official visit, this marvellous museum is a blend of Portugal, Arabia, India and China. Each room is filled with authentic period pieces: heavily carved Indian furniture, huge paintings of Portuguese heroes, ornate chandeliers, tapestries, carpets, jewellery, and sedan chairs. The kitchen looks like it could still produce a banquet on the immaculately laid table for 22 in the dining room. And with so few tourists on the island at any given time, you'll probably have the museum entirely to yourself. The adjoining **Chapel of Sao Paulo** still has its original Chinese carved pulpit, and behind the palace is the **Church of the Misericordia** and the **Museum of Sacred Art**, displaying religious paintings and carvings. Opening hours are 08h00–12h00 and 14h00–17h00 and someone is usually happy to show you around – although it would help if you could speak Portuguese (no entrance fee, but donations are appreciated). The museum also contains the offices of the excellent **Tourist Information Bureau**. The pleasant staff here are most helpful with info on accommodation, public transport and anything else

The underground cisterns in the Fort of São Sebastião still supply water to the island.

The Chapel of Nossa Senhora de Baluarte on the northern tip of Ilha.

pertaining to the island. They offer short tours of the Fort of São Sebastião or whole-day tours of the island, and are open 09h00–12h00 and 14h00–17h00 everyday. For information, tel: 26-61-0081, fax: 26-61-0082.

For such a small island, there is much of interest to see on Ilha de Moçambique, and many thick layers of history too – like the **Fort of São Sebastião** on the northern tip of the island (S15°01.737 E40°44.571). This formidable old fortress has not only withstood sieges and attacks by the Dutch and Omanis, but more recently served as a Portuguese bastion during the Mozambique liberation struggle. It is remarkably intact for the oldest complete fort still standing in sub-Saharan Africa, and even the extensive underground cisterns are still used by the islanders for their daily fresh water needs. There is no entrance fee and you are free to wander about the ram-

parts with their many old cannons, and explore the rooms in the courtyard. Just outside the walls, on the extreme tip of the island, is the **Chapel of Nossa Senhora de Baluarte**. Built in 1522, it is considered the oldest European-built structure in the southern hemisphere, and is the last resting place of many of the 16th- and 17th-century Portuguese bishops.

The little protected bay on the southeast corner of the island is a good place to watch the busy comings and goings of the fishing dhows, and there is always at least one boat being built or repaired on the beach – the ancient tools and methods used are fascinating. Another old craft practised on Ilha is that of the silversmith. Difficult to find in the warren of reed huts in Makuti Town (down the steps, right, off the central road), José Orievas works with four apprentices to create delicate and fine pieces. In a dark room with the only light coming through an open door (no wonder José's glasses are so thick), silver wire is melted, cast, drawn through holes in small plates and hammered on makeshift anvils. Their methods may be crude – smelting is achieved by blowing through a straw across a paraffin flame – but the chains, bracelets and pendants are beautiful, and not very expensive either.

Visit the fish market on the west of the island, just beyond the green mosque. The selection of fresh fish and crustaceans might not make your mouth water (when cooked they will), but you'll get a few good photographs. A little further north (S15°02.100 E40°43.908) is the beach where dhows come and go to Cabaceira Grande (cost 5 MT) and Cabaceira Pequena (3 MT), destinations across the bay. Whether you just want to watch and photograph these ancient crafts being executed, or actually take a trip, drop by at high tide. Unfortunately, the islanders use the beaches as a toilet, so swimming is not an option here. There is, however, one small beach that is reasonably clean, with beautiful white sand. Situated on the north of the island between Centro Nautico and the Fort of São Sebastião, it is popular with the locals who often exercise and play soccer there in the evenings.

Overnight on Ilha

I struggled to find accommodation on Ilha during my first visit in 1997, but now the visitor is spoilt for choice. The most up-market hotel is definitely the **Hotel Omuhipiti**, set apart from the crowded Stone Town on the northern tip of the island just outside the walls of the famous fort. Newly renovated to a very high standard and well staffed, the comfortable rooms offer air-con and satellite TV at a cost of 1500 MT single and 1725 MT double (including breakfast). It also has an excellent restaurant and safe off-street parking. For more information, tel: 26-61-0101, fax: 26-61-0105, website: www.intur.co.mz. The next most expensive establishment is **Casa do Gabriel**, a quaint little place in Rua do Celeiro, across the road from the green mosque. This guesthouse has been imaginatively designed and renovated by its Italian architect-owner and is beautifully decorated with local furniture and crafts. The rooms look out over a small plunge pool and intimate garden courtyard, and feature unique ideas like a bed suspended from the ceiling and a roof that opens for stargazing. A large self-contained room for two costs 720 MT, a family room for four, 1200 MT, and the rooms without *en-suite* bathrooms cost 500 MT single and 600 MT double. Your car will have to sleep outside, but there is a guard. For bookings, tel: 26-61-0090 or 82-419-7610, website: www.patiodosquintalinhos.com

My choice for comfort, position and value-for-money is **Escondidinho**. Over looking a small square in the centre of Ilha, this restored double-storeyed guesthouse has a laid-back atmosphere and big, airy rooms. It also has a wonderful unpretentious restaurant where I had one of my best seafood meals in Mozambique (nine queen prawns followed by fillet of parrot fish – the bill, 250 MT). The swimming pool is set in a pretty garden and displays of dancing by local school children are organised for some evenings. Double rooms with *en-suite* facilities are 600 MT and without are 480 MT. Parking is in the street but, again, there is a car guard. Contact Escondidinho, tel: 26-61-0078 or 82-674-8420, e-mail: ilhatur@itservices.co.mz, website: www.ilhatur.co.mz. The rest of the accommodation on Ilha de Moçambique consists of at least 10 small guesthouses spread around the island, but the following are just a few worth mentioning:

One of the oldest and most popular establishments is **Casa Branca** on the eastern side of the island behind the statue of Louis Camoes. There are three high-ceilinged rooms that overlook the sea and catch the cooling breeze. There are no private bathrooms, but breakfast is included at 400 MT single and 500 MT double. Flora, the proprietress, is a real go-getter and is busy renovating two more houses inland towards the museum that will offer a small self-contained family unit for 1 000 MT a night or double *en-suite* rooms for 500 MT. Let me know how they turn out. For more details, tel: 26-61-0076 or 82-454-3290, fax: 26-61 0089.

Casa Himo is a little way up the street from Branca (between the disused cinema and 25 de Junho school) and also faces the sea. This old, established guesthouse is clean and neat and has offstreet parking in the yard. Rooms are without private bathroom and cost 400 MT double and 200 MT single.

Unesco, tel: 26-61-0126, is my favourite of the 'cheapies' in the Old Town, as no other place evokes the feeling of going back in time as this place does. A big old merchant's house just up the road from the museum, it has storerooms that open to the beach below and bedrooms above that overlook the channel. It is also the offices of UNESCO, who are coordinating a lot of the island's restoration, and contains some valuable (but unrestored) antiques. With shared ablutions, rooms cost 200 MT single and 300 MT double.

You can't, however, get more central than **Oikos** guesthouse, tel: 26-61-0096, opposite the museum and in the same block as the Ancora d'Ouro. A bit tatty and no *en-suites* available, breakfast is nevertheless included at 240 MT single, 480 MT twin beds and 360 MT 'married' (double bed).

The last guest house in the Old Town is **Orrera Sana**, over the road from Escondidinho. Owned by the lovely lady, Regina, who runs the general-dealer store under the arches, and managed by her very knowledgeable son Hugo (both of whom speak English well), they have one single room and two doubles, all *en-suite* and inclusive of breakfast. There are fans in each room, and you have the use of the kitchen for self-catering. Hugo is a very good guide around the island too. The single *en-suite* room costs 400 MT, the two-bedder 450 MT and the double-bed room 500 MT. Contact Regina or Hugo on tel: 26-61-0136, e-mail: gimota@hotmail.com

I think the best of the Makuti Town bunch of guesthouses is the friendly **Casa Naju**, tel: 26-61-0008, which you will find north of the green mosque and the fish market. Painted in green trim, Naju's is a family business run by a mother and daughter and consists of a general shop and family residence. The rooms are part of the main house and have the neat, clean and tidy touch that only a woman can bring to an accommodation establishment. No private bathrooms here, but good value at 250 MT single and 500 MT double. Up the central Av 25 de Junho, on the right, just before the Igreja da Saude church, is **Copacabana**. With a busy bar and restaurant in the front, the rooms in this guesthouse might be noisy at night. A double-bedded *en-suite* room costs only 250 MT, and without bathroom costs 200 MT a person, breakfast included. Up to the church corner and around to the right is the difficult-to-find (come to think of it, they're all rather difficult to find) **Residencial Meia Lua**. Recognisable by its orange-painted trim, this rather neat little free-standing house offers a double bed (for married couples only!) in an air-conditioned room for 400 MT. The single room has no air-con, but costs only 200 MT. They all share the same nicely tiled bathroom.

Continuing across to the east coast and up a couple of blocks, you will find the very basic **Karo's Guest House**,

The former Governor's Palace is now a fascinating, well-stocked museum.

tel: 26-61-0034. For what you're getting – water only in buckets – it's probably a little overpriced at 250 MT single and 400 MT double. Breakfast is another 50 MT. The only place on Ilha where you can camp – and then only in little one- or two-man tents – is **Casa de Luis** (aka Private Gardens). A basic backpackers' joint in the middle of the Makuti *barrio*, it is impossible to describe how to get there – asking for '*O Makutini, Travessa dos Fornos'* will help. Set in a rather damp, smelly yard, at least the rooms are clean and you can use the kitchen. There are three rooms, each with two beds at a cost of 200 MT a bed, while camping is 100 MT a person.

Eating out on Ilha

You should be able to find somewhere to stay among that lot, and you could also eat at some of them, but there are some great restaurants with an island style, laid-back atmosphere on Ilha. The best, and one you must visit, is **Reliquias**. Decorated with relics (hence the name) of shipwrecks and treasures from the deep, they offer a full menu, daily specials and a busy bar. You can dine indoors or out in the garden right above the beach. It's popular with tourists and locals alike, so you may have to book – to do so, tel: 26-61-0092. For a pleasant local dining experience, try **O Paladar**, which you will find on the back corner of the block that houses the central market. Hostess, Kiu-Kiu, will welcome you for tea, coffee, light snacks, drinks, or a variety of genuine local dishes (it's so difficult to find anything other than grilled chicken, steaks and seafood in most restaurants). Food

is specially prepared, so order an hour ahead by calling tel: 82-455-9850.

I've already mentioned the fabulous food that can be enjoyed at the **Escondidinho Restaurant**, but it deserves another mention. Cooked with care and flair and enjoyed on a cool open-sided veranda, it's especially pleasant on an evening when they've organised the local school dance troupe to perform. For bookings, tel: 26-61-0078. **Centro Nautico** is more of a bar than a restaurant, but they do serve snacks and light meals to go with the cold drinks that you will sip on their rooftop patio as you watch the sun go down over the channel (life is a slow, easy pleasure on Mozambique Island!). Although the **Ancora d'Ouro** was closed when I was last there, I'm sure it will open again. Its wonderfully central position opposite the Church of the Misericordia in the old Stone Town entices you to just sit and watch the world go by, as the time goes by…

Out and about on Ilha

There are few shops on the island, with the only cluster being 'under the arches' in the Rua de Arcos. This is a long building with an arched façade housing a pharmacy, Missinga curios and a small general dealer run by Regina, who also owns the Orrera Sana guesthouse. The most central bakery is unmarked, but on the opposite corner from Ancora d'Ouro and the Church of the Misericordia. They bake in the early morning and close when they've sold out, so don't go looking for bread or rolls in the late afternoon. In the same block as Ancora is a gallery selling art and jewellery. Other supplies can be bought at the central market or at a couple of small shops, where it is said you can also change money. The official currency exchange is at the branch of **Banco Comercial de Moçambique** (S15°02.117 E40°43.959) in a beautifully restored and panelled building on Av Amilcar Cabral, but no traveller's cheques are accepted.

There is an Internet service available at the **TDM** offices just north of the museum. They have two terminals and charge 1 MT per minute. International calls on a good clear line can also be made from here. You will find Joachim Meier (aka Yoyo) one block behind TDM. He came to Ilha to work in underwater archeology and has stayed on to open a dive school. He is busy renovating his premises and things are a little chaotic, but there is all the scuba gear, fishing rods and reels and even mountain bikes for hire. Contact Yoko, tel: 82-438-5070.

In case of a medical emergency, it is probably best to see Dr Rino Scuccato who runs the Escondidinho guesthouse. He has retired from the medical profession, but is very experienced and well connected. If necessary, he can arrange for a transfer to the hospital in Nampula or an airlift out.

The service station on the island side of the causeway will probably not have fuel, but you can buy from hawkers out of cans if you are desperate. In the market behind the service station, small mechanical and tyre repairs can also be undertaken. Minibuses leave from the mainland side of the causeway for various destinations.

There are at least four smaller islands offshore from Ilha de Moçambique – Ilha de Sete Paus, Ilhas Injaca, Ilha de Goa and Ilha das Cobras. All are uninhabited and most of them are still growing slowly as their coral multiplies. The **Baia de Mossuril** (in which Ilha de Moçambique lies) is ringed with mangroves and small fishing villages, while beautiful sandy beaches such as **Praia da Carrosca** grace the northern peninsula. Down south past Ponta Bajone there is **Baia de Lunga** and more uninhabited coast with inviting beaches. All of this is best reached by boat and the tourism office at the museum would be glad to assist with more information and help in organising a sailing dhow to take you there.

The Church of Santo Antonio.

21 North to Pemba

To continue your journey north, you have to retrace your steps to Monapo and then Namialo. Turn north at the intersection (S14°55.421 E39°58.879) onto the EN106. The tarred road here is reasonable, although some sections do have bad potholes. Nacaroa lies 65 kilometres from Namialo and at around 120 kilometres, you'll pass some weirdly shaped granite hills.

Careened fishing boats are repaired at Paquitequete, Pemba.

PEMBA

to Russells Place / Blackfoot Bar 2 km (S12°57,952 E40°04,040)

Baía de Pemba

WIMBI

Wimbi
Pemba
Dolphin
Wimbi Beach
Pemba Dive
Complexo Caraçol
Casino & Complexo Nautilus
Anchor Traffic Circle
Kaskazini Tourist Information and CI Divers

Avenida de Marimal

Sethy Nissan
S12°59,361 E40°31,693
to Macomia, Nampula
DHL
Moti Rent-a-car
Embondeiro Transport Stand

0   200   400   600 m
0 (1 cm)   168 metres

Pemba Beach
S12°57,873 E40°31,672

CARIACÓ

Market
WW1 Memorial Circle
S12°58,076 E40°30,723
Globe Circle
Osman Transport
CeeBee Pemba Curios
Setec Auto
Bank
Toyota

Dhows across Bay
PAQUITEQUETE
Mosque
Market
Port
City Hall
Governor's Mansion
Escarpment Viewpoint
Cabo Delgado
TDM / M-Cell

Baía de Pemba

PAQUITEQUETE

0   50   100 m
0 (1 cm)   75 m

Fishermen's Village
Pensão Maritime
Banco Comercial de Moçambique
Market
Farmácia Pemba
Restaurant 556
Conselho Municipal City Hall
Immigration
Ave 16 de Julho
Ave 25 de Setembro
Ave 1 de Maio
Governor's Mansion
Escarpment Viewpoint
Ave Eduardo Mondlane
BIM Expresso
Ceconur
Pensão Baía
Cabo Delgado
TDM / M-Cell
Banco Standard
Viatur
LAM - Pemba Takeaway and Bottle Store
Pastelaria
Residencial Lys
Flor d'Avenida
Market
Port
Rua do Comércio

Baía de Pemba

Namapa is 146 kilometres from Namialo, and you are able to refuel here. A couple of kilometres further you will cross the important Lurio River, a colourful sight of wide, sandy streams crowded with people washing clothes and enjoying themselves in the sun. At 186 kilometres, at the town of Chiore, carry on straight (do not take the left fork) and you will reach a major T-junction at Metoro (S13°06.345 E39°52.341). On your left is a new tarred road that stretches as far as Montepuez (the centre of a new fragrance industry), which then deteriorates and eventually goes all the way west to Lichinga. You take the road right (east) and head for Pemba on a good tar road.

After 13 kilometres on the east-bound road, you pass the turn-off north to Macomia and on to the Tanzanian border and another 53 kilometres further is the dirt-road turn-off north to Metuge, Quissanga and the jump-ing-off place for Ibo Island. But, keeping to the tar, you carry on straight towards Pemba (the general speed limit is 80 kph, with 50 kph through the towns), and at S12°59.361 E40°31.693 you reach the Pemba airport terminal building (rumour has it that a lion was shot recently on one of the runways!).

Introducing Pemba

A right turn at the airport will take you down to Wimbe Beach, but carry on straight into Pemba for a full circuit of the town and back to Wimbe. Making your way down the hill, you will reach the traffic circle with the globe in the middle. A right turn here leads down to the seafront at the war memorial traffic circle and the very up-market Pemba Beach Hotel, but head straight to the main intersection in town (you will know it by the Standard Bank, Hotel Cabo Delgado and mCell offices). Turn left here, head up the hill, turn right

Locals trek-fish off the beach at Pemba.

and stop at the monument to view one of the deepest, most protected bays in the world. The road winds down to the old town and the small dockyard. Head through to the point and stop again for a view and photograph of the low-lying, reed-hutted village on the beach. Swing right and around the point – the road passes this village with all its fishing and boat-building activities to come out at the entrance of the vast bay (I was fortunate enough to spot whales here). Follow the seafront to the World War I memorial traffic circle and carry on to pass the Pemba Beach Hotel. You then reach another traffic circle (with a large anchor in the middle) where a right turn would take you back to the airport. Straight on takes us past the Complexo Nautilus and the beautiful palm-studded beaches of Wimbe. This is where tourists and travellers relax and enjoy the best of Mozambique. You carry on past the restaurants and accommodation to the end of the tar, and after 2 kilometres of sandy dirt road (keep left at the fork), you reach Russell's Place (S12°57.952 E40°04.040).

Overnight in Pemba

Russell's Place (aka Cashew Camp) is one of my favourite camp sites in Mozambique – away from from the hustle and the hustlers; a great beach across the road; an easy-going owner always available to assist; tasty, wholesome meals; and the Blackfoot Bar. The pub acquired its name in the days before its floor was cemented and everyone's feet were blackened by the dark soil. Now it's much more comfortable, but with the same buzzy vibe and beau-

> ### Your most useful contact
> for all tourism services and bookings of accommodation, car rental, watersports, island trips, cultural events and even hunting is Kaskazini, Complexo Nautilus, Wimbe Beach, tel: 82-309-6990, e-mail: kaskazini@teledata.mz. They are also a mine of information and have an excellent website that covers Pemba and surrounds: www.kaskazini.com

tifully carved bar. There is a pool table, dartboard, notice board and sports TV – in fact, you might never want to leave! The dish of the day (cost 120 MT) is usually pizza, calamari or fish and comes as a generous self-service buffet. Camping under the trees costs 120 MT, dorm beds 170 MT, two-bedded A-frames 400 MT, three-bedded 500 MT and four-bedded 600 MT. All share the same rustic, but scrupulously clean ablutions, where hot showers are from a bucket on a charcoal burner, and the toilets are long-drop. Mains water and electricity should be arriving soon and then everything will be upgraded. For more information, tel: 82-686-2730, e-mail:russellbott@yahoo.com.au,website: www.pembamajic.com

Heading back into town from Russell's, on the left just before the anchor traffic circle, is **Complexa Turistico Caracol**, which offers smart, new, clean and comfortable rooms across the road from the main Wimbe beach, bars and restaurants. All double suites have sea views, air-cons, *en-suite* bathrooms and verandas for 1 000 MT.

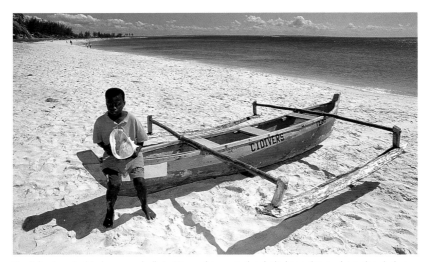

Don't be tempted to buy sea shells in Mozambique. Rather help keep them where they belong – living on the underwater reefs.

A suite of two bedrooms, lounge and bathroom, with additional TV and fridge, costs 1 920 MT. There is a small adjoining restaurant called Tipico. For details, tel: 27-22-0147 or 82-688-7430, fax: 27-22-0108, e-mail: sulemane@teledata.mz, website: www.centroturisticocaracol.com. Across the road – and on the beach – is **Complexo Nautilus**, which has thatched bungalows under the palms, each with bathroom, fridge and air-con. There is a new pool, bar and restaurant and the choice of two diving operations. A new casino has also opened on the premises. A two-sleeper luxury bungalow costs 1 500 MT, a luxury four-sleeper 2 300 MT, and a standard four-sleeper bungalow 1 300. Contact Nautilus, tel: 82-460-8640, e-mail: nautilushtl@teledata.mz

Continuing along the seafront on the Av de Marginal we reach the magnificent new **Pemba Beach Hotel** (S12°57.873

E40°31.672). From the moment you enter the gates of the extensive grounds and feast your eyes on the bougainvillea-covered main building, you know this is going to be a stylish visit. Huge Zanzibar doors set the mood as East African chic, while bubbling fountains, potted palms and cool, jazzy piped music slow you down to island time. Of course, the art is original, the carpets hand woven and the staff pleasant, friendly and efficient, for this is not just one of the best hotels in Mozambique, but one of the best in Africa. Within the complex is a sports club with swimming pool, tennis courts, gym and a newly constructed small-craft harbour. The Bar Niassa and Quirimba Restaurant are understandably the best in Pemba. The rooms simply have everything you could wish for at a cost of 3 000 MT single and 4 000 MT double. The suites are even more opulent and cost 6 000 MT single and 8 000 MT double. Within the estate are spacious free-standing villas for longer-term stays – 5 000 MT a day, 20 000 MT a week, and 65 000 MT a month. For reservations, tel: 27-22-1770, fax: 27-22-1779, website: www.pembabeach.com

From the World War I memorial traffic circle, head up into town and turn right into the main street at the globe traffic circle. The **Hotel Cabo Delgado** is very centrally situated on the corner of Av 25 de Setembro and Av Eduardo Mondlane. Although it looks a little run-down from the outside, the rooms are large and clean. Some have aircon, but others have water in buckets. Singles cost 480 MT , doubles 720 MT and a two-roomed suite 1 152 MT. For details, rel: 27-22-0558, fax: 27-22-1552. One block up Av Eduardo Mondlane, turn left to get to the **Residential Lys**. On a quiet side street, recently painted, and always with running water, this is better value than the Cabo Delgado. Rooms with private bathroom and air-con cost 500 MT single and 600 MT double; private bathroom and fan costs 350 MT and 450 MT, and fan and shared facilities costs 250 MT and 350 MT. To book, tel: 27-22-0951, fax: 27-22-0108, e-mail: suleman@teledata.mz. If you were to turn right instead of left off Av Eduardo Mondlane, you would find the **Pensão Baia** at 289 Av 1 Maio. Also in a quiet neighbourhood, the rooms are clean and neat and there is a cheap restaurant and shady patio. A room with two beds and shared facilities costs 350 MT and an air-conditioned room with bathroom costs 400 MT single and 500 MT double. Contact, tel: 27-22-0153.

Eating out in Pemba

Other than the restaurants at the hotels listed earlier, there are more options for eating out. The best is **Restaurant 556** on the edge of the hill as you drive down to the harbour. With air-conditioning, a great view of the bay, soft lights and a cosmopolitan atmosphere, this is the place for a smart evening meal. Prices range from half a chicken 180 MT, rump steak 250 MT to pizza 270 MT. The best place for daytime pastries, coffee and light lunches is the **Pastelaria Flor d'Avenida**, just up from Hotel Cabo Delgado on Av Eduardo Mondlane. There is also a bakery next door selling rolls, bread and pastries. The newest and most popular spot to eat and drink on Wimbe Beach is the **Pemba Dolphin**, just past the Complexo Nautilus. It's more of a beach bar than a restaurant, but they do serve good snacks in a beautiful setting under the palm trees. There are two other restaurants on Wimbe Beach. Heading away from Pemba Dolphin in the direction of Russell's, you will first reach the **Restaurant Wimbe**, which is more of a nightclub really, and then there's the **Restaurant Aquilo Romano**, serving predominantly Italian dishes. For takeaways, drop in at **Pemba Takeaways** at the intersection at Hotel Cabo Delgado.

Out and about in Pemba

There are a couple of diving options in Pemba. **CI Divers** has a shop in the main Complexo Nautilus building, and offers resort diving courses for 4000 MT, open-water courses for 6400 MT and divemaster for 11700 MT. A guided dive with their equipment costs 880 MT and only half of that if you have your own gear. Contact Pieter or Gi-Gi Jacobs, tel: 82-682-2700, tel/fax: 27-22-0102, e-mail: cidivers@teledata.mz, website: www.cidivers.com. **Pemba Dive's** offices are on the beach just past Pemba Dolphin. They are a smaller operation and a little cheaper, and also rent out paddle-skis and fishing rods. Call Brenda Franck, tel: 27-22-0820. Peter and Colleen Leube run fishing charters on their boat *Tenacious*. A full day's fishing (maximum seven hours and no more than four people) costs 7700 MT, and a half-day 4400 MT. They also do sunset cruises (two hours, six people) for 2200 MT. Contact the Leubes, tel: 82-428-9880, e-mail: peterleube@yahoo.com or through Pemba Dive. Martin Visagie runs a sport fishing and diving operation based on his 34-foot boat *St Lazarus*. Whether it's day trips or five- and seven-day packages, he has the gear, tackle and 40 years of experience to tailor an itinerary to suit your needs. Contacts are in South Africa, tel: +27-(0)35-571-0104 or +27-(0)82-936-3599, fax: +27-(0)35-571-0089, e-mail: worldcharters@iafrica.com, website: www.world-charters.com.

The intersection of 25 de Setembro and Eduardo Mondlane has a few other attractions too. Across from the the Hotel Cabo Delgado, you will find the Standard Bank, then the offices of airline LAM, bottle store and Pemba Takeaways. On the other corner is TDM for public telephones, and mCell for mobile phones and recharge vouchers. Up the road from the Cabo Delgado is a small supermarket, auto-spares, tyres and gas shop, as well as a pharmacy. Behind LAM is the **Viatur** travel agency, tel: 27-22-3431, fax: 27-22-2249, e-mail: viatur@emilmoz.com, and Omar Rent-a-car. Up the road, on the same side, is the Pastelaria Flor d'Avenida.

Another busy part of town is the section of the main road past the globe traffic circle. There's a garage on the right at the circle and then, a little further on the left, is the fascinating handicraft centre **Cee Bee Pemba**. This is a treasure house of Makonde carvings, jewellery, mats and baskets, all marked at reasonable prices. Further down the road on the right are a few motor-spares shops and the big, well-stocked Osman Jacob Supermarket. Across the road is Toyota de Moçambique, tel: 27-22-0551, fax: 27-22-0813, e-mail: toyotapmb@teledata.mz. Next up is a bank, and further down on the right is another good bakery.

The old town down near the dockyard used to be a hive of activity, but now it's just a traffic jam of trucks ferrying Mozambique's precious hardwood forests to hungry foreign ships. Maybe it's because the old Maritimo Hotel is closed for renovations, but the few remaining shops and bars are mostly deserted. The market is still alive and kicking, and the main post office is still open, but there is not much to keep a traveller down here.

Boats dry out at low tide in Paquitequete, Pemba, the largest town in the north.

At the airport (just off the main road as you come into Pemba) you will find DHL and the offices of **Moti Rent-a-Car**. They have a range of pick-ups to hire, from a Toyota 4x2 at 1 000 MT a day and 6 MT per km, to a 4x4 Mitsubishi Colt for 1 700 MT a day and 10 MT per km. Contact Moti, tel 27-22-1687, fax: 27-22-1688. The airport hosts domestic flights by LAM to Beira and Maputo as well as some charter flights, and in 2005 there were scheduled international flights between Pemba and Mayotte in the Comores. A Portuguese pilot, Louis de Faria, was also advertising a weekly return service to Mtwara, just across the border in Tanzania, in a small eight-seater plane. The one-hour flight left Pemba every Friday at 11h00, returned from Mtwara at 13h00 and cost 2 000 MT one way. Contact Viatur Travel Agency (see page 158).

Shortly after the airport, on your right going into Pemba, is Sethy Nissan, tel: 27-22-1521, fax: 27-22-0079, e-mail: sethy1@teledata.mz. Further on into town is the big new Galp service station for fuel and puncture repairs, where they also have a surprisingly well-stocked minimarket (food, booze and toiletries). Galp also refills gas cylinders, as do Vida Gas near the port and Ceconur in the main avenue in town. For general auto repairs, try **Setec Auto**, tel: 27-22-0323.

There is a private clinic just up the hill from the Hotel Cabo Delgado in Av Eduardo Mondlane and a provincial hospital in Av Base Moçambique (carry on through Cabo Delgado intersection). For medical assistance, tel: 27-22-1701. You can be tested for malaria at the Centro de Saude de Natite Clinic near Mbangula market. This clinic also has a Cuban dentist with lots of anaesthetic!

There are a couple of Internet options in town. The more appealing one is in the Cee Bee Pemba handicraft shop on the main road into Pemba (1.5 MT a minute) and the other is Cabine Telefonica on the road through Wimbe Beach (2 MT a minute).

22 Ibo Island and north to Tanzania

The history of Ibo Island and the Querimbas Archipelago is similar and linked to that of Ilha de Moçambique. First settled by Muslim traders, the islands were part of a commercial network that started in the Gulf of Oman and stretched down the East African coast – Mogadishu, Kismayo, Lamu, Zanzibar and Kilwa to the north, and Ilha de Moçambique and Sofala to the south. Large trading dhows would sail down the coast, using the northerly winds during November to April, and sail back again on the southerly winds from May to October – the Trade Winds.

The crumbling entrance to the Fort of São João on Ibo Island.

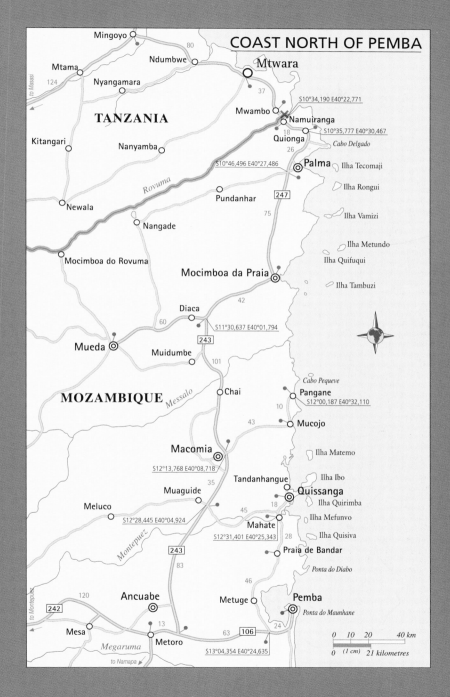

COAST NORTH OF PEMBA

Mingoyo

Mtama

Ndumbwe

Nyangamara

Mtwara

80

37

to Masasi

124

TANZANIA

Kitangari

Nanyamba

Mwambo

S10°34,190 E40°22,771

Namuiranga

S10°35,777 E40°30,467

Quionga

Cabo Delgado

18

26

S10°46,496 E40°27,486

Palma

Ilha Tecomaji

Rovuma

Pundanhar

247

Ilha Rongui

Newala

75

Ilha Vamizi

Nangade

Ilha Metundo

Mocimboa do Rovuma

Ilha Quifuqui

Mocimboa da Praia

Ilha Tambuzi

42

Diaca

60

S11°30,637 E40°01,794

243

Mueda

Muidumbe

101

MOZAMBIQUE *Messalo*

Chai

Cabo Pequeve

Pangane

S12°00,187 E40°32,110

10

43

Mucojo

Macomia

Ilha Matemo

S12°13,768 E40°08,718

Tandanhangue

Ilha Ibo

35

Muaguide

Quissanga

Meluco

45

18

Ilha Quirimba

S12°28,445 E40°04,924

Mahate

Ilha Mefunvo

S12°31,401 E40°25,343

28

Ilha Quisiva

Montepuez

243

Praia de Bandar

83

Ponta do Diabo

46

to Montepuez

120

242

Ancuabe

Metuge

Pemba

24

Ponta do Maunhane

Mesa

13

63

106

Metoro

Megaruma

S13°04,354 E40°24,635

to Namapa

0 10 20   40 km

0 (1 cm) 21 kilometres

The old, disused warehouses that line the small harbour at Ibo attest to a more prosperous past.

Ivory and slaves were the main commodities when the Portuguese muscled their way in during the 16th century. As Ibo rose in importance under the Portuguese, a fort was constructed and the island's prosperity peaked in the late 18th century as it became the major supplier of slaves to the sugar plantations of France's Indian Ocean Islands. It's decline in the early 1900s was mainly due to the lack of a decent deep-sea harbour, and trading operations moved to the nearby harbour of Porto Amelia (as Pemba was then known). So the island has slumbered for the last 100 years, left to the local fisherfolk who have no use for the grand abandoned villas and administrative buildings.

En route to Ibo Island

Recently incorporated into the new **Parque National das Querimbas**, along with a large stretch of the coastline, the archipelago offers a unique opportunity to experience the history and natural beauty of this part of the African coast. Go and enjoy the time-warp that is Ibo Island.

Zero your tripmeter at the airport and travel for 24 kilometres towards Metoro, then turn right (S13°04.354 E40°24.635) to Metuge. Carry on straight along a deeply rutted and potholed dirt road (very bad when wet). At 70 kilometres you will pass Praia de Bandar; keep left here and follow the signs to Quissanga. Little villages rattle by and you might spot bush hunters armed with nothing more than bows and arrows. With the speedo on 92, you will cross a long Bailey bridge and, a couple of kilometres further, enter the little town of Mahate. There is a sign-boarded intersection in the middle of town (S12°31.401 E40°25.343) indicating Pemba 102 (from where you've come), Macomia 47 (to the left) and Quissanga 15 (straight on, to where you're going). Continue until you reach an incongruous traffic circle around a small monument (you will recognise the spot by a large concrete cross in the area). Turn left to Bairro de Tandanhangue. Cross a couple of dodgy little wooden bridges, drive through Tandanhangue village (ignore the 'Safe Parking' signs) and cross the tidal flats until, three hours and 116 kilometres from Pemba, you reach Baobab Beach, the jumping-off place for Ibo Island.

Since 1997, when I first visited this charmed place, they have improved the road and built a few mud huts on the beach, housing a small shop, bar and eating place. There is even overnight accommodation (very basic) in case you miss the last boat across to the island. But the fishermen still skilfully sail their dhows in through the mangrove trees and land their catches here, the women and children still flock around to see what has been caught and opportunistic birds still scavenge the shore – a

---

PAINTED LADIES

On Ibo, and other islands and towns along the north coast, you are likely to see young women with their faces painted white. This tradition is known as *musiro* and is used primarily to protect, soften and beautify the skin. The paste for this mask is made by grinding a branch of the msiro tree with a little water and is left on for the day. A painted white face is sometimes also an indication of the woman's marital status, or whether her husband is away for a while!

---

little piece of unspoilt Africa. The huts cluster around the enclosed compound of **Wildlife Adventures**, who run the Bela Vista Lodge on Ibo. Here you can camp for 50 MT a person (in your own tent), 100 MT (in their tent) or leave your car safely enclosed and guarded for 50 MT a day. *Chapas* run between here and Pemba for about 70 MT and a dhow ride across to Ibo should cost about the same – less if you bargain well. These days, some boats are powered by outboard motors, but for the ultimate island-hopping adventure try to take a sailing dhow.

Boats leave from the beach at high tide and then only sporadically, so be patient and watch what the local travellers do. When it's time to go, you will have to wade out to the dhow, so take your shoes off and be prepared to get wet. Alternatively, you might be offered a ride out in a small dinghy, but this will cost you extra. Find a dry spot in the boat to stow your gear and choose a seat where you won't get too drenched by spray (but you'll still get wet). Depending on the wind, you might be poled or rowed out through the channel in the mangroves, but when you hit the open bay, a tatty old sail will be unfurled, ancient frayed ropes pulled tight and suddenly you'll be skimming over the water as efficiently as on any playboy's million-dollar yacht. Dolphins will cavort under your bow and you might take a short cut through a mangrove swamp to suddenly come upon the little harbour of Ibo. There's more getting wet here, but when you're on dry land, put your shoes on again as there are lots of thorns about.

Overnight on Ibo

Accommodation on Ibo Island is limited – the best, by far, is the bright and breezy **Bela Vista Lodge** overlooking the channel (walk straight along the sea wall from the jetty, and it's on your right). A golden yellow bougainvillea frames the building, large high-ceilinged rooms catch the cool ocean breeze, and Amber, the ridgeback, slumbers in the shade. Dining is on the wide front veranda – fresh pancakes for breakfast and, if you're lucky, giant lobster for dinner. There are no private bathrooms, and a single room costs 875 MT, a double 1 250 MT and a dorm bed 375 MT (including breakfast). For info and bookings contact Wildlife Adventures in South Africa, tel: +27-(0)21-461-2235, fax: +27-(0)21-461-2068, e-mail: sales@wildlifeadventures. co.za, website: www.wildlifeadventures. co.za, or in Mozambique, tel: 27-24-3001 or call Laura, tel: 82-669-9430.

Casa Janine (aka Vila Ruben) was until recently the only accommodation on Ibo, and is situated just past Bela Vista on the Rua Basilio PO Seguro. French-speaking Janine, who has been on the island for over 15 years, offers camping for 100 MT per person, dorm beds for 150 MT and rustic *en-suite* bungalows for 360 MT per person. The place is a bit run-down but serves cold beers, good home-cooked seafood meals and island-grown coffee, all at very reasonable prices. Contact Janine, tel: 27-22-0800 or 82-629-7950. The third option is the unmarked, TDM-owned guesthouse in town overlooking the harbour. It is hardly ever open, but the manager can usually be found in the bar/restaurant across the street. An *en-suite* single costs 700 MT and rooms without bathrooms cost 300 MT single and 400 MT double.

Out and about on Ibo

The best way to get a feel for the island is to take a walk around the town. We start at the jetty that juts out into the little harbour. Young boys might be playing on the beach, just as they do all over the world – a bit loutish and loud and showing off with cartwheels and somersaults in the sand. Boats waiting for the tide to rise will be loading passengers and goods before being poled out into deeper water – they'll hoist the boom, the lateen sail will billow and fill, and then they're gone. A walk along the sea wall at low tide will reward you with sightings of a good variety of waders and seabirds as the tidal flats begin to dry out.

Passing the Bela Vista Lodge on your right, you have the beach on your left (only swimmable at high tide). Once smart, but now decaying houses line this Rua Basilio PO Seguro, casuarina trees whisper in the wind, and you pass Casa Janine on your left. Carry on and you soon reach the old Portuguese **Fort of São João**. Perfectly shaped as a five-pointed star and dating back to 1791, it is in reasonable condition. Cannons protrude from the ramparts over the sea below and big spreading trees shade the courtyard. The entry fee is a bit opportunistic at 30 MT, but it does allow you to observe and photograph the silversmiths at work there. Some of their jewellery is on display and for sale at bargain prices.

Continuing around the perimeter of the island will bring you to fishermen's huts and some interesting boatbuilding activity, but we still have to explore the town, so head out of the gates of the fort and walk up the Rua de Fortaleza towards town. The old cement courts of the Discoteca Tenis will catch your eye, although it is now just a local bar. Keep left up the Rua Dona Maria Pia, past row upon row of once-quaint cottages and shops, in the direction of the concrete water tower on the hill. You may come across a 'painted lady' and it could cost 5 MT to photograph her. Don't expect to find much in the way of supplies at the small municipal market (or for that matter on the rest of the island). Just past the market is another, smaller fort, which dates back to 1841. Turn right here and head down to the water's edge.

The small run-down dwelling at the harbour wall houses another silversmith where you can watch the process of jewellery-making and also purchase pieces. Swing right to stroll the promenade back into the centre of town, passing the newly renovated but unmarked TDM guesthouse. Keep on the street closest to the water to pass old shops and trading houses with back yards that open onto the harbour for loading and unloading. One of these buildings is being converted into a small hotel that looks like it might be something very special when finished.

The road now widens into an open square surrounded by police station, district administration and frangipani-framed governor's office. Dusty public gardens with broken benches attest to a much grander era when ladies and gents paraded in their finery, but at least the nearby post office and school are still in use. Keeping left, you pass the big old church and a beautifully ornate building covered with fine decorative cast-iron work. The final building of note on your walkabout is the ruin of the little Fort of São José, which predates the larger São João fort. A few more steps, and you're back at the jetty.

You will have noticed on your walk that there are no bars (the Muslim influence) and no restaurants (no demand), so your only options are Bela Vista and Janine's. It's a good idea to bring a supply of bottled water and anything else you may require, as there is very little that you can buy on the island (sometimes fishermen will sell you the pick of their catch). And because there is no mains electricity on the island and only a few small generators, nothing much happens at night. In fact, the same is true of the day, so bring a thick book to read (and a torch!). I met Florian who was planning to start up a dive operation, so hopefully this will offer an alternative to reading. Although the whole archipelago has been declared a national park, I hope the sealife survives the wholesale poaching that takes place. When I was there, a large Spanish factory ship was blatantly anchored inshore off Ibo and was cleverly not fishing, but buying up all the seafood it could from the local fishermen – thus encouraging and corrupting the islanders to poach their own heritage and reserves. Local politicians were reputed to be benefiting.

Back to the mainland

To return to the mainland, first check when the tide will be high. Make sure you are already packed, but leave your luggage at your accommodation and go down to the jetty a couple of hours before high tide. Negotiate a price (50 MT to 75 MT seems fair) and then fetch your luggage just before leaving. The procedure is the same as when we came across – wade out, stow luggage, settle in, wait for last-minute stragglers and sail off. If you arrive back at Baobab Beach late in the afternoon and need to get back to Pemba by public transport, it is probably wiser to stay over on the beach rather than sqeeze aboard an overloaded pick-up and tackle the rough road back in the dark.

There is another, much more up-market and expensive option in the Querimbas Archipelago. The small, previously uninhabited **Quilalea Island** has a luxury resort where you can be pampered in blissful isolation. Rates include all meals, picnics, teas, and watersports, but it must be the most expensive accommodation in the country: 7000 MT a person sharing (they do offer special deals sometimes). For more information contact Quilalea Island, tel: +27-(0)11-447-9422, e-mail: quirimbas@plexusmoz.com, website: www.quelalea.com

The alternative is to retrace your incoming route through **Tandanhangue** village (1.3 kilometres), the **Quissanga** traffic circle (6 kilometres) to the signposted intersection in Mahate (19.8 kilometres). This time, turn right onto the **Macomia** road to continue your quest northwards. The road is rough with potholes, ruts and sand, but at the main tarred road (S12°28.445 E40°04.924), turn right and head north to Macomia, another 35 kilometres on. This is the point (S12°13.768 E40°08.718) at which you can turn off east down to the coast to visit Pangane's idyllic palm-fringed beaches. Macomia has a lively market, diesel from the pumps and petrol in cans. You can also get a meal and drink in Chung's Bar at the intersection, where all the buses stop.

Cannons point out from the ramparts of the Fort of São João.

A rough dirt road runs for 43 kilometres from the above-mentioned intersection down to the coast at **Mucojo**. Carry on through this village and up the coast along a very soft sandy track (engage 4x4 and deflate your tyres). Thousands of palms cover this stretch of the coast and the fronds and husks of these trees are used to cover the worst patches of the track to make it passable. Another little village, **Nambo**, is passed and, after another 10 kilometres from Mucojo, you reach Pangane.

Pangane

Casa Suk (S12°00.187 E40°32.110) seems to be the centre of the village and the most solid building – the rest of the village is made up of the reed huts of local fishermen. Casa Suk has a block of neat, clean rooms in the back yard and good vehicle security.

They charge 200 MT a person in a basic room with shared ablutions. There is no bar/restaurant, but they will cook for you on order. Across the track on the beach is a small fenced-off area, grandly called **The Pangane Beach Bar and Restaurant**, where you can sit and enjoy basic food and drinks (fish, rice and beer).

But you only came down here for one reason, and that was to stay at **Ashim's**. Ashim and his charming family run a small camp right at the end of the beach (the solid blue-and-white house stands 1 kilometre beyond Casa Suk). Out on a coral headland and almost surrounded by sea and beach, Ashim offers a choice of three tiny unfurnished coral-and-reed huts, or camping. The huts do not even have cemented floors, but are adequate if you have your own mattresses and other camping gear. They cost 250 MT each and camping is

MOCIMBOA DE PRAIA

Dockyard and Jetty

Immigration

(Tele) TDM

Austral Bank $

Ave 7 Marco

Market

Camping (under construction)

Ave Edward Mondlane

Ave Samora Machel

(W)

Ave Graça Machel

Abandoned Club de M de Praia

District Office

Monument (Star)

Estrela

Pensao Magid

Pensao Saber Viver

Carlos

Pensao Leeta

S11°21,409 E40°21,015

to Palma and Ruvuma

to Airport

to Pemba

150 MT per tent. The cold showers and flush toilets (with a bucket of sea-water) are communal reed enclosures – it sounds bad, but it's attractively done.

The fishing is good around. Lateen-rigged sailing dhows bring in the catches, *kapenta* dries on the sand and octopus hang out on racks. If you're looking for a place to unwind, this is it.

On to Mocimboa

Back at Macomia, you swing northward again on a road that is partly reasonable gravel, and partly bad tar. After 101 kilometres, you reach an intersection (S11°30.637 E40°01.794) where the road splits – left on a brand-new tarred road to Mueda and then rough tracks to Montepuez and eventually Lichinga, or right to Mocimboa da Praia. (If you are driving in the opposite direction, from Mocimboa da Praia south to Pemba, take care here. It is very easy to carry straight on past the turn-off and head for Mueda. You need to turn left here to get to Pemba.) It is 42 kilometres of reasonable tar to Mocimboa, which is entered via a traffic circle. The right turn leads to the aerodrome, the left to Palma, and road straight ahead on into town.

Mocimboa is entered via a long dual-carriage road (another Av Samora Machel) and within a kilometre you encounter almost all the accommodation the town has to offer. The first is **Pensão Leeta**, a scruffy double-storeyed building on the right. The ablutions are shared, the shower is cold and the toilet flushes with a bucket of water, but a double bed in a room costs only 200 MT. Contact Manuel,

tel: 27-28-1147. Further down, also on the right, is the much better **Pensão Saber Viver**. Tightly run by a Muslim father and son, this is a quiet place with no bar and no drinking allowed. The rooms are even cheaper at 150 MT and have a double bed and private bathroom with a bucket shower (toilets are outside and are shared). There is a safe yard for your vehicle, but they rather cheekily charge 50 MT a night for your car. Contact Rajabo, tel: 27-28-1160. The **Carlos Resthouse and Discoteca** across the road cannot be recommended, even though their grubby double rondavels are only 100 MT a night (I think they are more often rented by the hour – or half-hour!). The smelly toilets are a hole in the floor and the place is very noisy from the all-night bar and disco. Further on down the road, on the left, is the long-established **Pensão Residencial Magid**. Run-down, dirty and with a noisy bar, it at least serves decent cheap food. A room with two beds and shared facilities costs 175 MT, a room with double bed and *en-suite* bucket bathroom is 200 MT. Parking is in a back yard. Telephone Jusinto, tel: 27-28-1099.

Just past Magid is an unfinished service station that sells diesel from a road tanker at 17 MT per litre, and beyond that a star monument and the district offices. Across the road is the pleasant **Estreda** bar and restaurant, and then the abandoned Club de Mocimboa de Praia on the left (oh, how that must have partied here in the 'old days'). There is another fuel station just down Av Eduardo Mondlane, but if we stay on Samora Machel we will find a cluster of shops selling general goods. On the right-hand side of the road is the bright new Tekawey (take-away) Shahista, named after this newly arrived Indian couple's young daughter. There is a selection of Indian delicacies, a small stock of groceries and freshly baked bread, cake and biscuits. A small open-air market on the left is where you can buy the bare necessities, and then the road swings off to the right and heads for the beach. To carry on straight from the market would bring you to the harbour where you would be shocked to see how much timber is being shipped out. How much longer can it continue?

Rather swing right and continue on down Av 7 Marco. The TDM (telephones) is on your left, followed by the Austral Bank. Across the road is another bakery and then you hit the beach and The Miramar. **The Miramar** is a collection of three bungalows on the beach. Grubby and run-down, with no security,

it does however have a popular bar/restaurant pleasantly presided over by the hugely obese and non-moving Bebe, who rules from her bedroom-cum-kitchen. There is one more accommodation establishment, still being built, that will cater for the upper market. **Chez Natalie** (S11°19.901 E40°21.184) is out on the north side of town and overlooks the mangrove-circled mouth of the Mpanga River. Bungalows are raised up for a better view, and water, electricity and even Internet access is promised on a 24-hour basis. I hope they complete this sorely needed facility. For up-to-date info, tel: 21-49-8497, e-mail: natalie@teledata.mz

The turn-off north opposite Pensão Saber Viver is from where the *chapas* pick-ups leave to go to Palma and on to the Tanzanian border on the Rovuma River. Enquire the night before and ask to be picked up at your hotel, as they leave very early (around 04h00).

The sun sets over the Rovuma River while Tanzania beckons in the distance.

To the Tanzania border

You've come so far from first crossing the border into Mozambique at Ponta do Ouro that you are now close to reaching the northern border with Tanzania. Just 120 kilometres left to go. Leaving Mocimboa da Praia, turn north to **Palma** at the aerodrome traffic circle (S11°21.409 E40°21.015) and zero your tripmeter. This dirt road is rough and potholed, and very bad in wet conditions. It goes through small villages with well-known names like Maputo and Quelimane. At 49 kilometres, there is a turn-off right to the village of **Olumbi**, but carry on straight. After about 1 hour and 40 minutes, you will reach an important intersection at 78 kilometres (S10°46.496 E40°27.486). To the right, it is 2 kilometres into Palma town – don't bother going down, I could find nothing of interest – and to the left is a very rough track that loops back around to **Mueda**. Straight across the intersection is the route to Tanzania.

Passing a big new church on your right as you leave the intersection, the track narrows to a single lane and deteriorates into deep sand. Visibility is bad, with high grass and dense bush on either side, so be careful of the speeding *chapas* pick-ups that ply this section of road. At 100.5 kilometres another track comes in from the right. This is the direct route from Palma town and one to avoid if you were coming from the north. There are reputed to be many elephants in the area and, although I didn't see any, there was plenty of fresh dung on the track. The sand becomes thicker and softer with a high 'island' in the middle and the bush crowds in closer – all 4x4 driving. The village of **Quionga** is reached at 104 kilometres. Keep right at the well (S10°35.777 E40°30.467) and go down the main street, with its old lampposts. Pass the flagpole and admin buildings and bear left at the end of the village.

The river you see now is not yet the Rovuma, but forms a tidal flat that is tricky to negotiate. The Mozambican border post of **Namiranga** is reached at 122 kilometres (S10°34.190 E40°22.771). There is a little settlement here with a shop selling basic groceries, food and beer and even rough accommodation is available at the **Selamani Moosa Border Guest House** (a room with two beds costs 100 MT). The border is a cluster of mud huts, although they are building a smart new post, and it is hassle-free, as most isolated border posts are. To get to the banks of the Rovuma and the ferry, turn right at the border and take an extremely rough track for 5.5 kilometres to a cluster of huts (S10°35.694 E40°30.529).

What a spot! Of course, the real reason anything is here, and why you are here, is the ferry. Owned and based on the Tanzanian side of the Rovuma, it is supposed to operate all year round. In reality, however, it sometimes breaks down, or the crew takes a holiday because of low demand, or flooding makes it too dangerous to operate. It is therefore a good idea to check first with Captain Philip Mtupa in Tanzania, tel: +255-744-762222. Able to carry four cars or two trucks, it costs 300 MT for a car. If you do not have a vehicle, small boats run across regularly and charge 50 MT a person.

23
West through Malawi to Tete and Cahora Bassa

As you are up in the north of Mozambique, you may want to take a detour… I suggest a route from Nampula, via Cuamba, to Blantyre in Malawi, and then the short run to Tete. Zero the trusty speedo at the train station in **Nampula** and head out east on the Av de Trabalho towards Alto Molocue.

Cahora Bassa Dam and the hydroelectric plant dominate the gorge at Songo.

After just 4.2 kilometres (S15°06.685 E39°13.661), turn right to **Ribaue** and **Cuamba**. The rocky pinnacles and domes that dot the countryside here are a challenge to any mountaineer, but the gravel road is not too demanding until you pass through **Rapale** (at 20 kilometres). Now it deteriorates and crisscrosses the railway line that runs parallel. Dusty in the dry and wet and slippery when wet, it passes through the bustling little market town of **Nomigonha**.

On to Malema

At a higher altitude and away from the coastal humidity, **Ribaue** was once a popular refuge from lowland heat. Still a pretty town with tree-lined avenues, there is an old derelict 1930s hotel on the road out of town that must have once been the last word in luxury. A cellphone tower has just been erected, so try your phone here. The road east continues through town and out past the Canam Cotton Factory. At 161 kilometres, there is an unsignposted turn-off to the left, but keep straight and, after another 4 kilometres, there is a fork (S14°58.371 E38°03.717) in the road. Keep right towards **Cuamba** (left will take you down south to Alto Molocue). This is pleasant hilly countryside with many kopjes and inselbergs. **Malema** is reached at 240 kilometres, so turn left at the station (S14°56.859 E37°24.948). The town and its amenities come as a surprise out here in the dusty bush. Heading away from the station, and all on your left, you will find **Pensão Malema**, which has a limited restaurant and basic *en-suite* rooms, costing

50 MT for a single and 80 MT a double. Then there's the TDM for public phones and Internet, followed by a shop and the municipal market behind it. Next up is a bar, then the **Residencial Cave Negra**, a dirty, noisy place with rooms (shared facilities) for 100 MT single and 150 MT double. At the end of the road is the smart, but weirdly out-of-place **N&F Lodge** (Complexo Malaya). It is a lot more expensive than the other places in town, but is clean, comfortable, secure, motel-like establishment with bar/restaurant and even a hairdresser on the premises. Accommodation is in four-bedroomed, self-contained bungalows where each double room is *en-suite* with satellite TV and 24-hour electricity. The cost is 450 MT per room. Across the road is a fuel station and shop; swing right here to leave town, passing the hospital on your right.

A jagged range of inselbergs looks like the scaly spine of a monstrous dinosaur off on the left, as the road deteriorates further. A traffic circle with a statue of the Madonna (S14°52.730 E37°00960) is reached at 286 kilometres, where the left turn leads to Gurue (see Chapter 21). Carry on straight and pass the impressive stone gates of the Mutuali Secondary School and, a little further on, the large and incongrous old tsetse fly control building. The road now has sharp, deep potholes and is badly rutted, so slow down to 40 kph. When you cross the Lurio River into the Niassa province, the road improves and you can maintain 80 kph. The mountains just keep getting bigger and better. Fortunately, there is no mountain driving, as these

CUAMBA

Cuamba Station

Open Square

District Administration

Windmill

Amaramba Cinema

Narisqueira

Eduardo Monpalane

Pensão Namaacha

Naboa

Commercial

Auto Niassa

Rua Liberade

Park

Big Shop

Av. Samora Machel

Market

Post and Telecommunication

S14°48,067 E36°32,367

BIM Expresso Bank and ATM

Pensão São Miguel

Statue of Madonna

Frelimo Monument

Cyclo Holdings Auto Spares

School

Vision 2000

Residencial Formosa

to Intre Lagos and Mandimba

giants rise up sheer from the flat countryside, like the giant sheer-sided monster of a mountain 20 kilometres before Cuamba. With a round cupola dome on top and waterfalls down the sides, this is the best of the bunch. Finally, 350 kilometres from Nampula and a hard day's ride, we reach Cuamba.

Cuamba

Cuamba is an important junction town. The railway line from the coast at Nacala forks east into Malawi and north to the towns of Lichinga, while roads fan out to Lichinga, Malawi, Gurue and Nampula.

As the economic hub of the Niassa province and because of its proximity to Malawi, Cuamba is a bustling town and has a lively market. Water in the taps, however, only runs for an hour in the early morning and again for an hour in the early evening.

The town is entered along Av Eduardo Mondlane, the main street, and the first feature, just past the school, is an intersection on the left with a statue of the Madonna in the centre. Remember this spot, as this is the way out. Across the road, opposite the school, is a BP service station that doesn't always have fuel. Then there is the BIM Bank and Expresso ATM and, moving on along Eduardo Mondlane, there is a park on your right. Two blocks further on your right is a little cluster of a bar/restaurant, shop and bakery, a disused cinema and a fuel pump that almost always has diesel and sometimes petrol. Across the open square on your left is the railway station and at the end of the road is the general hospital.

Driving back along Av Eduardo Mondlane, turn down left into Rua Liberade just before the park. The **Pensão Namaacha** on your left might have closed down by the time you read this, as it was definitely on its way out when I saw it. Very shabby, with bombed-out bathrooms and dirty bedrooms, they charge only 150 MT a room. Whether that includes your pick of the girls that hang about there, I can't say. Facing the park on your right is a large general dealer and, if you continue on down Rua Liberade, you will find another bank. One more block down, on your left is Auto Niassa for vehicle repairs, and then the market on your right. A right turn at Auto Niassa into Av Samora Machel will bring you to Cyclo Holding Auto Spares.

Cuamba's best accommodation is at the **Hotel Vision 2000** in Av 3 de Fevereiro, down from the BP station on the main road as you come into town. First-floor double rooms with bathroom and fan cost 660 MT. Second-floor double rooms have bathroom, air-con, fridge and satellite TV for 1000 MT, including breakfast. With a pleasant outdoor bar under thatch and a restaurant serving reasonably priced meals, this is the place to eat and drink. For details, tel: 27-16-2632, fax: 27-16-2713, e-mail: h-vision2000@teledata.mz. Cheaper is the **Pensão Sao Miguel**, just west of Vision 2000. Owned and run by a Portuguese settler, it also boasts a small bar/restaurant and has secure parking in the back yard. Double rooms with shared facilities cost 300 MT, with bathroom 400 MT, and with bathroom, TV and air-con 450 MT.

The road to Cuamba is rugged and lonely, but boasts fantastic scenery.

A first-class passenger train runs between Nampula and Cuamba on alternate days, except Mondays. At 05h00 on Tuesday morning, it leaves Cuamba and takes 10 hours to reach Nampula. On Wednesday, it returns to Cuamba, and so it goes back and forth between the two towns until Sunday. Tickets cost 400 MT, which includes lunch. Another train runs on the days that the first-class train is not running and charges 100 MT for second-class and 54 MT for third-class tickets. There is also a slow goods train that runs from Cuamba to the Malawian border at Entre Lagos (open flatbeds or closed cattle trucks for about 22 MT). You will then have to walk across the border and board a train at Nayuchi in Malawi for the ride to Liwonde. This can take more than 24 hours and is very rough, but it is also one of Africa's more exciting train rides. Although I've done this trip, don't ask me about timetables!

On to Liwonde

To drive to **Liwonde** in Malawi from Cuamba you have two options; the obvious – and considerably easier – but longer route (325 kilometres) north via Mandimba and Mangochi, or the obscure, rough, but shorter track (190 kilometres) directly west via the border at Nayuchi. I suggest the latter, but what follows is a brief description of the northern route…

Go to the Madonna intersection in Cuamba (S14o48.067 E36o32.367), turn south and cross the railway line. Make your way through this reed-hut part of town, with its buses and trucks loading passengers and goods for the long haul ahead. A sprawling market on the outskirts of town sells mainly bright plastic ware and shiny new bicycles. Pass under the railway bridge and carry straight on (a left turn here would take you along the shorter Nayuchi route). A reasonable dirt road follows the railway line for more than 100 kilometres, and then swings west to cross the Lugenda River at about 150 kilometres. At just short of 200 kilometres, you reach **Mandimba**, where you can turn north to Lichinga. Carry on through town and head for the border, which should be easy, but make sure you have insurance for your vehicle in Malawi, as you will be stopped and asked for it. Hold on to your Mozambican vehicle insurance (hopefully it will still be valid), because you will need it when you re-enter Mozambique at Zobue to get to Tete. Then it's just over 50 kilometres to **Mangochi**, which you will enter across the new bridge over the wide Shire River. Get onto the M3 heading south (you could nip up north to Cape Maclear on Lake Malawi first) and, after approximately 75 kilometres, you will reach the intersection where the M6 from Lilongwe joins up. Turn left, cross the Shire River again and you've reached Liwonde. Continue on the M3 through Zomba to reach **Blantyre**.

The shorter route via **Entre Lagos** and **Nayuchi** also starts at Cuamba's Madonna intersection, crosses the railway line, passes the market, under the railway line again and then turns immediately left at S14°48.256 E36°31.550. A decent 80-kph dirt road runs west for 86 kilometres to a bridge at **Vila de Insaca** – but don't cross the bridge or enter the town. Turn right just before the bridge (S15°11.029 E35°52.662) onto a rapidly deteriorating narrow track. This is a 40-kph road and probably impassable when wet. You will pass through many little villages until, 23 kilometres from the bridge, you cross the railway

tracks again; turn left here, and arrive in Entre Lagos. If you're doing this route in reverse – in other words, coming from Entre Lagos and heading for Cuamba – then be sure to turn right across the railway line at S14°59.501 E35°53.716.

Entre Lagos is a dump and the sooner you get through it the better. Customs and immigration are at the station (you can't miss them) and are fast and efficient. If you are unfortunate enough to be stuck here, ask the customs officials to help (they have a spare house), or make your way to the **Pensão Destino**, which faces the tracks a little further on. Run-down, with dirty, shared toilets, there is no food or drink, but their beds don't look too bad and only cost 40 MT each. The New Rest House around the corner is much the same.

Having completed the formalities for leaving Mozambique, follow the railway line along a sandy track for 1.5 kilometres and pass through the barrier that forms the border with Malawi. Less than 1 kilometre further is the Nayuchi border post, also in their railway station. Again, the formalities are simple and pleasant, although I think it's unfair to charge $11 for the processing of the vehicle's temporary import permit. I must mention that this border crossing has one major problem if you are crossing from Mozambique with your own car – you cannot buy Malawian vehicle insurance here, so unless you have valid insurance, perhaps from an earlier visit, you will be in trouble when you are asked for it at a roadblock. A letter from the border officials might help, but with no letter or insurance, I had to use all my negotiating skills to avoid paying a fine on my way down to Blantyre.

Nayuchi has the same basic non-amenities as Entre Lagos, so head out as soon as you can (it's quite easy to travel between Cuamba and Blantyre in a day).

The area is dotted with lakes that form part of Malawi's Ramsar-declared wetlands, so the birdlife is good – as is the fishing, judging by the number of boats being built and used on the small lakes alongside the road. (Entre Lagos is so named as it lies between the lakes of Chiuta in the north and Chilwa to the south). About 43 kilometres from the Nayuchi border post, you will reach a tarred road (S14°59.881 E35°29.473), turn left towards Liwonde. This is where you might encounter a police roadblock. They will check for two triangles, the vehicle's temporary import permit and insurance, as well as your driver's licence. Another 32 kilometres brings you to Liwonde, where you need to turn south onto the M3 and head for Blantyre via Zomba (with possibly more roadblocks).

Blantyre

Approaching Blantyre, you will first encounter its large suburb, or sister city, **Limbe**. Keep right at the first major traffic intersection and make your way onto the Kamuzu Highway, through the Independence Arch and across the intersection with Makata Road. The sprawling Chichiri Mall on your left has a huge, well-stocked Shoprite supermarket as its main tenant and also boasts fashion shops, banks, a phar-

---

THE ZOMBA PLATEAU

If you are not in a hurry to reach Blantyre, you might want to explore the Zomba Plateau. Situated high above Zomba town, it is one of Malawi's most popular walking and hiking areas – the indigenous forests and interesting birdlife are the main attractions. Turn off right in the town and go up past the golf club. There are guest lodges and two camp sites: the forestry camp and another at the Kuchawe trout farm.

---

macy, takeaways, a branch of Soche Tours, and a PostNet agency for phone, Internet, copying and DHL.

Carry on down Kumuzu Highway through the industrial area (for motor spares and workshops, as well as gas refills) to the circle at the bottom – you will recognise it by the clock tower (S15°47.275 E35°00.817). Carry on straight into the city centre or turn right at the clock tower for the recommended accommodation.

Turn right into Chileke Road at the clock-tower circle and pass under the railway bridge. Take the first left turn, drive through the busy Wenela bus station, and you will end up in front of **Doogle's Backpacker Lodge** (S15°47.031 E35°00.898). A favourite stopover for travellers crossing Africa, the facilities include a swimming pool, TV lounge, good Internet connection, reasonably priced meals and the most popular bar in Blantyre – all set in a secure garden environment. Camping is $3 a person, dorm beds $5 and comfortable double rooms are $15 a night – all share the same clean, spacious bathrooms with a never-ending supply of hot water. Billy and Mark are always willing to assist and can provide info on any travel matter. For enquiries, tel: +265-(0)1-62-1128, e-mail: doogles@africa-online.net

The top hotel in Blantyre is the centrally situated **Mount Soche Hotel** on Glyn Jones Road. With a swimming pool, satellite TV, 24-hour room service, a business centre and two very good restaurants, its rooms range from standard at $190/220 single/double to superior suites at $330 double. For details, tel: +265-(0)1-62-0588, fax: +265-(0)1-62-0154, e-mail: Mountsoche@lemeridienmalawi.co.mw. **Ryalls Hotel**, down the road, is brand new, but a little cheaper. For information, tel: +265-(0)1-62-0955. Another recommended place to stay is **Kabula Lodge**, in the quiet suburb of the same name (follow the signs past Mount Soche Hotel). Family run and popular with volunteer workers on extended stays, it offers a range of accommodation from $7 for basic singles to $20 for self-contained doubles and use of the well-equipped kitchen. For information, tel: +265-(0)1-621216. For takeaways, visit Nando's (or maybe you've had enough peri-peri chicken) on the corner of Henderson Street and Haile Selassie Road, and for a good vibey pub try Cactus, down Slater Road.

There is a Mozambican Consulate on Kamuzu Highway, near to the Masalima post office. Transit visas (for passage through the Tete Corridor) are issued on the same day for $11, or overnight for $7. Proper tourist visas cost $20 and take three days to process. Any one of the many banks in town will change money for you, or better still, use one of the private forex bureaux in the city centre, close to the Mount Soche Hotel. The new **Mwaiwathu Hospital** in Chileka Road just above the bus station (as well as Doogle's) offers a comprehensive medical service and is open all hours. Contact the hospital, tel: +265-(0)1-62-2999. Many travellers go on the free tour offered by **Carlsberg Brewery** (tel: +265-(0)1-67-0222) on Wednesdays at 14h30, more for the free beer swilling than an interest in the brewing process, I'm sure…

Malawi has a good bus network, and buses run in all directions from the bus station near Doogle's. Different levels of luxury and speed determine the price and departure times – ask at Doogle's or the bus station. Blantyre is also internationally very well connected by luxury coach to Zimbawe and South Africa. Lines such as City-to-City, Vaal Africa and Linking Africa have depots in the city and run to Harare and Johannesburg. Fuel is freely available all over town and costs $0.88 per litre for petrol (watch out for the ethanol blend, which has a very low octane rating) and $0.82 per litre for diesel.

On to Tete

To get out of Blantyre and on your way to Tete, make your way up Glyn Jones Road from the clock-tower traffic circle and turn right at the next intersection (Oilcom service station is on your right). Travel for 8 kilometres to a traffic circle and go straight across. Another 50-odd

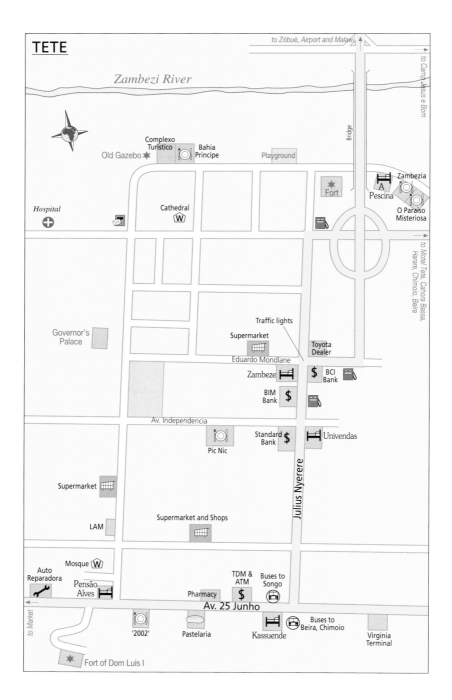

TETE

Zambezi River

to Zóbuè, Airport and Malawi

to Cama Jesus e Bom

Bridge

to Motel Tete, Cahora Bassa, Harare, Chimoio, Beira

Complexo Turistico
Old Gazebo
Bahia Principe
Playground

Zambezia

Fort
Pescina
O Paraiso Misteriosa

Hospital
Cathedral

Governor's Palace

Traffic lights
Supermarket
Toyota Dealer
Eduardo Mondlane
Zambeze
BCI Bank
BIM Bank

Av. Independencia

Pic Nic
Standard Bank
Univendas

Supermarket

Julius Nyerere

Supermarket and Shops
LAM

Mosque

Auto Reparadora
Pensão Alves

TDM & ATM
Buses to Songo

Pharmacy

Av. 25 Junho

to Market

'2002'
Pastelaria
Kassuende
Buses to Beira, Chimoio
Virginia Terminal

Fort of Dom Luis I

kilometres of excellent tar brings you to the bridge across the Shire River, and on the other side is a right turn to Lilongwe. Carry on straight to **Mwanza** (another 46 kilometres of good road) and refuel before crossing the border back into Mozambique (fuel is cheaper in Malawi). The crossing should be trouble free and not too expensive if you still have valid Mozambican vehicle insurance. Immigration will cost you 30 MT per person and there is another 45 MT for your vehicle's temporary import permit.

Moatize is about 100 kilometres from the border and has most amenities, but with Tete less than 20 kilometres down the road, it's not worth stopping here. Cross the Revubue River, pass the airport on the right and just past the mCell tower is the turn-off north to eastern Zambia. Carry on to the impressive 540-metre concrete suspension bridge across the Zambezi that carries you into Tete.

Tete, like so many old towns of Mozambique, predates the arrival· of the Portuguese. If you want to camp here, turn off left just before the bridge and drive downstream for less than a kilometre to **Jesus e Bom Campsite** (S16°09.318 E33°36.018). Laid out on the banks of the mighty Zambezi, with a great view of the bridge and town, this grassy spot offers the only camping in Tete. There is electricity, and flush toilets, but the showers are cold (there is no need for hot water in this temperate, often stuffy, climate). The charge is 40 MT a person, plus 60 MT a vehicle a night. Contact Riaan Terblanche, tel: 25-22-0195.

Be careful when rejoining the main road at the bridge. If you want to head away from Tete towards Malawi, drive under the bridge and right, to come up pointing away from the town. If you're going to cross the Zambezi into Tete, don't go under the bridge, but turn right just before it and swing up to face the town. The *transitos* on duty at the bridge love catching and fining motorists who take the wrong option, or cross the solid white line in the road. There is a 5-MT toll to cross the bridge. To carry on towards the Zimbabwean border without driving into the centre of Tete, take the first turn left across the bridge to get out of town. You will pass the **Motel Tete** (S16°09.889 E33°35.933) on the banks of the Zambezi as you leave. This motel has 20 clean and neat rooms built and furnished to a high standard. There is a good restaurant, safe parking and no noisy bar. A double *en-suite* room with TV, air-con and fridge costs 800 MT a night. For info, tel: 25-22-3467 or 25-22-3498.

To enter the centre of Tete and explore, carry on straight over the bridge and turn right – but watch out for one-way streets. Make your way down Av Eduardo Mondlane to the traffic lights, passing the BP garage on your left. On the corners of this intersection with Av Julius Nyerere is a bank, the Hotel Zambeze and the main **Toyota** dealer, tel: 25-22-2847, fax: 25-22-2391, e-mail: toyota.tete@teledata.mz. Turn left into Julius Nyerere to pass more banks and, on the next corner (with Av Independencia), is the Univendas Store for hardware, tools and spares – upstairs, above the shop, are rooms to let. Down the side streets is an assortment of shops, but keep going till you run into the T-junction of Av 25 Junho. Turn right into this street, which is abuzz with buses, *chapas*, bars, restaurants and the Kassuende Hotel on your left. There's the TDM (for public telephones) and a pharmacy on your right and a bakery on your left. Further down, on the right-hand corner, is the Pensão Alves and, on your left, the road up to the Fort of Dom Luis. Further on is the covered market and an auto-repair works.

Now head down to the road along the banks of the Zambezi. Starting upstream, you will come across an isolated old gazebo perched in the middle of the mud – a favourite spot for the Portuguese colonials to enjoy their sundowners. Lower down, you pass the Complexo Turistico Bahia Principe, then a children's playground and another fort. This riverside drive passes under the bridge to the A Piscina and Zambeze O Paraiso Misterioso bar/restaurants.

Overnight in Tete

After the Motel Tete, the next best accommodation in town is the **Hotel Zambeze** on the corner of Av Eduardo Mondlane and Julius Nyerere. It's a bit tatty, but very central, and at five storeys (fortunately the lift works), there are great views, especially from the excellent rooftop restaurant. The rooms are all *en-suite* and range in price from 250/350 MT single/double to 500/650 MT single/double with air-con and 1000/1 200 MT with air-con, TV and fridge (breakfast included in all). For information, tel: 25-22-3100.

The next best place to stay is **Predio Univendas**, a neat, low-key collection of rooms and apartments above the Univendas Store on Av Julius Nyerere. All rooms have air-con and are large and airy, with very good security – there is a private yard for your car. Rates are 400/550 MT single/double with shared facilities, 600/750 MT with *en-suite* facilities, while the larger two-roomed suites cost 750/900 MT. For details, tel: 25-22-3198.

The **A Piscina**, tel: 25-22-3084, offers accommodation in a pleasant garden setting below the bridge on the banks of the Zambezi. A little dilapidated and almost always full, plain double rooms using shared ablutions cost 400 MT a night, *en-suite* single/double 300/500 MT. But most people rather visit A Piscina for the popular bar and restaurant. Moving down the accommodation scale, there is the **Pensão Alves**, tel: 25-22-2523, at the end of Av 25 Junho. It's a bit of a dump with a noisy but reasonably priced bar and restaurant. Plain single rooms cost 350 MT and doubles 400 MT, but the nightly disco will probably keep you awake. Back along Av 25 Junho, around where the buses rev and hoot, is the **Hotel Kassuende**, cheap at 200 MT single and 220 MT double, *en-suite* air-conned doubles cost 370. For bookings and info, tel: 25-22-2531. All intercity buses congregate in this area on Av 25 Junho and you will find transport to Beira, Malawi and Zimbabwe.

Eating out in Tete

Other than the bars and restaurants attached to hotels already mentioned, there are two comfortable eateries on the banks of the river, where it is pleasant to sit and sip and sup while the mighty Zambezi drifts by. The **Complexo Turistico Bahia Principe** is upstream near the gazebo and the **Zambezi a Pariaso Misteriosa** is just below the bridge. A good place in town for light meals and refreshments is the **Pic Nic Bar and Restaurant** on Av Independencia. Their prego rolls are 25 MT and hamburgers 40 MT, and can be enjoyed indoors or out on the patio.

In and around Tete

You should also check out the two forts in town. A really far-flung outpost during the early colonial days, Tete relied on the defences of the fort that stands on the water's edge. The other one, the **Fort of Dom Luis I**, was where they housed the slaves that were in transit down to the coast. Situated up the hill from Pens[a]o Alves in Av 25 Junho, you will have to tread carefully when exploring, as it is now used as the neighbourhood toilet.

Cahora Bassa

An interesting excursion from Tete is a visit to the **Cahora Bassa** dam. Taking your distance from the bridge in town, drive out past Motel Tete on good tar for 20 kilometres until you reach the turn-off right at S16°18.399 E33°31.054 (signposted to Songo). The road north to Cahora Bassa is also good tar, and 136 kilometres from Tete, you will pass the left turn (S15°38.898 E32°47.708) to Ugezi Tiger Lodge, the best accommodation in the area. Songo town is just 5.5 kilometres straight ahead, up a winding road through the hills.

Songo is a typical company town and exists mainly for the construction and electricity companies – everything and everyone belongs to them. Pretty and well laid out, it has good schools and a hospital. The main intersection in town is at S15°36.727 E32°46.352, where you turn left to enter the small town centre. Here you will find a decent supermarket, banks, service station, pharmacy, TDM and post office.

The Fort of Dom Luis I, which overlooks Tete, used to house slaves but is now derelict.

A drive down and across a bougain-villea-covered traffic circle will bring you to the unmarked **Pensão Sete Montes**, a neat, tidy and quiet place with secure parking, but no bar or restaurant. They have 16 *en-suite* double rooms with fridges for 400 MT a night and one larger suite with TV and air-con for 600 MT. For information, tel: 82-865-0070, fax: 25-28-2341.

If you turn right at the town's main intersection, you'll pass the airport and hospital, and heading up right you will find the **Club Centro Social** (S15°35.767 E32°45.787). Still beauti-fully maintained among lush gardens, this was once the hub of the construc-tion company's social life. Now priva-tised and known as Teles' Club, it offers a well-stocked bar, elegant restaurant, large swimming pool and comfortable accommodation. Single rooms cost 600 MT a night and double suites 700 MT – all have air-con, and some have TV. Contact the club, tel: 25-28-2497.

Continuing out of town, you pass through the old construction camp and suddenly the dam wall is below you. The road winds down a switch-back series of hairpin bends with many opportunities and spots to stop and enjoy the view of the narrow gorge. At the bottom is a boom that blocks your way to the wall, so turn left here and continue along this tarred road around to even more excellent lookout points. The best is up a steep, stony 4x4 track to a hilltop that rewards you with a great view of the expanse of the lake. Carry on around the lake shore until, at S15°37.188 E32°42.645, you come to the turn-off to **Ugezi Tiger Lodge**. It's

a short, rough dirt road down past the *kapenta* fish drying plants to the lodge. Nestled in the hills and bays above the dam, the stone and thatch buildings blend in perfectly. Grassed, shaded and with stunning views, the camp sites and chalets are most welcoming and the small swimming pool (there are too many hippos and crocs in the dam) offers relief from the heat. This is a fisherman's paradise, and the bar and restaurant are decorated with mounted and stuffed, record-breaking fish and trophies. Groups fly in, rent boats and tackle, and go back home with broad smiles on their faces.

Camping in your own tent costs 120 MT a person, and the lodge's tent (with bed) 200 MT. Attractive double *en-suite* stone chalets are 700 MT and deluxe four-bed chalets 1 600 MT. Set-menu suppers are a reasonable 180 MT. For further information contact Emelio or Annetjie in Mozambique, tel: 25-28-2049 or 82-599-8410, or in South Africa, +27-(0)82-539-6411.

From Cahora Bassa, head back to the Tete road and turn right (south). From this intersection, it is 71 kilome-tres to the unsignposted traffic circle at Luenha (S16°50.182 E33°16.464). Turn right and it's another 48 kilo-metres to the Zimbabwean border at Nyamapanda and then another 235 kil-ometres to Harare. Carry on straight at the circle for 258 kilometres of reason-able (but narrow) tar, through Guro and Catandica, to connect with the EN6 highway. Once you reach the EN6, you can, of course, head west into Zimbabwe, east down to Beira or south on the EN1 to Maputo.

CAHORA BASSA, SONGO

Cahora Bassa Dam

Dam wall

View point

Lookout

Boom

Steep stoney track

Ugezi Tiger Lodge

Lookout

1,5 km

Construction Camp Buildings

S15°35,767 E32°45,787

S15°37,188 E32°42,645

Pensao Sete Montes

SONGO
Hospital

Tele's Club Centro Social

Pharmacy

Airport

10,5 km

S15°36,727 E32°46,352

5,5 km

S15°38,898 E32°47,708

136 km
to Tete

24

Portuguese
words and phrases

Fancy phrase books list dozens of rules and even more exceptions, but you'll be just fine if you remember that 's' is usually pronounced *sh*, 'c' is pronounced *s*, and 'm' as *n*. To get a feel of for the language, listen to people speaking around you -- and then give it a try. Don't be afraid to make mistakes, Mozambicans are very understanding.

While Mozambicans speak mostly Portuguese, the locals are generally friendly and hospitable, and many are well able to converse in English.

Counting

1 *um/uma* (one beer = *uma cerveja*)
2 *dois/duas*
3 *tres*
4 *quatro*
5 *cinco*
6 *seis*
7 *sete*
8 *oito*
9 *nove*
10 *dez*
11 *onze*
12 *doze*
13 *treze*
14 *catorze*
15 *quinze*
16 *dezasseis*
17 *dezassete*
18 *dezoito*
19 *dezanove*
20 *vinte*
21 *vinte e um*
30 *trinta*
40 *quarenta*
50 *cinquenta*
60 *sessenta*
70 *setenta*
80 *oitenta*
90 *noventa*
100 *cem*
500 *quinhentos*
1 000 *mil*
2 000 *dois mil*
10 000 *dez mil*

Greetings and pleasantries

Hello   *Hola*
Goodbye   *Ciao*
Friend   *Amigo*
Good morning   *Bom dia*
Good afternoon   *Boa tarde*
Good evening/night   *Boa noite*

How are you?   *Como esta?*
I am well   *Estou bem*
Yes   *Sim*
No   *Nao*
Please   *Por favor*
Thank you   *Obrigado*
You're welcome   *De nada*
Sorry   *Desculpe*
I am a poor traveller   *Eu sou viajante pobre*
My name is…   *Me chamou…*
I don't speak Portuguese   *nao falo Portugues*
I don't know   *Nao sei*
I don't understand   *Nao compreendo*
No problem!   *Nao faz mal!*
Okay   *Tudo bem*

Questions

What is your name?   *Como se chama?*
How much (cost)?   *Quanto custa?*
What?   *Que?*
When?   *Quando?*
When does that bus leave?   *Quando sai esta machimbombo?*
Right now?   *Agora mesmo?*
Where?   *Onde?*
Here?   *Aqui?*
There?   *Ali, la?*
How far?   *Quantos kilometros?*
Have you got…?   *Tem…?*
Where from?   *Donde?*
Where is…?   *Onde fica esta?*
Who?   *Quem?*
Do you know?   *Voce sabe?*
May I (take a photo)?   *Da licenca…?*

Time

Yesterday   *Ontem*
Today   *Hoje*
Tomorrow   *Amanha*
Day   *Dia*

Morning *Manha*
Night *Noite*
Now *Agora*
Before *Antes*
After *Depois*
Never *Nunca*
Sunday *Domingo*
Monday *Segunda-feira*
Tuesday *Terca-feira*
Wednesday *Quarta-feira*
Thursday *Quinta-feira*
Friday *Sexta-feira*
Saturday *Sabado*

Descriptions
Good *Bom/Boa* (m/f)
Large *Grande*
Small *Pequeno/a* (m/f)
A lot *Muito/a* (m/f)
A little *Pouco/a* (m/f)
Nothing *Nada*
Enough *Bastante*
That's enough! *Basta!*

Eating and drinking
Restaurant *Restaurante*
Roadside *Restaurante quiosque*
To eat *Comer*
Menu printed/hand-written *Cardapio/ementa*
Set menu *Menu*
Breakfast *Matabicho*
Lunch *Almoco*
Dinner *Jantar*
Meat *Carne*
Beef *Carne de vaca*
Steak *File bife*
Well done/medium/rare *Bem passado/medio/mal passado*
Kebab *Espetada*
Steak roll *Prego*
Pork *Carne de porco*

Eggs *Ovos*
Chicken *Frango*
Peri-peri fried chicken *Galinha frita com peri-peri*
Fish *Pescado*
Crab *Caranguejo*
Crayfish *Lagostim*
Lobster *Lagosta*
Prawns *Camarao*
Calamari *Lulas*
Fresh *Fresco*
Fruit *Fruta*
Rice *Arroz*
Pasta *Massa*
Chips *Batatas fritas*
Maize porridge *Nsima*
Vegetables *Legumes*
Bread *Pao*
Coffee *Café*
Tea *Cha*
Milk *Leita*
Water *Agua*
Mineral water *Agua mineral*
Beer *Cerveja*
Spirits *Aguardente*
The bill *Conta*
Cheap *Barato*
Fair price *Bom preco*
Too expensive *Muito caro*

In town...
City/town *Cidade*
Road *Estrada*
Left *A esquerda*
Right *A direita*
House *Casa*
Shop *Loja*
Supermarket *Supermercado*
Market *Mercado*
For sale *Vende-se*
Bank *Banco*
Money *Dinheiro*

Change   *Cambio*
Traveller's cheques   *Cheques de viagem*
Black market   *Candonga*
Hotel   *Hotel*
Small hotel   *Pensão*
Room   *Quarto*
Single/double   *Simples/duplo*
Room for married couples   *Casal*
   Bed Cama
Bathroom/toilet   *Casa de banho*
Ladies   *Senhoras*
Gents   *Senhors*
Shower   *Chuveiro*
Wash   *Lavar*
Nightclub   *Boite*
Doctor   *Medico*
Bus   *Machimbombo*
Truck   *Camiao*
Train   *Comboio*
Ticket   *Bilhete*

And for the desperate…

I feel sick *Estao enjoado*
Take me to the hospital *Levar-me para
   hospital*
My car has broken down *Meu carra
   esta quebrado*
I need a mechanic *Queru um mecanico*

Adeus, boa viagem!

Index